BUS

Real-Resumes For Engineering Jobs

...including real resumes used to change careers
and resumes used to gain federal employment

Anne McKinney, Editor

PREP PUBLISHING

FAYETTEVILLE, NC

PREP Publishing

1110 ½ Hay Street
Fayetteville, NC 28305
(910) 483-6611

Copyright © 2004 by Anne McKinney

All rights reserved under International and Pan-American Copyright Conventions. No part of this book may be reproduced or copied in any form or by any means–graphic, electronic, or mechanical, including photocopying, taping, or information storage and retrieval systems– without written permission from the publisher, except by a reviewer, who may quote brief passages in a review. Published in the United States by PREP Publishing.

Library of Congress Cataloging-in-Publication Data

Real-resumes for engineering jobs : ...including resumes used to change careers and resumes used to gain federal employment / Anne McKinney.
        p. cm. -- (Real-resumes series)
    ISBN 1-885288-42-5 (trade paper)
    1. Engineers--Employment. 2. Resumes (Employment) I. McKinney, Anne, 1948- II. Series.

    TA157.R35 2004
    650.14'2--dc22   2004053406

Printed in the United States of America

PREP Publishing

Contents

Real-Resumes For Engineering Jobs

Anne McKinney, Editor

A WORD FROM THE EDITOR:
ABOUT THE REAL-RESUMES SERIES

Welcome to the Real-Resumes Series. The Real-Resumes Series is a series of books which have been developed based on the experiences of real job hunters and which target specialized fields or types of resumes. As the editor of the series, I have carefully selected resumes and cover letters (with names and other key data disguised, of course) which have been used successfully in real job hunts. That's what we mean by "Real-Resumes." What you see in this book are *real* resumes and cover letters which helped real people get ahead in their careers.

We hope the superior samples will help you manage your current job campaign and your career so that you will find work aligned to your career interests.

The Real-Resumes Series is based on the work of the country's oldest resume-preparation company known as PREP Resumes. If you would like a free information packet describing the company's resume preparation services, call 910-483-6611 or write to PREP at 1110½ Hay Street, Fayetteville, NC 28305. If you have a job hunting experience you would like to share with our staff at the Real-Resumes Series, please contact us at preppub@aol.com or visit our website at www.prep-pub.com.

The resumes and cover letters in this book are designed to be of most value to people already in a job hunt or contemplating a career change. If we could give you one word of advice about your career, here's what we would say: Manage your career and don't stumble from job to job in an incoherent pattern. Try to find work that interests you, and then identify prosperous industries which need work performed of the type you want to do. Learn early in your working life that a great resume and cover letter can blow doors open for you and help you maximize your salary.

As the editor of this book, I would like to give you some tips on how to make the best use of the information you will find here. Because you are considering a career change, you already understand the concept of managing your career for maximum enjoyment and self-fulfillment. The purpose of this book is to provide expert tools and advice so that you *can* manage your career. Inside these pages you will find resumes and cover letters that will help you find not just a job but the type of work you want to do.

Overview of the Book

Every resume and cover letter in this book actually worked. And most of the resumes and cover letters have common features: most are one-page, most are in the chronological format, and most resumes are accompanied by a companion cover letter. In this section you will find helpful advice about job hunting. Step One begins with a discussion of why employers prefer the one-page, chronological resume. In Step Two you are introduced to the direct approach and to the proper format for a cover letter. In Step Three you learn the 14 main reasons why job hunters are not offered the jobs they want, and you learn the six key areas employers focus on when they interview you. Step Four gives nuts-and-bolts advice on how to handle the interview, send a follow-up letter after an interview, and negotiate your salary.

The cover letter plays such a critical role in a career change. You will learn from the experts how to format your cover letters and you will see suggested language to use in particular career-change situations. It has been said that "A picture is worth a thousand words" and, for that reason, you will see numerous examples of effective cover letters used by real individuals to change fields, functions, and industries.

The most important part of the book is the Real-Resumes section. Some of the individuals whose resumes and cover letters you see spent a lengthy career in an industry they loved. Then there are resumes and cover letters of people who wanted a change but who probably wanted to remain in their industry. Many of you will be especially interested by the resumes and cover letters of individuals who knew they definitely wanted a career change but had no idea what they wanted to do next. Other resumes and cover letters show individuals who knew they wanted to change fields and had a pretty good idea of what they wanted to do next.

Whatever your field, and whatever your circumstances, you'll find resumes and cover letters that will "show you the ropes" in terms of successfully changing jobs and switching careers.

Before you proceed further, think about why you picked up this book.
- Are you dissatisfied with the type of work you are now doing?
- Would you like to change careers, change companies, or change industries?
- Are you satisfied with your industry but not with your niche or function within it?
- Do you want to transfer your skills to a new product or service?
- Even if you have excelled in your field, have you "had enough"? Would you like the stimulation of a new challenge?
- Are you aware of the importance of a great cover letter but unsure of how to write one?
- Are you preparing to launch a second career after retirement?
- Have you been downsized, or do you anticipate becoming a victim of downsizing?
- Do you need expert advice on how to plan and implement a job campaign that will open the maximum number of doors?
- Do you want to make sure you handle an interview to your maximum advantage?

- Would you like to master the techniques of negotiating salary and benefits?
- Do you want to learn the secrets and shortcuts of professional resume writers?

Using the Direct Approach

As you consider the possibility of a job hunt or career change, you need to be aware that most people end up having at least three distinctly different careers in their working lifetimes, and often those careers are different from each other. Yet people usually stumble through each job campaign, unsure of what they should be doing. Whether you find yourself voluntarily or unexpectedly in a job hunt, the direct approach is the job hunting strategy most likely to yield a full-time permanent job. The direct approach is an active, take-the-initiative style of job hunting in which you choose your next employer rather than relying on responding to ads, using employment agencies, or depending on other methods of finding jobs. You will learn how to use the direct approach in this book, and you will see that an effective cover letter is a critical ingredient in using the direct approach.

The "direct approach" is the style of job hunting most likely to yield the maximum number of job interviews.

Lack of Industry Experience Not a Major Barrier to Entering New Field

"Lack of experience" is often the last reason people are not offered jobs, according to the companies who do the hiring. If you are changing careers, you will be glad to learn that experienced professionals often are selling "potential" rather than experience in a job hunt. Companies look for personal qualities that they know tend to be present in their most effective professionals, such as communication skills, initiative, persistence, organizational and time management skills, and creativity. Frequently companies are trying to discover "personality type," "talent," "ability," "aptitude," and "potential" rather than seeking actual hands-on experience, so your resume should be designed to aggressively present your accomplishments. Attitude, enthusiasm, personality, and a track record of achievements in any type of work are the primary "indicators of success" which employers are seeking, and you will see numerous examples in this book of resumes written in an all-purpose fashion so that the professional can approach various industries and companies.

Using references in a skillful fashion in your job hunt will inspire confidence in prospective employers and help you "close the sale" after interviews.

The Art of Using References in a Job Hunt

You probably already know that you need to provide references during a job hunt, but you may not be sure of how and when to use references for maximum advantage. You can use references very creatively during a job hunt to call attention to your strengths and make yourself "stand out." Your references will rarely get you a job, no matter how impressive the names, but the way you use references can boost the employer's confidence in you and lead to a job offer in the least time.

You should ask from three to five people, including people who have supervised you, if you can use them as a reference during your job hunt. You may not be able to ask your current boss since your job hunt is probably confidential.

A common question in resume preparation is: "Do I need to put my references on my resume?" No, you don't. Even if you create a references page at the same time you prepare your resume, you don't need to mail, e-mail, or fax your references page with the resume and cover letter. Usually the potential employer is not interested in references until he meets you, so the earliest you need to have references ready is at the first interview. Obviously there are exceptions to this standard rule of thumb; sometimes an ad will ask you to send references with your first response. Wait until the employer requests references before providing them.

An excellent attention-getting technique is to take to the first interview not just a page of references (giving names, addresses, and telephone numbers) but an actual letter of reference written by someone who knows you well and who preferably has supervised or employed you. A professional way to close the first interview is to thank the interviewer, shake his or her hand, and then say you'd like to give him or her a copy of a letter of reference from a previous employer. Hopefully you already made a good impression during the interview, but you'll "close the sale" in a dynamic fashion if you leave a letter praising you and your accomplishments. For that reason, it's a good idea to ask supervisors during your final weeks in a job if they will provide you with a written letter of recommendation which you can use in future job hunts. Most employers will oblige, and you will have a letter that has a useful "shelf life" of many years. Such a letter often gives the prospective employer enough confidence in his opinion of you that he may forego checking out other references and decide to offer you the job on the spot or in the next few days.

With regard to references, it's best to provide the names and addresses of people who have supervised you or observed you in a work situation.

Whom should you ask to serve as references? References should be people who have known or supervised you in a professional, academic, or work situation. References with big titles, like school superintendent or congressman, are fine, but remind busy people when you get to the interview stage that they may be contacted soon. Make sure the busy official recognizes your name and has instant positive recall of you! If you're asked to provide references on a formal company application, you can simply transcribe names from your references list. In summary, follow this rule in using references: If you've got them, flaunt them! If you've obtained well-written letters of reference, make sure you find a polite way to push those references under the nose of the interviewer so he or she can hear someone other than you describing your strengths. Your references probably won't ever get you a job, but glowing letters of reference can give you credibility and visibility that can make you stand out among candidates with similar credentials and potential!

The approach taken by this book is to (1) help you master the proven best techniques of conducting a job hunt and (2) show you how to stand out in a job hunt through your resume, cover letter, interviewing skills, as well as the way in which you present your references and follow up on interviews. Now, the best way to "get in the mood" for writing your own resume and cover letter is to select samples from the Table of Contents that interest you and then read them. A great resume is a "photograph," usually on one page, of an individual. If you wish to seek professional advice in preparing your resume, you may contact one of the professional writers at Professional Resume & Employment Publishing (PREP) for a brief free consultation by calling 1-910-483-6611.

Part One: Some Advice About Your Job Hunt

What if you don't know what you want to do?

Your job hunt will be more comfortable if you can figure out what type of work you want to do. But you are not alone if you have no idea what you want to do next! You may have knowledge and skills in certain areas but want to get into another type of work. What *The Wall Street Journal* has discovered in its research on careers is that most of us end up having at least three distinctly different careers in our working lives; it seems that, even if we really like a particular kind of activity, twenty years of doing it is enough for most of us and we want to move on to something else!

That's why we strongly believe that you need to spend some time figuring out *what interests you* rather than taking an inventory of the skills you have. You may have skills that you simply don't want to use, but if you can build your career on the things that interest you, you will be more likely to be happy and satisfied in your job. Realize, too, that interests can change over time; the activities that interest you now may not be the ones that interested you years ago. For example, some professionals may decide that they've had enough of retail sales and want a job selling another product or service, even though they have earned a reputation for being an excellent retail manager. We strongly believe that interests rather than skills should be the determining factor in deciding what types of jobs you want to apply for and what directions you explore in your job hunt. Obviously one cannot be a lawyer without a law degree or a secretary without secretarial skills; but a professional can embark on a next career as a financial consultant, property manager, plant manager, production supervisor, retail manager, or other occupation if he/she has a strong interest in that type of work and can provide a resume that clearly demonstrates past excellent performance in *any* field and *potential* to excel in another field. As you will see later in this book, "lack of exact experience" is the last reason why people are turned down for the jobs they apply for.

> Figure out what interests you and you will hold the key to a successful job hunt and working career. (And be prepared for your interests to change over time!)

How can you have a resume prepared if you don't know what you want to do?

You may be wondering how you can have a resume prepared if you don't know what you want to do next. The approach to resume writing which PREP, the country's oldest resume-preparation company, has used successfully for many years is to develop an "all-purpose" resume that translates your skills, experience, and accomplishments into language employers can understand. What most people need in a job hunt is a versatile resume that will allow them to apply for numerous types of jobs. For example, you may want to apply for a job in pharmaceutical sales but you may also want to have a resume that will be versatile enough for you to apply for jobs in the construction, financial services, or automotive industries.

> "Lack of exact experience" is the last reason people are turned down for the jobs for which they apply.

Based on more than 20 years of serving job hunters, we at PREP have found that your best approach to job hunting is **an all-purpose resume** and **specific cover letters tailored to specific fields** rather than using the approach of trying to create different resumes for every job. If you are remaining in your field, you may not even need more than one "all-purpose" cover letter, although the cover letter rather than the resume is the place to communicate your interest in a narrow or specific field. An all-purpose resume and cover letter that translate your experience and accomplishments into plain English are the tools that will maximize the number of doors which open for you while permitting you to "fish" in the widest range of job areas.

Your resume will provide the script for your job interview.
When you get down to it, your resume has a simple job to do: Its purpose is to blow as many doors open as possible and to make as many people as possible want to meet you. So a well-written resume that really "sells" you is a key that will create opportunities for you in a job hunt.

This statistic explains why: The typical newspaper advertisement for a job opening receives more than 245 replies. And normally only 10 or 12 will be invited to an interview.

But here's another purpose of the resume: it provides the "script" the employer uses when he interviews you. If your resume has been written in such a way that your strengths and achievements are revealed, that's what you'll end up talking about at the job interview. Since the resume will govern what you get asked about at your interviews, you can't overestimate the importance of making sure your resume makes you look and sound as good as you are.

> Your resume is the "script" for your job interviews. Make sure you put on your resume what you want to talk about or be asked about at the job interview.

So what is a "good" resume?
Very literally, your resume should motivate the person reading it to dial the phone number or e-mail the screen name you have put on the resume. When you are relocating, you should put a local phone number on your resume if your physical address is several states away; employers are more likely to dial a local telephone number than a long-distance number when they're looking for potential employees.

If you have a resume already, look at it objectively. Is it a limp, colorless "laundry list" of your job titles and duties? Or does it "paint a picture" of your skills, abilities, and accomplishments in a way that would make someone want to meet you? Can people understand what you're saying? If you are attempting to change fields or industries, can potential employers see that your skills and knowledge are transferable to other environments? For example, have you described accomplishments which reveal your problem-solving abilities or communication skills?

> The one-page resume in chronological format is the format preferred by most employers.

How long should your resume be?
One page, maybe two. Usually only people in the academic community have a resume (which they usually call a *curriculum vitae*) longer than one or two pages. Remember that your resume is almost always accompanied by a cover letter, and a potential employer does not want to read more than two or three pages about a total stranger in order to decide if he wants to meet that person! Besides, don't forget that the more you tell someone about yourself, the more opportunity you are providing for the employer to screen you out at the "first-cut" stage. A resume should be concise and exciting and designed to make the reader want to meet you in person!

Should resumes be functional or chronological?
Employers almost always prefer a chronological resume; in other words, an employer will find a resume easier to read if it is immediately apparent what your current or most recent job is, what you did before that, and so forth, in reverse chronological order. A resume that goes back in detail for the last ten years of employment will generally satisfy the employer's curiosity about your background. Employment more than ten years old can be shown even more briefly in an "Other Experience" section at the end of your "Experience" section. Remember that your intention is not to tell everything you've done but to "hit the high points" and especially impress the employer with what you learned, contributed, or accomplished in each job you describe.

Once you get your resume, what do you do with it?

You will be using your resume to answer ads, as a tool to use in talking with friends and relatives about your job search, and, most importantly, in using the "direct approach" described in this book.

When you mail your resume, always send a "cover letter."

A "cover letter," sometimes called a "resume letter" or "letter of interest," is a letter that accompanies and introduces your resume. Your cover letter is a way of personalizing the resume by sending it to the specific person you think you might want to work for at each company. Your cover letter should contain a few highlights from your resume—just enough to make someone want to meet you. Cover letters should always be typed or word processed on a computer—never handwritten.

Never mail or fax your resume without a cover letter.

1. Learn the art of answering ads.

There is an "art," part of which can be learned, in using your "bestselling" resume to reply to advertisements.

Sometimes an exciting job lurks behind a boring ad that someone dictated in a hurry, so reply to any ad that interests you. Don't worry that you aren't "25 years old with an MBA" like the ad asks for. Employers will always make compromises in their requirements if they think you're the "best fit" overall.

What about ads that ask for "salary requirements?"

What if the ad you're answering asks for "salary requirements?" The first rule is to avoid committing yourself in writing at that point to a specific salary. You don't want to "lock yourself in."

There are two ways to handle the ad that asks for "salary requirements."

What if the ad asks for your "salary requirements?"

First, you can ignore that part of the ad and accompany your resume with a cover letter that focuses on "selling" you, your abilities, and even some of your philosophy about work or your field. You may include a sentence in your cover letter like this: "I can provide excellent personal and professional references at your request, and I would be delighted to share the private details of my salary history with you in person."

Second, if you feel you must give some kind of number, just state a range in your cover letter that includes your medical, dental, other benefits, and expected bonuses. You might state, for example, "My current compensation, including benefits and bonuses, is in the range of $30,000-$40,000."

Analyze the ad and "tailor" yourself to it.

When you're replying to ads, a finely tailored cover letter is an important tool in getting your resume noticed and read. On the next page is a cover letter which has been "tailored to fit" a specific ad. Notice the "art" used by PREP writers of analyzing the ad's main requirements and then writing the letter so that the person's background, work habits, and interests seem "tailor-made" to the company's needs. Use this cover letter as a model when you prepare your own reply to ads.

Date

Exact Name of Person
Exact Title
Exact Name of Company
Address
City, State, Zip

Dear Exact Name of Person (or Dear Sir or Madam if answering a blind ad):

With the enclosed resume, I would like to express my interest in exploring employment opportunities with your organization.

As you will see from my resume, I have excelled in a track record of promotion with a company involved in the manufacturing of distribution and control products. I have earned a reputation as a gifted problem solver while performing as a Senior Engineering Technician, Design Engineer, and Product Line Engineer. Although I excelled in the engineering field, I did so without the benefit of formal education in engineering for several years. In 2000, I returned to college to earn my engineering degree in the evenings, and I will receive my B.S. in Electrical Engineering *summa cum laude* this May.

Although I am held in high regard by my current employer, the company is closing the plant where I work and relocating its product lines to a facility in Alabama. I have been offered a senior management position at the Alabama facility, but I am selectively exploring opportunities in other organizations. I would appreciate your holding my interest in your company in confidence at this time.

I believe that my success in the engineering field thus far has been due to my ability to look at each problem I encounter with a creative yet practical problem-solving approach. To use the vernacular, I am able to "think outside the box." I take pride in the numerous contributions I have made to my employer's bottom line, and I offer an ability to work effectively with others at all organizational levels.

I hope you will call or write me soon to suggest a time convenient for us to meet and discuss your current and future needs and how I might serve them. Thank you in advance for your time.

Sincerely,

Jared Coolidge

Alternate last paragraph:
I hope you will welcome my call soon to arrange a brief meeting to discuss your current and future needs and how I might serve them. Thank you in advance for your time.

Employers are trying to identify the individual who wants the job they are filling. Don't be afraid to express your enthusiasm in the cover letter!

2. Talk to friends and relatives.

Don't be shy about telling your friends and relatives the kind of job you're looking for. Looking for the job you want involves using your network of contacts, so tell people what you're looking for. They may be able to make introductions and help set up interviews.

About 25% of all interviews are set up through "who you know," so don't ignore this approach.

3. Finally, and most importantly, use the "direct approach."

The "direct approach" is a strategy in which you choose your next employer.

More than 50% of all job interviews are set up by the "direct approach." That means you actually mail, e-mail, or fax a resume and a cover letter to a company you think might be interesting to work for.

To whom do you write?

In general, you should write directly to the *exact name* of the person who would be hiring you: say, the vice-president of marketing or data processing. If you're in doubt about to whom to address the letter, address it to the president by name and he or she will make sure it gets forwarded to the right person within the company who has hiring authority in your area.

How do you find the names of potential employers?

You're not alone if you feel that the biggest problem in your job search is finding the right names at the companies you want to contact. But you can usually figure out the names of companies you want to approach by deciding first if your job hunt is primarily geography-driven or industry-driven.

In a **geography-driven job hunt,** you could select a list of, say, 50 companies you want to contact **by location** from the lists that the U.S. Chambers of Commerce publish yearly of their "major area employers." There are hundreds of local Chambers of Commerce across America, and most of them will have an 800 number which you can find through 1-800-555-1212. If you and your family think Atlanta, Dallas, Ft. Lauderdale, and Virginia Beach might be nice places to live, for example, you could contact the Chamber of Commerce in those cities and ask how you can obtain a copy of their list of major employers. Your nearest library will have the book which lists the addresses of all chambers.

In an **industry-driven job hunt,** and if you are willing to relocate, you will be identifying the companies which you find most attractive in the industry in which you want to work. When you select a list of companies to contact **by industry,** you can find the right person to write and the address of firms by industrial category in *Standard and Poor's, Moody's,* and other excellent books in public libraries. Many Web sites also provide contact information.

Many people feel it's a good investment to actually call the company to either find out or double-check the name of the person to whom they want to send a resume and cover letter. It's important to do as much as you feasibly can to assure that the letter gets to the right person in the company.

On-line research will be the best way for many people to locate organizations to which they wish to send their resume. It is outside the scope of this book to teach Internet research skills, but librarians are often useful in this area.

What's the correct way to follow up on a resume you send?

There is a polite way to be aggressively interested in a company during your job hunt. It is ideal to end the cover letter accompanying your resume by saying, "I hope you'll welcome my call next week when I try to arrange a brief meeting at your convenience to discuss your current and future needs and how I might serve them." Keep it low key, and just ask for a "brief meeting," not an interview. Employers want people who show a determined interest in working with them, so don't be shy about following up on the resume and cover letter you've mailed.

STEP THREE: Preparing for Interviews

But a resume and cover letter by themselves can't get you the job you want. You need to "prep" yourself before the interview. Step Three in your job campaign is "Preparing for Interviews." First, let's look at interviewing from the hiring organization's point of view.

What are the biggest "turnoffs" for potential employers?

One of the ways to help yourself perform well at an interview is to look at the main reasons why organizations *don't* hire the people they interview, according to those who do the interviewing.

Notice that "lack of appropriate background" (or lack of experience) is the *last* reason for not being offered the job.

The 14 Most Common Reasons Job Hunters Are Not Offered Jobs (according to the companies who do the interviewing and hiring):

1. Low level of accomplishment
2. Poor attitude, lack of self-confidence
3. Lack of goals/objectives
4. Lack of enthusiasm
5. Lack of interest in the company's business
6. Inability to sell or express yourself
7. Unrealistic salary demands
8. Poor appearance
9. Lack of maturity, no leadership potential
10. Lack of extracurricular activities
11. Lack of preparation for the interview, no knowledge about company
12. Objecting to travel
13. Excessive interest in security and benefits
14. Inappropriate background

Department of Labor studies have proven that smart, "prepared" job hunters can increase their beginning salary while getting a job in *half* the time it normally takes. (4½ months is the average national length of a job search.) Here, from PREP, are some questions that can prepare you to find a job faster.

Are you in the "right" frame of mind?

It seems unfair that we have to look for a job just when we're lowest in morale. Don't worry *too* much if you're nervous before interviews. You're supposed to be a little nervous, especially if the job means a lot to you. But the best way to kill unnecessary

It pays to be aware of the 14 most common pitfalls for job hunters.

fears about job hunting is through 1) making sure you have a great resume and 2) preparing yourself for the interview. Here are three main areas you need to think about before each interview.

Do you know what the company does?
Don't walk into an interview giving the impression that, "If this is Tuesday, this must be General Motors."

Research the company before you go to interviews.

Find out before the interview what the company's main product or service is. Where is the company heading? Is it in a "growth" or declining industry? (Answers to these questions may influence whether or not you want to work there!)

Information about what the company does is in annual reports, in newspaper and magazine articles, and on the Internet. If you're not yet skilled at Internet research, just visit your nearest library and ask the reference librarian to guide you to printed materials on the company.

Do you know what you want to do for the company?
Before the interview, try to decide how you see yourself fitting into the company. Remember, "lack of exact background" the company wants is usually the last reason people are not offered jobs.

Understand before you go to each interview that the burden will be on you to "sell" the interviewer on why you're the best person for the job and the company.

How will you answer the critical interview questions?
Put yourself in the interviewer's position and think about the questions you're most likely to be asked. Here are some of the most commonly asked interview questions:

Anticipate the questions you will be asked at the interview, and prepare your responses in advance.

Q: *"What are your greatest strengths?"*
A: Don't say you've never thought about it! Go into an interview knowing the three main impressions you want to leave about yourself, such as "I'm hard-working, loyal, and an imaginative cost-cutter."

Q: *"What are your greatest weaknesses?"*
A: Don't confess that you're lazy or have trouble meeting deadlines! Confessing that you tend to be a "workaholic" or "tend to be a perfectionist and sometimes get frustrated when others don't share my high standards" will make your prospective employer see a "weakness" that he likes. Name a weakness that your interviewer will perceive as a strength.

Q: *"What are your long-range goals?"*
A: If you're interviewing with Microsoft, don't say you want to work for IBM in five years! Say your long-range goal is to be *with* the company, contributing to its goals and success.

Q: *"What motivates you to do your best work?"*
A: Don't get dollar signs in your eyes here! "A challenge" is not a bad answer, but it's a little cliched. Saying something like "troubleshooting" or "solving a tough problem" is more interesting and specific. Give an example if you can.

Q: "What do you know about this organization?"

A: Don't say you never heard of it until they asked you to the interview! Name an interesting, positive thing you learned about the company recently from your research. Remember, company executives can sometimes feel rather "maternal" about the company they serve. Don't get onto a negative area of the company if you can think of positive facts you can bring up. Of course, if you learned in your research that the company's sales seem to be taking a nose-dive, or that the company president is being prosecuted for taking bribes, you might politely ask your interviewer to tell you something that could help you better understand what you've been reading. Those are the kinds of company facts that can help you determine whether or not you want to work there.

Q: "Why should I hire you?"

A: "I'm unemployed and available" is the wrong answer here! Get back to your strengths and say that you believe the organization could benefit by a loyal, hard-working cost-cutter like yourself.

In conclusion, you should decide in advance, before you go to the interview, how you will answer each of these commonly asked questions. Have some practice interviews with a friend to role-play and build your confidence.

STEP FOUR: Handling the Interview and Negotiating Salary

Now you're ready for Step Four: actually handling the interview successfully and effectively. Remember, the purpose of an interview is to get a job offer.

Eight "do's" for the interview

According to leading U.S. companies, there are eight key areas in interviewing success. You can fail at an interview if you mishandle just one area.

1. **Do wear appropriate clothes.**

You can never go wrong by wearing a suit to an interview.

2. **Do be well groomed.**

Don't overlook the obvious things like having clean hair, clothes, and fingernails for the interview.

3. **Do give a firm handshake.**

You'll have to shake hands twice in most interviews: first, before you sit down, and second, when you leave the interview. Limp handshakes turn most people off.

4. **Do smile and show a sense of humor.**

Interviewers are looking for people who would be nice to work with, so don't be so somber that you don't smile. In fact, research shows that people who smile at interviews are perceived as more intelligent. So, smile!

5. **Do be enthusiastic.**

Employers say they are "turned off" by lifeless, unenthusiastic job hunters who show no special interest in that company. The best way to show some enthusiasm for the employer's operation is to find out about the business beforehand.

Go to an interview prepared to tell the company why it should hire you.

A smile at an interview makes the employer perceive of you as intelligent!

6. Do show you are flexible and adaptable.

An employer is looking for someone who can contribute to his organization in a flexible, adaptable way. No matter what skills and training you have, employers know every new employee must go through initiation and training on the company's turf. Certainly show pride in your past accomplishments in a specific, factual way ("I saved my last employer $50.00 a week by a new cost-cutting measure I developed"). But don't come across as though there's nothing about the job you couldn't easily handle.

7. Do ask intelligent questions about the employer's business.

An employer is hiring someone because of certain business needs. Show interest in those needs. Asking questions to get a better idea of the employer's needs will help you "stand out" from other candidates interviewing for the job.

8. Do "take charge" when the interviewer "falls down" on the job.

Go into every interview knowing the three or four points about yourself you want the interviewer to remember. And be prepared to take an active part in leading the discussion if the interviewer's "canned approach" does not permit you to display your "strong suit." You can't always depend on the interviewer's asking you the "right" questions so you can stress your strengths and accomplishments.

Employers are seeking people with good attitudes whom they can train and coach to do things their way.

An important "don't": Don't ask questions about salary or benefits at the first interview.
Employers don't take warmly to people who look at their organization as just a place to satisfy salary and benefit needs. Don't risk making a negative impression by appearing greedy or self-serving. The place to discuss salary and benefits is normally at the second interview, and the employer will bring it up. Then you can ask questions without appearing excessively interested in what the organization can do for you.

Now...negotiating your salary
Even if an ad requests that you communicate your "salary requirement" or "salary history," you should avoid providing those numbers in your initial cover letter. You can usually say something like this: "I would be delighted to discuss the private details of my salary history with you in person."

Once you're at the interview, you must avoid even appearing *interested* in salary before you are offered the job. Make sure you've "sold" yourself before talking salary. First show you're the "best fit" for the employer and then you'll be in a stronger position from which to negotiate salary. **Never** bring up the subject of salary yourself. Employers say there's no way you can avoid looking greedy if you bring up the issue of salary and benefits before the company has identified you as its "best fit."

Don't appear excessively interested in salary and benefits at the interview.

Interviewers sometimes throw out a salary figure at the first interview to see if you'll accept it. You may not want to commit yourself if you think you will be able to negotiate a better deal later on. Get back to finding out more about the job. This lets the interviewer know you're interested primarily in the job and not the salary.

When the organization brings up salary, it may say something like this: "Well, Mary, we think you'd make a good candidate for this job. What kind of salary are we talking about?" You may not want to name a number here, either. Give the ball back to the interviewer. Act as though you hadn't given the subject of salary much thought and respond something like this: "Ah, Mr. Jones, I wonder if you'd be kind enough to tell me what salary you had in mind when you advertised the job?" Or ... "What is the range you have in mind?"

Don't worry, if the interviewer names a figure that you think is too low, you can say so without turning down the job or locking yourself into a rigid position. The point here is to negotiate for yourself as well as you can. You might reply to a number named by the interviewer that you think is low by saying something like this: "Well, Mr. Lee, the job interests me very much, and I think I'd certainly enjoy working with you. But, frankly, I was thinking of something a little higher than that." That leaves the ball in your interviewer's court again, and you haven't turned down the job either, in case it turns out that the interviewer can't increase the offer and you still want the job.

Salary negotiation can be tricky.

Last, send a follow-up letter.

Mail, e-mail, or fax a letter right after the interview telling your interviewer you enjoyed the meeting and are certain (if you are) that you are the "best fit" for the job. The people interviewing you will probably have an attitude described as either "professionally loyal" to their companies, or "maternal and proprietary" if the interviewer also owns the company. In either case, they are looking for people who want to work for *that* company in particular. The follow-up letter you send might be just the deciding factor in your favor if the employer is trying to choose between you and someone else. You will see an example of a follow-up letter on page 16.

A follow-up letter can help the employer choose between you and another qualified candidate.

A cover letter is an essential part of a job hunt or career change.

Many people are aware of the importance of having a great resume, but most people in a job hunt don't realize just how important a cover letter can be. The purpose of the cover letter, sometimes called a **"letter of interest,"** is to introduce your resume to prospective employers. The cover letter is often the critical ingredient in a job hunt because the cover letter allows you to say a lot of things that just don't "fit" on the resume. For example, you can emphasize your commitment to a new field and stress your related talents. The cover letter also gives you a chance to stress outstanding character and personal values. On the next two pages you will see examples of very effective cover letters.

A cover letter is an essential part of a career change.

Please do not attempt to implement a career change without a cover letter. A cover letter is the first impression of you, and you can influence the way an employer views you by the language and style of your letter.

Special help for those in career change

We want to emphasize again that, especially in a career change, the cover letter is very important and can help you "build a bridge" to a new career. A creative and appealing cover letter can begin the process of encouraging the potential employer to imagine you in an industry other than the one in which you have worked.

As a special help to those in career change, there are resumes and cover letters included in this book which show valuable techniques and tips you should use when changing fields or industries. The resumes and cover letters of career changers are identified in the table of contents as "Career Change" and you will see the "Career Change" label on cover letters in Part Two where the individuals are changing careers.

Date

Addressing the Cover Letter: Get the exact name of the person to whom you are writing. This makes your approach personal.

Exact Name of Person
Title or Position
Name of Company
Address
City, State, Zip

Dear Exact Name of Person: (or Dear Sir or Madam if answering a blind ad.)

First Paragraph: This explains why you are writing.

I would appreciate an opportunity to talk with you soon about how I could add value to your organization through my versatile skills in both engineering and management.

Second Paragraph: You have a chance to talk about whatever you feel is your most distinguishing feature.

Since receiving my B.S. degree in Engineering, I have excelled in jobs related to product design, manufacturing engineering, process engineering, and product engineering while earning a reputation as a resourceful technical problem solver who works well with people. I offer a strong "bottom-line" orientation and, in my most recent job, I generated new product margins and cost reductions which contributed more than $7.5 million annually. I have acquired expertise related to risk management legislation, patents and trademarks, UL/CSA certification procedures, and OSHA standards, and I have handled responsibility for OSHA, EPA, hazardous wastes, energy management systems, and computerized communication systems.

Third Paragraph: You bring up your next most distinguishing qualities and try to sell yourself.

With a reputation as an engineer who works well with others and who can "translate" complex technical concepts into language non-engineers can understand, I am respected for my integrity and "common sense." I can provide outstanding personal and professional references.

Fourth Paragraph: Here you have another opportunity to reveal qualities or achievements which will impress your future employer.

In today's marketplace, I believe it makes sense for professionals to have as many areas of expertise as possible, and I can certainly offer you expert skills in both engineering and management. I sincerely enjoy working with people while handling the challenge of solving stubborn technical problems. A fast learner with the ability to rapidly master new bodies of knowledge in our fast-changing world, I would welcome the opportunity to help you carve out new niches and solve problems in emerging technologies as well as existing ones.

Final Paragraph: He asks the employer to contact him. Make sure your reader knows what the "next step" is.

I hope you will write or call me soon to suggest a time at your convenience when we could discuss your current and future needs and how I might serve them. Thank you in advance for your time.

Sincerely yours,

Christopher Bailey

Alternate Final Paragraph: It's more aggressive (but not too aggressive) to let the employer know that you will be calling him or her. Don't be afraid to be persistent. Employers are looking for people who know what they want to do.

Alternate last paragraph:

I hope you will welcome my call soon to see if you could set aside some time for us to discuss your current and future needs and how I might serve them. Thank you in advance for your time.

Date

Exact Name of Person
Title or Position
Name of Company
Address
City, State, Zip

Dear Exact Name of Person: (or Dear Sir or Madam if answering a blind ad.)

I would appreciate an opportunity to talk with you soon about how I could contribute to your organization through my versatile experience as an engineer in product engineering, product marketing, and project management.

As you will see from my resume, I have excelled in a track record of accomplishment with Pisgah Corporation since graduating with my B.S. degree in Mechanical Engineering (Industrial concentration).

I started my employment with the company as a Design Engineer in Asheville, NC, and earned an Engineering Recognition Award in 2001. I have developed multiple control designs for use in several industries. I became a Product Marketing Manager in 2002 and received a prestigious award in 2003 for Excellence in Marketing. As a Product Marketing Manager, I played a key role in producing a gross sales increase of $22.6 million over a two-year period.

In 2004 I was specially selected to act as a Product Engineering Manager and relocated to Charlotte, NC where I have handled a wide range of tasks related to the strategic and tactical transfer of products from an assembly plant in Asheville to a Custom OEM assembly plant in Charlotte. I have set up the engineering department, standardized product production of $20 million in sales, communicated with outside sales professionals and customers during the phase-in process, and created documentation related to the manufacture and assembly of products. While supervising a team of nine design engineers and two drafts people in developing new products and planning production methods, we have added $3.4 million in revenue through recent product development programs.

I am approaching your company because I believe my versatile experience in project management, product development, marketing analysis and sales, and engineering design could be of value to you. I can provide outstanding personal and professional references at the appropriate time.

If you can use a superior performer with a strong bottom-line orientation and an ability to think strategically, I hope you will contact me to suggest a time when we might meet to discuss your needs and how I might help you achieve them. Thank you in advance for your time.

Sincerely,

Patrick Hendersen

This accomplished professional is responding to an advertisement. He analyzed the job vacancy opening very closely and he has made sure that he has tailored his letter of interest to the areas mentioned in the vacancy announcement.

Date

Exact Name of Person
Title or Position
Name of Company
Address (number and street)
Address (city, state, and zip)

Follow-up Letter

A great follow-up letter
can motivate the
employer
to make the job offer,
and the salary offer may
be influenced by the
style and tone of your
follow-up
letter, too!

Dear Exact Name:

I am writing to express my appreciation for the time you spent with me on December 9, and I want to let you know that I am sincerely interested in the position of Senior Metallurgical Engineer which we discussed.

I feel confident that I could skillfully interact with your staff, and I would cheerfully relocate to Tennessee, as we discussed.

As you described to me what you are looking for in the person who fills this position, I had a sense of "déjà vu" because my current employer was in a similar position when I went to work for them. The general manager needed someone to come in and be his "right arm" and take on an increasing amount of his management responsibilities so that he could be freed up to do other things. I have played a key role in the growth and success of the organization, and my supervisor has come to depend on my sound advice as much as well as my proven ability to "cut through" huge volumes of work efficiently and accurately. Since this is one of the busiest times of the year for my employer, I feel that I could not leave during that time. I could certainly make myself available by mid-January.

It would be a pleasure to work for your organization, and I am confident that I could contribute significantly through my strong qualities of loyalty, reliability, and trustworthiness. I am confident that I could quickly learn your style and procedures, and I would welcome being trained to do things your way.

Yours sincerely,

Jacob Evangelisto

In this section, you will find resumes and cover letters of professionals seeking employment, or already employed, in the engineering world. How do these individuals differ from other job hunters? Why should there be a book dedicated to people seeking jobs in engineering organizations? Based on more than 20 years of experience in working with job hunters, this editor is convinced that resumes and cover letters which "speak the lingo" of the field you wish to enter will communicate more effectively than language which is not industry-specific. This book is designed to help people (1) who are seeking to prepare their own resumes and (2) who wish to use as models "real" resumes of individuals who have successfully launched careers in engineering organizations or advanced in those organizations. You will see a wide range of experience levels reflected in the resumes in this book. Some of the resumes and cover letters were used by individuals seeking to enter the field; others were used successfully by senior professionals to advance in the field.

Newcomers to an industry sometimes have advantages over more experienced professionals. In a job hunt, junior professionals can have an advantage over their more experienced counterparts. Prospective employers often view the less experienced workers as "more trainable" and "more coachable" than their seniors. This means that the mature professional who has already excelled in a first career can, with credibility, "change careers" and transfer skills to other industries.

Newcomers to the field may have disadvantages compared to their seniors. Almost by definition, the inexperienced professional—the young person who has recently entered the job market, or the individual who has recently received respected certifications—is less tested and less experienced than senior managers, so the resume and cover letter of the inexperienced professional may often have to "sell" his or her potential to do something he or she has never done before. Lack of experience in the field she wants to enter can be a stumbling block to the junior employee, but remember that many employers believe that someone who has excelled in anything—academics, for example—can excel in many other fields.

Some advice to inexperienced professionals...
If senior professionals could give junior professionals a piece of advice about careers, here's what they would say: Manage your career and don't stumble from job to job in an incoherent pattern. Try to find work that interests you, and then identify prosperous industries which need work performed of the type you want to do. Learn early in your working life that a great resume and cover letter can blow doors open for you and help you maximize your salary.

Special help for career changers...
For those changing careers, you will find useful the resumes and cover letters marked "Career Change" on the following pages. Consult the Table of Contents for page numbers showing career changers.

CAREER CHANGE

Date

Exact Name of Person
Title or Position
Exact Name of Company
Address
City, State, Zip

**ADVISOR &
ENGINEERING
ANALYSIS
SUPERINTENDENT**
This individual has
served his country in
the U.S. Air Force
and wishes to
embark on a civilian
career.

Dear Exact Name of Person: (or Sir or Madam if answering a blind ad.)

I would appreciate an opportunity to talk with you soon about how I could contribute to your organization through my outstanding managerial and supervisory abilities as well as through my reputation as a professional who can be counted on for personal integrity, resourcefulness, and dedication to excellence in everything I attempt.

You will see from my enclosed resume that I have been serving my country in the U.S. Air Force and have built a track record of results while becoming highly skilled in managing human and material resources for maximum effectiveness. I have applied my initiative and knowledge to bring about results while planning, coordinating, and managing training and operations.

I offer a reputation for possessing the ability to take a group of poor performers and turn them into respected teams of disciplined and effective professionals. I am persistent in my search for innovative ways to improve quality and bring about increases in productivity, knowledge, and results.

Through my history of achieving results, building teams, and bringing about needed improvements, I am the type of mature professional who would be of benefit to any organization which values initiative, drive, and self-confidence.

I hope you will welcome my call soon to arrange a brief meeting to discuss your current and future needs and how I might serve them. Thank you in advance for your time.

Sincerely,

Theodore Ramsey

Alternate last paragraph:
I hope you will call or write me soon to suggest a time convenient for us to meet and discuss your current and future needs and how I might serve them. Thank you in advance for your time.

THEODORE RAMSEY

1110½ Hay Street, Fayetteville, NC 28305   •   preppub@aol.com   •   (910) 483-6611

OBJECTIVE

To benefit an organization that can use an innovative thinker and results-oriented professional who offers superior team building, problem-solving, and managerial abilities along with the confidence to make tough decisions and insist on quality.

EDUCATION

Earned a **Bachelor of Sciences in Engineering degree**, Middle Tennessee State University, Murfreesboro, TN, 2004.
- Maintained a 3.92 GPA while simultaneously excelling in critical Air Force jobs.

EXPERIENCE

Advanced in a track record of accomplishments with the U.S. Air Force:

ADVISOR and **ENGINEERING ANALYSIS SUPERINTENDENT.** Arnold AFB, TN (2004-present). Described as **"a powerhouse of drive and initiative,"** brought about numerous improvements which increased the effectiveness of engineering support activities for a 150-person organization; serve as senior advisor for computer and information security.
- Monitored manpower requirements and acted as the mentor for mid-level supervisors.
- Implemented an innovative program for tracking employee performance: developed a questionnaire which earned positive comments from evaluators and subjects.
- Led efforts which produced guidelines for each team and career field and a welcome packet for new employees to help their transition run more smoothly.

HUMAN RESOURCES MANAGER. Arnold AFB, TN (2001-03). As the first person to hold this position, managed scheduling, training, and staffing for six mobile support teams as well as providing guidance to a senior executive on manpower utilization, database administration, and operations for a 200-person organization filling worldwide assignments.
- Simplified human resource management reports used by staff members making decisions on how personnel were to be integrated during a complex reorganization project.
- Increased customer satisfaction through development of a customer service database.
- Put together teams and managed participation in six major exercises.
- Converted a database to a spreadsheet; reduced hours needed for compilation by 50%.
- Was named **Manager of the Year** for a 1,000-person organization.

SENIOR SUPERVISOR. Ramstein AB, Germany (2000-01). Provided leadership and supervision for 75 people in 10 career paths and controlled a $2 million inventory of equipment.

SUPERVISOR FOR TRAINING AND OPERATIONS. Ramstein AB, Germany (1998-00). Handled multiple simultaneous responsibilities including advising the operations supervisor, planning and overseeing career progression of technical specialists, administering and documenting training, and reviewing quality control reports.

FLIGHT OPERATIONS SUPERVISOR. Shaw AFB, SC (1997-98). Worked closely with Army and Navy counterparts while setting up procedures, writing operating instructions, and supervising a multimillion-dollar ground portion of an information downlinking system.

OPERATIONS SUPERVISOR. Shaw AFB, SC (1994-97). Evaluated as a solid and versatile performer, handled support activities for an information gathering organization including issuing instructions, maintaining a database, and managing improvements.

PERSONAL

During a distinguished career, was honored with three Meritorious Service Medals, three Air Medals, two AF Commendation Medals, and six Good Conduct Medals and was an honor student in every military training program attended. Hold Top Secret SBI security clearance.

CAREER CHANGE

Date

Exact Name of Person
Exact Title of Person
Company Name
Address
City, State zip

**ADVISOR &
TRAINING SPECIALIST**

This individual hopes to
leave military service
and land a highly paid
position with a civilian
contractor working in
the Middle East.

Dear Exact Name of Person: (or Dear Sir or Madam if answering a blind ad.)

I would appreciate an opportunity to talk with you soon about how I could contribute to your organization through my skills and experience related to engineering, law enforcement, and security.

As you will see from my resume, I offer experience in dealing with people of all cultures, and I am knowledgeable of customs in many different countries.

My management skills are extensive. In one job I excelled as Air Operations Manager involved in planning and managing numerous missions to Iraq with total success. Among the many medals and awards I have received have been the Armed Forces Expeditionary Medal for the War on Terror.

HAZMAT qualified and an expert with several weapons, I have taught various foreign and domestic light weapons. While in Iraq I taught patrolling to Iraqi police and organized law enforcement activities after participating in the disarming, retraining, and re-arming of Iraqi police. During the War on Terror I used my explosives expertise to blow up ammunitions dumps and bunkers, and as a Special Forces Engineer I have contributed my expertise of explosives during civil engineering projects throughout the Middle East.

You would find me in person to be a congenial individual with excellent communication skills. I can provide outstanding references. I am single and willing to relocate according to your needs.

I hope you will welcome my call soon to arrange a brief meeting at your convenience to discuss your current and future needs and how I might serve them. Thank you in advance for your time.

Yours sincerely,

Francis Riley

Alternate last paragraph:
I hope you will call or write me soon to suggest a time convenient for us to meet and discuss your current and future needs and how I might serve them. Thank you in advance for your time.

FRANCIS RILEY

1110½ Hay Street, Fayetteville, NC 28305   •   preppub@aol.com   •   (910) 483-6611

OBJECTIVE
To offer a broad base of experience in supervising and leading personnel, the ability to work under pressure and deadlines, and a high degree of initiative and self motivation to an organization that can use a mature professional who sets the standard.

EXPERIENCE
Earned a reputation as a dedicated and selfless individual who could be counted on for the difficult jobs and for strong leadership under pressure, U.S. Army:
ADVISOR and **TRAINING SPECIALIST.** Fort Benning, GA (2004-present). Was the subject matter expert on my Special Forces Detachment for planning engineering and demolitions operations while also training/advising American, allied, and foreign national personnel; instructed 80 indigenous personnel in light infantry techniques.
- Managed combat/civil engineering projects.

SPECIAL PROJECT: **SPECIAL FORCES ENGINEERING SERGEANT & TRAINING SUPERVISOR.** Iraq (2002-03). Earned an Army Achievement Medal and was evaluated as a team player with extremely high standards while supervising and instructing operations including infiltration and return from special areas by air, land, or sea; trained, advised, and led local national personnel when working outside of the U.S.
- Developed logistical and supply support plans for a six-month mission in Iraq and achieved important results in a variety of areas: supervised repair of 30 pieces of heavy road repair equipment, organized a sanitation department for the country's third largest city, trained and supervised 100 road crew workers, returned with no losses of equipment, and worked with non-government agencies to provide civil support.
- Taught patrolling to Iraqi police and organized law enforcement activities; disarmed, retrained, and re-armed Iraqi police; assisted in a weapons buy-back program.

SPECIAL FORCES ENGINEER and **TRAINING SPECIALIST.** Fort Campbell, KY (2000-02). Planned, supervised, and personally conducted training for both American and foreign students in specialized subject matter which included foreign internal defense.
- Earned the respect and praise of superiors as an effective and skilled instructor while leading classes including engineering, demolitions, land navigation, and marksmanship.
- Awarded Special Forces Tab, August 2000.

COMBAT ENGINEER. Fort Drum, NY (1997-99). Received an Army Commendation Medal for my accomplishments.

EDUCATION & TRAINING
Completing requirements for an associate's degree in Liberal Arts.
Excelled in a broad range of training programs which included the following:
Primary Leadership Development Course   U.S. Army Airborne School
Combat Engineer Training   Combat Lifesaving Course
Special Forces Engineering Course for Supervisory Personnel
Air Movement Operations and Air Transportation of Hazardous Materials Course

SPECIAL SKILLS
Qualified as expert with M16 and M4 rifles and M9 Barretta pistol.
HAZMAT qualified; PADI certified as Open Water Diver; logged 20 hours as a private pilot.

PERSONAL
Have traveled extensively. Physically fit and enjoy active sports such as kayaking and skiing. Secret security clearance. Have earned numerous medals including the Armed Forces Expeditionary Medal for Korea and War on Terror.

Date

Exact Name of Person
Exact Title
Exact Name of Company
Address
City, State, Zip

Dear Exact Name of Person (or Dear Sir or Madam if answering a blind ad):

I would appreciate an opportunity to talk with you soon about how I could contribute to your organization through my distinguished background of accomplishments and experience in the management of maintenance, construction, and renovation projects.

As you will see from my enclosed resume, I offer a strong history of reducing costs, bringing projects in on time, and handling the complexities of large-scale domestic and off-shore construction and renovation projects. In my most recent position as Senior Facilities Engineer for Mandell Products in San Diego, I oversaw all phases of physical plant expansion and renovation projects for this 1,400-employee manufacturing plant.

Earlier as the Manager for Facilities Engineering for Fruit of the Loom in San Diego, I provided expertise during a period of major growth and expansion for this consumer goods manufacturer with 65 sites. I managed construction projects of up to 100,000 square feet in the Pacific Islands to include developing methods for reducing property insurance costs while guaranteeing the quality and timeliness of renovation and building activities. Prior to my promotion to that position, as a Senior Facilities Engineer I managed a $3.5 million asbestos abatement program, developed maintenance management training programs, reduced maintenance expenses, and managed multiple plant projects.

If you can use a positive, results-oriented manager who enjoys challenges and meets deadlines with precision and enthusiasm, I hope you will contact me soon so that we might discuss your needs. I can assure you in advance that I have an excellent reputation and would quickly become a valuable asset to your company.

Sincerely,

Leonard Robinson

LEONARD ROBINSON

1110½ Hay Street, Fayetteville, NC 28305 • preppub@aol.com • (910) 483-6611

OBJECTIVE

To offer a strong background of distinguished accomplishments in the areas of equipment and facilities construction, maintenance, and renovation to an organization that can benefit from my management experience in project engineering and maintenance.

EDUCATION

B.S., Aircraft Maintenance Engineering, University of San Diego, San Diego, CA, 1996.

EXPERIENCE

Have built a reputation as a hard-charging and innovative management professional:
SENIOR FACILITIES ENGINEER and **MAINTENANCE MANAGER.** Mandell Products, San Diego, CA (2002-present). After two years as the manager of 17 electrical and mechanical technicians completing plant maintenance and capital renovations, was promoted to oversee all phases of improvements to the physical plant including expansion and renovation projects.

- Administer on-going renovations to an 800,000 square-foot non-union plant with 1,400 employees producing automotive air and oil filters for both original equipment and aftermarket customers.
- Apply my expertise with EPA regulations, fire protection, and safety while reducing property insurance costs and increasing employee safety through renovations to the fire and emergency alarm systems.
- Negotiate fees and make spot purchases which reduced expenses for utilities.
- Assisted in the completion and start up of a 500,000-square-foot distribution center.
- As Maintenance Manager from 2002-04, was interim manager of the electrical and environmental departments and organized the maintenance department.
- Develop and implement long-range plans for plant HVAC, lighting, and roofing installations.

MANAGER FOR FACILITIES ENGINEERING. Fruit of the Loom, San Diego, CA (1988-02). Was promoted to manage three engineers and oversee the construction and renovation of facilities for this rapidly growing and expanding organization after approximately eight years as Senior Facilities Engineer.

- Made vital contributions which allowed this consumer goods manufacturer to expand to 65 plants; as manager for construction projects in the Pacific Islands, oversaw a $10 million operational budget for the company in 2000. Developed innovative ideas which resulted in a $240,000 cost reduction for property insurance for the 65 facilities.
- Supervised engineers involved in construction, renovation, environmental, and maintenance projects in both domestic and off-shore facilities.
- As Senior Facilities Engineer from 1988-96, provided oversight for capital projects related to plant and equipment improvements including developing and implementing fire protection programs, production improvements, EPA compliance, and expansions.
- Managed a $3.5 million asbestos abatement program for domestic and offshore facilities.
- Reduced plant maintenance budgets by $200,000; developed maintenance management and training programs. Coordinated a waste incineration and steam generation installation and start up with the city of Scottsdale, AZ.

Highlights of other experience: Excelled in positions which included Director of Maintenance, Engineering, and Construction; Plant Industrial Engineer and Division Material Handling Engineer; Facilities Planning and Projects Engineer; and Field Engineer.

PERSONAL

Am available for relocation according to employer needs. Enjoy traveling and becoming familiar with other cultures. Respond to challenge with determination to excel.

Date

Exact Name of Person
Title or Position
Exact Name of Company
Address
City, State, Zip

Dear Exact Name of Person: (or Dear Sir or Madam if answering a blind ad.)

At the recommendation of Mr. Bob Grady, I am sending you a resume to indicate my interest in the position of Instructor at the Mercedes Performance Center.

As you will see from my resume, I offer an extensive background in the automotive industry and have specialized in Mercedes maintenance, service, and repair for the past eight years. I became associated with Mercedes because, while serving as an Automotive Mechanic and Heavy Equipment Mechanic Supervisor with the U.S. Army and U.S. Government, I bought a Mercedes while stationed in Germany. I quickly became acquainted with the superior abilities of this driving machine, and I decided that I would pursue employment with the Mercedes organization after leaving the military.

In my current position as a Mercedes Technician with San Jose Mercedes of CA, I have been recognized as one of Mercedes' most skilled technicians. I received a letter from the General Manager of Mercedes of the Western Region, commending me for achieving one of the company's highest Customer Satisfaction Index (CSI) scores in the Western Region.

Although I am excelling in my current position, I feel I could make significant contributions to Western in some capacity in which I am involved in training other technicians to "do it right, the first time." Prior to joining the Mercedes organization, I gained extensive experience as a Technical Instructor while serving in the U.S. Army and working for the U.S. Government. At Fort Belvoir, VA, and at locations in Germany, I provided formal classroom instruction as well as hands-on field training to military and civilian personnel at multiple sites. While earning numerous awards for technical expertise as well as safety achievements, I excelled in extensive technical training which included the U.S. Army Engineer School and the Heavy Equipment Mechanic School.

I would appreciate your advising me about the next step I should take in exploring the possibility of becoming an Instructor at the Mercedes Performance Center. I can provide outstanding references at the appropriate time.

Sincerely,

Nicholas Decker

NICHOLAS DECKER

1110½ Hay Street, Fayetteville, NC 28305   •   preppub@aol.com   •   (910) 483-6611

OBJECTIVE   To contribute to an organization that can use a highly skilled automotive troubleshooter and problem solver with specialized expertise related to Mercedes along with experience in training others in classroom and field settings.

CERTIFICATIONS ACT Certified Mercedes Master Technician; ASE Certified Master Technician

**MERCEDES
TRAINING**
Completed Mercedes of North America Service Training at the Mercedes Central Region Training Center and the Southern Region Training Center, 1998-present.
- Programs included classroom instruction in Mercedes theory and computer systems as well as hands-on experience in diagnosis, repair, and programming of Mercedes systems.

EDUCATION
Excelled academically (4.0 GPA) while completing more than two years of college course work at College of the Canyons, Golden State University, and Central Texas College.
Completed **Associate's degree equivalent in Automotive Service and Repair,** College City of San Francisco, CA, 1996-98.
- Two-year program included instruction in automotive theory and systems repair as well as experience in troubleshooting, repair, and rebuilding of automotive systems.

Completed extensive technical training sponsored by the U.S. Army including **U.S. Army Engineer School and Heavy Equipment Mechanic School;** gained skills related to performing general support-level repairs on military equipment including combustion-powered vehicles such as 1¼ ton thru 22½ ton trucks, truck tractors, semi trailers; combat and combat-support vehicles including personnel carriers and armored vehicle bridge launchers (AVLB).
- Became skilled in troubleshooting brakes, steering, fuel injection, and hydraulics using test measurement and diagnostic equipment (TMDE) such as pressure gauges, dial indicators, and specialized test equipment (STE/ICE).

EXPERIENCE
MERCEDES TECHNICIAN. San Jose, Santa Clara, and San Francisco, CA (1996-present). Have been recognized as one of Mercedes' most skilled technicians.
Reputation as a technical expert: Have become skilled at all aspects of troubleshooting, servicing, and repairing Mercedes as well as diagnosing, servicing, and repairing rear-wheel drive systems. Utilize DIS/TIS tester to aid in diagnosis process. Analyze, repair, and adjust two- and four-wheel alignment systems.

AUTOMOTIVE MECHANIC & HEAVY EQUIPMENT MECHANIC SUPERVISOR. U.S. Government, Germany and the U.S. (1989-95). Trained and supervised mechanics in performing the full range of overhaul, repair, and rebuild of vehicles and generators. Also delivered prepositioned equipment used for REFORGER to sites throughout Europe.
- Directed maintenance and inspection programs; performed repairs, overhauls, and rebuilds of 12-cylinder, 2000-hp engines requiring unusually precise repairing, fitting, and adjusting of moving parts. Trained and supervised dozens of mechanics.

TECHNICAL INSTRUCTOR & HEAVY EQUIPMENT MECHANIC. U.S. Government, Fort Belvoir, VA, and locations in Germany (1983-89). At a major training site for military personnel, provided formal classroom instruction as well as hands-on field training to military and civilian personnel at multiple sites.

PERSONAL
Resourceful problem solver. Strong personal initiative. Excellent references. Have been evaluated as a highly motivated leader whose technical competence surpasses expectations.

Date

Exact Name of Person
Title or Position
Exact Name of Company
Address
City, State, Zip

AVIATION MAINTENANCE CREW CHIEF

Dear Exact Name of Person: (or Dear Sir or Madam if answering a blind ad.)

With the enclosed resume, I would like to express my interest in exploring employment opportunities with your organization.

As you will see from my resume, I have excelled in the aviation engineering and maintenance field while serving my country in the U.S. Army. The recipient of numerous medals and awards recognizing my leadership and creativity as a manager, I was credited with saving time and money through procedures I established for maintenance and troubleshooting. In one position as a Quality Assurance Inspector, I maintained flawless accountability of $16 million in aircraft. In another position as a Helicopter Mechanic, I became proficient in keeping helicopters operational in the combat environment of Iraq. I was handpicked for my most recent position as Aviation Maintenance Crew Chief because of my technical expertise and strong supervisory skills.

I hope you will welcome my call soon to arrange a brief meeting to discuss your current and future needs and how I might serve them. Thank you in advance for your time.

Sincerely,

Tristen Hancock

Alternate last paragraph:
I hope you will call or write me soon to suggest a time convenient for us to meet and discuss your current and future needs and how I might serve them. Thank you in advance for your time.

TRISTEN HANCOCK

1110½ Hay Street, Fayetteville, NC 28305　　•　　preppub@aol.com　　•　　(910) 483-6611

OBJECTIVE

To contribute to an organization that can a skilled, knowledgeable aviation mechanic with the ability to motivate and supervise and effectively manage time and resources.

EDUCATION & TRAINING

College: Completed 1½ years of study, **Engineering**, Casper College, Casper, WY.
Technical Training: Received U.S. Army training which included the 15-week Attack Helicopter Repair Course as well as other programs in lifesaving.
Leadership Training: Completed the Army's **Primary Leadership Development Course** which emphasizes leadership, communication, resource management, and technical skills.

AIRCRAFT & TECHNICAL EXPERTISE

Through training and experience, have developed extensive knowledge which includes:
Aircraft: AH-64A Apache helicopter and UH-60 Blackhawk helicopter
Equipment and systems: Use Aviation Ground Power Unit (AGPU), Engine Flush Aviation Equipment, and work on GE 701-C engines (Apache helicopters)

EXPERIENCE

Advanced ahead of my peers to supervisory roles while serving in the U.S. Army:
AVIATION MAINTENANCE CREW CHIEF. Fort Rucker, AL (2004-present). Officially cited for my initiative, dedication, and self-motivation, supervised three associates in maintenance in support of eight Apache helicopters and equipment in excess of $60 million.
* Was credited with saving time and money by establishing procedures for cleaning vital bolts, washers, and other components which previously had been replaced.
* Supervised and replaced GE 701-C engines, transmissions, gear boxes, and blades.
* Earned respect for sound judgment and contagious enthusiasm for meeting short notices and ensuring aircraft are maintained and ready for service at all times.
* Continue to emphasize safety in the work place with the result that no unit ever suffered an accident or serious safety violation under my leadership.

MAINTENANCE TEAM LEADER & QUALITY ASSURANCE INSPECTOR. Germany (2003-04). Trained and supervised eight people in an Apache helicopter maintenance facility with responsibility for timely completion of scheduled as well as unscheduled maintenance.
* Controlled $250,000 in equipment in support of aircraft worth $16 million each.
* Provided 250- and 500-hour phase maintenance which included inspection as well as replacement of major components. Performed strict quality assurance inspections according to precise specifications; became known as an astute problem solver.

HELICOPTER MECHANIC. Fort Rucker, AL, and Iraq (1999-03). Built and refined my technical, mechanical, and leadership skills while becoming known as a reliable young professional who could be counted on no matter how dangerous or difficult the situation.
* Displayed my ability to work under pressure during an assignment in Iraq where 12-hour days were the norm in a war-torn area of operations.
* Became proficient in such activities as removing, re-installing, and replacing helicopter engines, transmissions, blades, auxiliary power units, main rotor heads, Environmental Control Units, hydraulic components, and structure panels.
* Used tools, power tools, wrenches, special tools, and pneumatic tools while working with hoists and up to 10-ton cranes; became familiar with corrosion control.
* As custodian of the unit tool room, played a significant role in recognition with Army Aviation Association "Unit of the Year" and "Masters of Readiness" awards in 1999.

PERSONAL

Earned several honors including U.S. Army Commendation and National Defense Service Medals and two Army Achievement Medals. Excellent work ethic and initiative.

Date

Exact Name of Person
Exact Title
Exact Name of Company
Address
City, State, Zip

Dear Exact Name of Person (or Dear Sir or Madam if answering a blind ad):

With the enclosed resume, I would like to express my interest in exploring employment opportunities with your organization.

As you will see from my resume, I gained experience in the biomedical engineering field while serving in the U.S. Army as a Biomedical Equipment Technician. In that capacity, I expertly used schematics and test equipment while examining equipment for defective parts, malfunctioning components, and broken connections.

After I left the Army, I joined a prominent organization in Delaware, and I developed and managed the first-ever biomedical equipment repair program for Milford Memorial Hospital. Subsequently as a Field Service Engineer I worked as a member of a six-person team of technicians in the electromedical division.

I was aggressively recruited by my current employer to represent the company to 27 hospitals throughout Delaware and New Jersey. Although I am excelling in my job which involves the sale of biomedical and imaging equipment, and I can provide outstanding references at the appropriate time, I am exploring opportunities to return to the technical and mechanical aspects of the biomedical equipment field. I hold an A.A.S. degree in Biomedical Engineering, and I was also the Distinguished Graduate of a 30-week course in advanced biomedical equipment repair.

I hope you will welcome my call soon to arrange a brief meeting to discuss your current and future needs and how I might serve them. Thank you in advance for your time.

Sincerely,

Dale Wheeler

Alternate last paragraph:
I hope you will call or write me soon to suggest a time convenient for us to meet and discuss your current and future needs and how I might serve them. Thank you in advance for your time.

DALE WHEELER

1110½ Hay Street, Fayetteville, NC 28305   •   preppub@aol.com   •   (910) 483-6611

OBJECTIVE

To apply my outstanding organizational skills and my proven ability to develop excellent customer relations through strong customer service, along with my specialized experience in the field of medical sales.

EXPERIENCE

IMAGING SALES SPECIALIST. Delaware Imaging Systems, Dover, DE (2001-present). Represent the company to 37 hospitals while covering all of Delaware and most areas of the state of New Jersey, selling and providing inservice support for cineradiographic film used in cardiac catheterization labs.
- Was singled out for "Outstanding Performance Awards" for the past few years for meeting corporate budget guidelines.
- Steadily increased territory sales to $1.7 million for 2004 from $1.5 million in 2003 in an area where the previous person's sales had only reached $1.1 million.
- Accomplished growth to become the third largest territory in the country while staying under budget in a time when some areas have seen declines in sales.
- Have earned the trust and confidence of my customers by always being available and able to solve any problems they encounter. Excelled in corporate training programs emphasizing professional sales and territorial management techniques.

FIELD SERVICE ENGINEER. American Medical Systems, Inc., Dover, DE (2000-01). As a member of a six-person team of technicians in the electromedical division, installed, repaired, and performed preventive maintenance on equipment including patent monitoring and operating room systems. Became known for my strong customer service and technical abilities.

CONSULTANT & BIOMEDICAL EQUIPMENT TECHNICIAN. Northeastern Medical Services, Newark, DE (1999-00). Developed and managed the first-ever biomedical equipment repair program for Milford Memorial Hospital in Milford, DE, as the liaison between the hospital and service company.
- Performed preventive maintenance, repairs, and electrical safety checks as well as researching and maintaining equipment repair histories.
- Set up a filing system and accounted for all equipment.

BIOMEDICAL EQUIPMENT REPAIR SPECIALIST & SHIFT SUPERVISOR. U.S. Army, Fort Stewart, GA (1997-99). At the nation's military bases, performed troubleshooting, repairs, and maintenance on state-of-the-art medical equipment; supervised technicians.
- Earned recognition for cheerfully contributing many hours of overtime.
- Was often singled out to provide advice and assistance.
- Examined equipment for defective parts, malfunctioning components, misalignments, and broken or loose connections. Used schematic diagrams and test equipment while troubleshooting. Maintained log books and prepared automated work orders.

BIOMEDICAL EQUIPMENT TECHNICIAN. U.S. Army, Fort Polk, LA (1995-97). Earned several awards for outstanding technical skills and job performance.
- Scored a perfect 100% on an occupational skills test, a rare achievement.

EDUCATION & TRAINING

A.A.S. degree in Biomedical Engineering, Delaware State University, Dover, DE, 1997.
- Was the Distinguished Graduate of a 30-week course in advanced biomedical equipment repair with a 96% GPA.

PERSONAL

Work well with others and offer outstanding communication and interpersonal skills.

Date

Exact Name of Person
Title or Position
Exact Name of Company
Address
City, State, Zip

CHEMICAL ENGINEER
with experience in
civil engineering &
construction program
management

Dear Exact Name of Person: (or Dear Sir or Madam if answering a blind ad.)

I would appreciate an opportunity to talk with you soon about how I could benefit your company through my superior background in engineering management, combined with my excellent problem-solving experience as a construction project manager.

While proudly serving my country in the U.S. Air Force, I progressed rapidly in leadership positions requiring keen problem-solving ability and analytical skills. I successfully managed construction projects working with $100 million-dollar budgets. I am very proud of my identification of fund duplication and ineffective programs which saved the government over four million dollars.

A chemical engineer and proven manager, I can offer you my ability to solve the toughest of problems, particularly where technical and mathematical abilities are crucial.

Innovative and determined, I won't give up until the job is done and I have developed a reputation as one who can be counted on to consistently exceed goals and do the "impossible" job.

I hope you will welcome my call soon to arrange a brief meeting at your convenience to discuss your current and future needs and how I might serve them. Thank you in advance for your time.

Sincerely yours,

Gregory Chapman

Alternate last paragraph:
I hope you will call or write me soon to suggest a time convenient for us to meet and discuss your current and future needs and how I might serve them. Thank you in advance for your time.

GREGORY CHAPMAN

1110½ Hay Street, Fayetteville, NC 28305   •   preppub@aol.com   •   (910) 483-6611

OBJECTIVE

To offer my chemical engineering expertise and management experience and problem-solving skills to an organization in need of a top-notch industrial manager and chemical engineer.

EXPERIENCE

In this "track record" of achievement with the U.S. Air Force, I have worked with budgets exceeding $100 million dollars while supervising staffs of more than 150 people in 16 different in job specialties.

ENGINEERING & CONSTRUCTION PROGRAM MANAGER. U.S. Air Force, Moron AB, Spain (2003-04). Coordinated an annual one billion-dollar program for the Army, Air Force, and Navy in Europe while serving as the "resident expert" on military construction laws and foreign currency.
*   Was instrumental in saving the government over $4 million.
*   Revised the method used for prioritizing engineering projects for all of Europe.

CHIEF OF CIVIL ENGINEERING OPERATION & AIRFIELD MAINTENANCE SUPERVISOR. U.S. Air Force, Robins AFB, GA (2001-03). Supervised 156 people in 17 different job specialties involved in operating and maintaining airfield pavements, buildings, and utility systems.
*   Implemented a model program on restoration and maintenance of heating, ventilating, and air conditioning which is now in use worldwide.
*   Transformed a substandard supply system, reducing average time to acquire supplies from 270 to 90 days.

COLLEGE INSTRUCTOR. Central Texas College campus at Robins AFB, GA (2000-01). Was recognized as one of the top instructors in physics and nuclear physics.

STRATEGIC PLANNER/REQUIREMENTS BRANCH CHIEF. U.S. Air Force, Moron AB, Spain (1997-99). Was promoted to this top-level strategic planning job supervising a staff of engineers and executives. Analyzed Air Force requirements for personnel and support programs.
*   Identified $4 billion in duplicated costs.
*   "Sold" the Air Force on innovative new budgeting procedures.

CONGRESSIONAL LIAISON & EUROPEAN CONSTRUCTION PROGRAM MANAGER. U.S. Air Force, Moron AB, Spain (1994-97). Worked closely with the Pentagon and Congressional staffs while analyzing and coordinating all Air Force construction throughout Europe.
*   Developed a new low-cost security system for executives' residences.
*   Advocated and obtained funding for a new renovation program.

Other experience: U.S. Air Force. Excelled in "line" and "staff" roles.

EDUCATION

M.S. degree, Engineering Management, University of Denver, CO, 1993.
*   Graduated with a perfect 4.0 grade point average.
B.S. degree, Chemical Engineering, University of Georgia, Athens, GA, 1985.

PERSONAL

Read, speak, and write Spanish. Am a problem solver who will not give up until the job is done. Am extremely knowledgeable about federal budget preparation and justification as well as defense contracting and supply procurement. Held a Top Secret security clearance. Easily adjust to new environments.

Exact Name of Person
Title or Position
Name of Company
Address
City, State, Zip

CHEMICAL ENGINEER
with experience as a
project director

Dear Exact Name of Person: (or Dear Sir or Madam if answering a blind ad.)

I would appreciate an opportunity to talk with you soon about how I could contribute to your organization through my expertise related to production management, project development and control, and computer expert systems and applications utilization.

Having attained the rank of Major in the U.S. Army, I offer a "track record" of accomplishments in positions of increasing responsibility requiring analytical, problem-solving, and decision-making skills.

In my present job as a Project Director, I conducted extensive research followed by planning a training program for 900 national guard personnel located in geographically separated locations. I planned for the most effective use of funds, oversaw the relocation of personnel to conduct the training, and am excelling in managing this complex project.

You will see by my resume that I have extensive experience in managing as many as 80 employees, multimillion-dollar inventories of high-tech equipment, and in applying my technical production and computer operations knowledge.

I hope you will welcome my call soon to arrange a brief meeting at your convenience to discuss your current and future needs and how I might serve them. Thank you in advance for your time.

Sincerely yours,

Tyler Chrisean

Alternate last paragraph:
I hope you will call or write soon to suggest a time convenient for us to meet and discuss your current and future needs and how I might serve them. Thank you in advance for your time.

TYLER CHRISEAN

1110½ Hay Street, Fayetteville, NC 28305 • preppub@aol.com • (910) 483-6611

OBJECTIVE

To apply my large-scale project development and management expertise acquired in a distinguished career as a senior military officer while contributing to an organization through my analytical and problem-solving abilities.

EDUCATION & TRAINING

M.S., Operations Research, Methodist College, Fayetteville, NC, 2003.
B.S., Chemical Engineering, Kettering University, Flint, MI.
Excelled in more than three years of training for military executives.

EXPERIENCE

PROJECT DIRECTOR. U.S. Army, Fort Stewart, GA (2004-present). Analyzed data which evaluated the requirements for a program supporting 900 national guard personnel.
*   Developed a comprehensive training project. Remained within a $2 million budget.

TECHNICAL CONTROL OPERATIONS MANAGER. U.S. Army, Fort Campbell, KY (2003-04). Gained experience working with multilevel staff and management while coordinating high-tech computerized operations. Excelled in high-pressure situations requiring "split-second" decisions. Developed complex and realistic computer simulations.

Advanced in Analysis/Program Development, U.S. Army, Fort Bragg, NC:
TECHNICAL ADVISOR. (2001-03). Learned how to deal effectively with civilian and military government officials while analyzing operational plans and determining that proposed combat scenarios met policy/capabilities standards.
*   Conducted a study impacting on design/safety standards for vehicles.

COMPUTER SIMULATION PROJECT ANALYST. (1999-01). Analyzed human and material resources acquisition and utilization data and developed methods and computer simulations used in planning future contingencies and operations.

Earned promotion in Management/Supervisory roles, U.S. Army, Korea:
GENERAL MANAGER. (1998-99). Controlled functional areas including maintenance, supply, and food service as well as supervising 100 employees maintaining $16 million in equipment. Applied time management skills and developed junior leaders which allowed the company to succeed despite severe personnel shortages.

MAINTENANCE MANAGER. (1996-98). Directed activities in a facility charged with maintaining 143 wheeled and 19 track vehicles; managed supply support, budgeting, inspections of facilities, and acquisitions. Maintained a 98% level of "on hand" repair parts.

PRODUCTION SUPERVISOR. Samsung Corporation, Richmond, VA (1994-95). Managed 10 employees on a mechanical production line in a facility producing multilayer circuit boards; ensured quality control standards were met. Evaluated performance and trained employees in the latest techniques. Designed a system for ensuring uniform thickness of circuit boards.

SPECIAL SKILLS & KNOWLEDGE

Offer extensive experience in developing computer modeling methods and applications as well as programming applications, and using simulations for training and in "real-world" situations.
Familiar with government contracting and procurement processes.

PERSONAL

Entrusted with a **Top Secret** security clearance. Was recognized with several medals for expertise as a technical analyst and researcher. Will relocate.

Exact Name of Person
Title or Position
Name of Company
Address
City, State, Zip

CHEMICAL ENGINEER

with experience as a
senior polymer &
adhesives chemist

Dear Exact Name of Person: (or Dear Sir or Madam if answering a blind ad.)

With the enclosed resume, I present my extensive experience and talent as a Chemical, Polymer, and Adhesive Specialist possessing exceptional technical abilities that have been proven in a wide variety of research laboratories and manufacturing environments.

I am currently excelling as a Senior Polymer & Adhesives Chemist for New Balance's Lawrence, MA manufacturing facility, where I formulate a broad range of chemicals and polymer adhesives used for bonding leather, nylon, polyester, cotton, and other fabrics to vulcanized rubber substrates to facilitate the manufacture of new product lines and to improve existing product lines.

In earlier positions, I have made substantial contributions in areas of technical knowledge advancement through applied research which improved efficiencies in existing products and processes, and also resulted in the introduction of newly developed products. I have extensive experience with customer service and technical support, both over the phone and at customer facilities. I am an accomplished problem-solver, innovative thinker, and hands-on, results-oriented individual. I possess extensive experience in project management, research benchwork, pilot scale-up to full production, and formulation design to meet specific end-use requirements. I have a capacity for accuracy and for detail, and I like to make systems and processes operate efficiently and precisely.

Although I am highly regarded by my present employer and can provide excellent personal and professional references at the appropriate time, I am interested in exploring career opportunities in a larger metropolitan area. I am not limiting my job search to one specific type of position, consequently I welcome opportunities to explore options in any field where my chemical, scientific, technical, business, manufacturing and people skills, knowledge, and experience can be fully utilized.

I can assure you in advance that I have an outstanding reputation and would quickly become a valuable asset to your operation. I am available to discuss employment opportunities at your earliest convenience.

Sincerely,

Clement Jackson

CLEMENT JACKSON

1110½ Hay Street, Fayetteville, NC 28305   •   preppub@aol.com   •   (910) 483-6611

OBJECTIVE   To technologically advance an organization seeking a talented Chemical, Polymer, and Adhesive Specialist with exceptional technical and managerial skills who is experienced in product/process improvement, manufacturing optimization, and innovative problem-solving.

EDUCATION   **B.S., Chemical Engineering, concentrations in Chemistry, Mathematics, Geology, and Life Science**, Drake University, Des Moines, IA, 1988.

EXPERIENCE   **SENIOR POLYMER & ADHESIVES CHEMIST.** New Balance Factory, Lawrence, MA (2004-present). Perform a variety of research and development, supervisory, and project management tasks while developing and producing water-based polymer adhesives for this large footwear manufacturer. Manage eight employees.

- Develop, manage, and implement multiple projects with emphasis on integrating new products and processes into the existing manufacturing system. Develop new latex polymer adhesives for bonding leather, nylon, polyester, cotton, and other fabrics to vulcanized rubber substrates.

RESEARCH & DEVELOPMENT MANAGER. New England Research Corporation, Hanover, MA (2001-04). Provided project management, supervisory oversight, formulation development, and customer support services for this busy custom formulator and compounder of latex polymer products. Created latex polymer formulations to customers' specifications.

SENIOR POLYMER CHEMIST. Big Apple Laboratories, Albany, NY (1999-01). Tasked with streamlining and updating chemical and polymer mixing processes, improving overall quality, and increasing production for this manufacturer of pharmaceutical polymer products.

- Developed process improvements and modifications in chemical and polymer formulations which resulted in a 35% increase in production yield rates.
- Determined the cause of and resolved a serious product defect, forestalling a massive product recall which would have cost the company millions of dollars.

TECHNICAL SERVICE REPRESENTATIVE. Goodyear Rubber & Latex Company, Philadelphia, PA (1994-98). Provided technical assistance to manufacturing customers who purchased plantation latex. Averted an impending lawsuit which could have cost Goodyear hundreds of thousands of dollars, by designing and directing comparative testing evaluations to demonstrate that product defects were not a result of defective latex supplied by Goodyear.

ASSISTANT TECHNICAL MANAGER. United National Corporation, Philadelphia, PA (1992-94). Responsible for chemical inventory control, formulation of polymer products, and ensuring that all needed materials were provided to keep production lines optimum for this large manufacturing facility, which produced 3 million specialty advertising balloons daily.

- Created a new line of elastic inks used for printing onto specialty advertising balloons. The inks were capable of stretching without cracking or chipping during balloon inflation.
- Developed an impermeable barrier coating for specialty advertising balloons that retained helium for seven days; latex balloons normally lose helium after only 8 to 12 hours.

ADHESIVES CHEMIST. American Latex & Chemical Corporation, Philadelphia, PA (1988-92). Contributed to this large custom formulating and compounding operation by formulating a diverse line of water-based polymer adhesives to meet customers' requirements.

PERSONAL   Excellent personal and professional references are available upon request.

CAREER CHANGE

Date

Exact Name of Person
Title or Position
Exact Name of Company
Address
City, State, Zip

CHIEF ENGINEER
A distinguished
military
professional is
making a career
change into the
private sector.

Dear Exact Name of Person: (or Dear Sir or Madam if answering a blind ad.)

I would appreciate an opportunity to talk with you soon about how I could contribute to your organization through my background as one of the U.S. Army's leading experts in nuclear weapons system maintenance, safety, operations, and training.

I have a unique background as a military officer who has become proficient in two distinct and highly technical career fields. Although over the past two years I have transferred to the field of marine engineering and rapidly advanced to Chief Engineer, you will see by looking at my enclosed resume that the bulk of my experience has been in the management of nuclear weapons transportation, inspection, operation, and technical assistance.

Widely recognized as an expert and called on for my advice by executives at high levels, I was personally involved in the large-scale project of removing chemical and nuclear weapons from Europe. This involved seeing to all the details of locating the proper containers, making the transportation arrangements, finding adequate storage sites, and overseeing the actual transfer.

You would find me to be a congenial person who offers an innate ability to work well with people and inspire them to peak performance. I believe strongly in leadership by example and excel in getting the most out of scarce resources.

I hope you will welcome my call soon to arrange a brief meeting at your convenience to discuss your current and future needs and how I might serve them. Thank you in advance for your time.

Sincerely yours,

Ryan Christensen

Alternate last paragraph:
I hope you will call or write me soon to suggest a time convenient for us to meet and discuss your current and future needs and how I might serve them. Thank you in advance for your time.

RYAN CHRISTENSEN

1110½ Hay Street, Fayetteville, NC 28305 • preppub@aol.com • (910) 483-6611

OBJECTIVE

To offer my technical expertise and leadership abilities to an organization that can use a mature professional who has excelled as a military officer in sensitive engineering operations.

EXPERIENCE

Earned advancement ahead of my peers and a reputation as one of the most knowledgeable experts in two highly technical career fields, U.S. Army:

CHIEF ENGINEER. Fort Bragg, NC (2004-present). Evaluated as having exceptional potential, was promoted and quickly mastered the demands of directing the operation, maintenance, repair, and overhaul of machinery and equipment valued in excess of $6 million.

- Inspected machinery and made decisions on the extent and nature of repairs, prepared maintenance reports/work orders, and directed the internal repair parts inventories.
- Maintained an exceptional 100% operational rate during a 230-day assignment to Iraq.

ENGINEERING OFFICER and **SUPPLY MANAGER.** Fort Bragg, NC (2003-04). Handled a wide range of activities for a 272-foot ocean-going logistics support vessel including guaranteeing safe and efficient operation of the engine department and machinery at sea.

- Maintained the ship's $4 million internal inventory of equipment, uniforms, and supplies.

SPECIAL WEAPONS TECHNICIAN. Italy (1999-02). Widely recognized as an expert in the field, provided senior executives with sound advice and guidance on matters related to the transportation, status reporting, and stockpile emergency verification of nuclear weapons.

- Personally ensured the success of automating nuclear logistics reporting by seeing that all Army units in Europe received applicable software and were on line and using it.
- Oversaw a major project upgrading chemical weapons systems in place throughout Europe: in just 11 weeks repaired 315 vehicles which allowed 600 to be in use.

DIRECTOR, NUCLEAR WEAPONS MAINTENANCE ACTIVITIES. Fort Snelling, MN (1997-99). In a position normally reserved for a higher-ranking professional, monitored training and operational readiness of personnel in the specialized nuclear weapons field including analyzing programs and proposing changes which would correct problem areas.

- Managed logistics support for at least 17 separate companies throughout the region.
- Coordinated a large-scale manpower study: used the results to revise guidelines.
- Was recognized as **the** Army expert on technical standards for nuclear-capable units. Managed the training programs for all nuclear weapons handlers for 144 companies.

NUCLEAR WEAPONS TECHNICIAN. Italy (1994-97). Became widely recognized as one of the most technically proficient and knowledgeable professionals in my field of training, evaluating, and assisting units throughout Germany and the Netherlands.

- Initiated a quarterly technical assistance visitation program which became an integral part of the parent organization's regular operations.

EDUCATION & TRAINING LICENSES

Completed three years of college course work in liberal arts.

Excelled in advanced training for military executives in areas including NATO Nuclear Policy, nuclear weapons surveillance (quality auditing), and Italian language and culture.

Licensed by the U.S. Army as a Chief Engineer for Class A1 vessels and as an Assistant Chief Engineer on Class A2 vessels.

Earned EPA certification as a Universal Technician for processing CFC/HCFC refrigerants.

PERSONAL

Awarded numerous medals for my accomplishments as an advisor, technical subject matter expert, and manager. Was entrusted with a Top Secret security clearance with BI.

CAREER CHANGE

Date

Exact Name of Person
Title or Position
Exact Name of Company
Address
City, State, Zip

CHIEF, ENGINEERING SERVICES BRANCH

This military professional has a targeted job campaign focused on Killeen, TX.

Dear Exact Name of Person: (or Dear Sir or Madam if answering a blind ad.)

Enclosed you will find my resume and a Town of Killeen application for the position of Director of Engineering Support Services. I would appreciate an opportunity to talk with you soon about how I could contribute to the Town of Killeen in this role through my strong interest in a position of this type as well as through my background of superior performance.

As you will see by my resume and application, my track record includes 20 years of service in the U.S. Army, culminating in executive roles as a Major. Through my military experience, I have refined the type of planning, analytical, public speaking, team and consensus building, and persuasive speaking skills you are seeking. Although frequent travel is necessitated by military life, I have always participated actively in sports and community activities. Now that I am retiring and am a resident of Killeen, I am able to be even more active in community affairs such as the "Killeen Beyond 2005 Committee" and community sports programs.

I understand that Killeen is in the midst of departmental reorganizations and realignments which will consolidate some departments and realign some personnel assignments within the town's government. Throughout my time in the Army, I was frequently involved in functional reorganization projects and in setting up new departments and administrative centers from scratch. I am very skilled at providing a strong leadership style which has been successful in ensuring these new entities are very quickly up to full operating speed and productivity.

I am a versatile professional able to adapt to rapid change, pressure, and deadlines while maximizing human and material resources to their fullest extent. I am proud of my reputation as an unquestionably honest individual and straightforward speaker. I have been successful in building teams of the highest quality by giving employees my trust and respect for their own abilities and decision-making skills.

I hope you will call or write me soon to suggest a convenient time for us to meet and discuss the town government's current and future needs and how I might serve them. Thank you in advance for your time.

Sincerely yours,

Robert Samson

Alternate last paragraph:

I hope you will welcome my call soon to arrange a brief meeting at your convenience to discuss your current and future needs and how I might serve them. Thank you in advance for your time.

ROBERT SAMSON

1110½ Hay Street, Fayetteville, NC 28305   •   preppub@aol.com   •   (910) 483-6611

OBJECTIVE

To benefit an organization in need of an experienced manager with a versatile background of expertise in engineering services planning and management who has refined public speaking, managerial, and supervisory skills as a military officer.

EDUCATION & EXECUTIVE TRAINING

M.S., Systems Management, Central Texas College, Killeen, TX, 2001.
B.S., Mathematics, Virginia State University, Petersburg, VA, 1985.
Earned certification in Operations Research/Systems Analysis.
Completed the military's graduate-level Command and General Staff College.

EXPERIENCE

Advanced in positions requiring a resourceful problem solver, U.S. Army:
CHIEF, ENGINEERING SERVICES BRANCH. Fort Hood, TX (2004-present). For a major military education center, develop and oversee all phases of planning and analyzing the effectiveness of training as well as managing inspections of graduates of the center's programs.
- Provided leadership and technical guidance during a period of turbulence caused by a functional reorganization.

DIRECTOR OF PLANNING, PROGRAMS, AND PROJECTS. Puerto Rico (2001-04). Promoted on the basis of my expertise displayed as the director of a new planning department, earned praise for my ability to handle multiple tasks under pressure while coordinating Special Operations plans throughout the region of Central and South America.
- Was often called on to supply my expertise and knowledge to similar organizations throughout the region and present briefings to embassy and higher levels.

Fort Hood, TX (1996-01). Consistently described as an exceptional performer, outstanding supervisor, and creative writer/speaker, excelled in three key positions during a period of change and reorganization:
- As a **General Manager,** expanded resources for sponsoring international students.
- As the **Chief of a Computer Simulation Center,** earned official praise as the catalyst for seeing this need and pushing through with the research and then managing this complex technologically advanced department.
- As the **Chief of Evaluation and Inspections,** supervised ten specialists in a department which evaluated the quality of training provided for seven instructional departments supporting 4,000 annually attending 50 courses. Directed a functional reorganization which included a new in-house training program, standard operating procedures guidelines, and a five-year evaluation plan.

ASSISTANT DIRECTOR FOR PERSONNEL AND OPERATIONS. Korea (1995-96). As second-in-command, oversaw administrative, logistical, and training programs while playing a major role in getting this new organization functioning quickly at a high level.
- Based on my skill in managing complex details in a rapidly changing environment, was handpicked to oversee a 10-week expedition into Thailand.

GENERAL MANAGER. U.S. Army, Fort Carson, CO (1994-95). Selected ahead of my peers to establish and train a team of 11 highly skilled specialists, led personnel through stressful and complex training in order to earn certification for worldwide assignments.

PERSONAL

Have traveled extensively and have a high degree of social and cultural awareness. Participated in organized sports as a player and coach throughout high school, college, and my years in the military.

Date

Exact Name of Person
Title or Position
Exact Name of Company
Address
City, State, Zip

Dear Exact Name of Person: (or Dear Sir or Madam if answering a blind ad):

With the enclosed resume, I would like to make you aware of my distinguished background of effectiveness in managing communications systems installation projects and of my strong knowledge of such diverse areas as technical school operations, procurement, and inventory control.

As you will see from my resume, I built a reputation as an adaptable professional while excelling in managing multiple simultaneous projects in demanding technical environments for the U.S. Air Force. I am accustomed to working under harsh weather conditions and within tight deadlines.

With a degree in Engineering Systems Technology, I also received extensive military training which emphasized management and leadership as well as techniques for effective instructors. In my final military assignment prior to retirement, I served as Chief of Communications Systems Engineering with the responsibility for planning, coordinating, and managing projects throughout the world. As operations director of a 55-person work center, I oversaw antenna and communications systems installation, enhances, and reconstruction projects which ensured continuous communications support for activities vital to national security.

Earlier jobs in quality assurance inspection, training program instruction and management, and engineering installation operations supervision allowed me to refine my reputation as a creative, energetic professional who could be counted on to complete projects on time and within budget. Cited on numerous occasions for solving difficult problems in ways which reduced expenditures and still allowed the project to be completed ahead of schedule, I was often sought out to provide technical guidance as well as counseling for subordinates.

If you can use an experienced communications technician with excellent time and resource management skills, I hope you will welcome my call soon when I try to arrange a brief meeting to discuss your goals and how my background might serve your needs. I can provide outstanding references at the appropriate time.

Sincerely,

Nathan Culver

Alternate last paragraph:
I hope you will write or call me soon to suggest a time when we might meet to discuss your needs and goals and how my background might serve them. I can provide outstanding references at the appropriate time.

NATHAN CULVER

1110½ Hay Street, Fayetteville, NC 28305 • preppub@aol.com • (910) 483-6611

OBJECTIVE

To offer a strong background in the management of communications systems installation and operations to an organization that can benefit from my leadership and expertise.

EDUCATION

A.S. in Engineering Systems Technology, Community College of the Air Force, 1993.

TECHNICAL SKILLS & KNOWLEDGE

Communications: use all cable locators and troubleshooting test equipment
Computers: am proficient in Windows; MS Word, Excel, Access, and PowerPoint
Construction equipment: operate trenchers, backhoes, line trucks, and tractor-trailers

EXPERIENCE

Advanced to manage worldwide communications systems, U.S. Air Force:
CHIEF OF COMMUNICATIONS SYSTEMS ENGINEERING. Pope AFB, NC (2001-04). Provided oversight to a team of 55 communications systems construction professionals, including 11 junior managers and 44 technicians; directed installation, enhancement, and reconstruction of antenna and communications systems in locations throughout the world.

- Planned, coordinated, and oversaw multiple simultaneous projects, including installation of a $9 million air traffic control system for ten FAA communications sites and an antenna installation project which saved $35,000 by using salvaged materials.
- Controlled a $3 million annual operating budget, handling inventory control, purchasing, and procurement; developed a preventive maintenance program for antenna systems.
- Expertly planned the removal of a major antenna system and its relocation without damage to structural steel, avoiding $50,000 in expenses.
- Located and corrected a design error in eight National Weather Service Next Generation Radar systems, reducing their vulnerability to lightning strikes.

DIRECTOR OF PLANS AND OPERATIONS. Pope AFB, NC (2000-01). Managed a technical school program, supervising a staff of three personnel providing instruction to over 300 students; developed lesson plans and coordinated training sites and materials; was handpicked to assist in rewriting skills tests for installation and maintenance managers.

QUALITY ASSURANCE INSPECTOR. Pope AFB, NC (1999). Supervised quality control instructors while managing quality initiatives and training programs emphasizing time management, customer service, and human relations; was cited as a "superb team leader."

ENGINEERING INSTALLATION SUPERVISOR. Pope AFB, NC (1998). Provided on-site supervision and safety guidance during antenna, steel tower, rigid radome, and associated systems installation, removal, and maintenance activities; earned promotion to QA Inspector based on results obtained in this position.

- Completed projects that included disassembly of a long-range radar facility in Alaska and a weather radar facility in Oklahoma in spite of severe weather delays.

CENTRALIZED ANTENNA SYSTEMS SUPERVISOR. Italy (1994-98). Managed 20 technicians maintaining more than $19.5 million worth of antenna systems at 85 NATO sites throughout Europe; oversaw scheduling of installation, repair, and maintenance.

- Supervised an eight-person team in a special project to install a three-antenna system at a bombing range in Italy, surveying, engineering, and correcting a potential hazard for flight training missions by resolving air-to-ground communications problems.

PERSONAL

Was entrusted with a Secret/NATO Secret security clearance. Am technically knowledgeable with a reputation for creativity and a high level of energy and enthusiasm.

CIVIL ENGINEER--a two-page resume

GEORGE WALKER

1110½ Hay Street, Fayetteville, NC 28305 • preppub@aol.com • (910) 483-6611

OBJECTIVE

To contribute to an organization needing a polished communicator and resourceful, strategic thinker offering vision, leadership, and team-building skills developed during a distinguished career in international environments.

EDUCATION

Master of Business Administration, University of South Carolina, 1987.
Bachelor of Science in **Civil Engineering**, Virginia Military Institute, 1982.
Excelled in rigorous and extensive graduate-level professional development training for military officers including the Air War College, Air Command and Staff College, and Squadron Officer's School.

CLEARANCE

Presently hold Top Secret (SCI) security clearance.

**EXPERIENCE
2003-04**

Rose to the rank of Lieutenant Colonel while serving in the U.S. Air Force:
OPERATIONS MANAGER. Hill Air Force Base, UT. Assisted in managing a $36.8 million budget and coordinating the activities of more than 1,000 people in five diverse organizations; ensured that all personnel were highly trained and integrated to accomplish wing mission. Instructor pilot for 240 officer aviators.

- Accomplished in-depth study of entire operations group's mission and processes; implemented changes to eliminate redundancy and reengineered internal systems to streamline resource allocation, vastly improving training quality and manpower efficiency.
- Institutionalized risk management throughout the operations group; principles utilized in every aspect of daily operations - enhanced safety.
- Led a runway extension project that will nearly double airlift capability; gained expertise in the Environmental Impact/Assessment Process and integrated civilian, environmental and military groups in "selling" the concept to the affected civilian communities.
- Cultivated teamwork and a winning attitude in a culturally diverse organization.

2001-03

CHIEF OF SAFETY. Hill Air Force Base, UT. Conceived, developed, and implemented risk management, safety, and mishap prevention programs affecting 5,000 people, a fleet of 91 aircraft, and aircraft operations. Directly supervised 12 executives while overseeing safety programs in 32 diverse organizations. Instructor pilot.

- Ran a program rated "outstanding" by Headquarters Air Mobility Command: 26,000 aircraft sorties handling 120,000 passengers and 3,600 cargo tons, and 65 major construction projects with no accidents.
- Oversaw research of bird/aircraft strike data that resulted in elimination of costly, ineffective risk control measures for Air Mobility Command C-130 aircraft.
- Proposed risk management strategies for flight and maintenance operations were incorporated into major command operating policy.
- Refined ability to "sell" and implement weapons, ground, and flight safety programs on macro scale - justified on a cost-benefits basis without tangible returns to users; result - no duty-related accidents.
- Developed a working knowledge of OSHA requirements and instituted Risk Management and safety programs throughout a large, diverse and fast-paced organization.

1997-00

OPERATIONS OFFICER. Kadena Air Base, Japan. Led squadron operations and maintenance of 19 combat-ready C-130 aircraft and over 430 personnel, including 85 officers implementing airlift operations throughout Asia, Europe, and the Middle East.

- Contingency expert – mentored or directed over 3,000 missions supporting NATO, non-NATO, and Partnership for Peace operations, including the insertion of Asian troops and humanitarian cargo into strife-torn Korea.
- Maximized resources executing an operations tempo exceeding the Air Combat Command C-130 utilization rate balancing mission tasking with maintenance capability – best maintenance indicators in 3 years.

1993-97   **BRANCH CHIEF.** Washington, DC. Handpicked by HQ U.S. Air Force for assignment to its Air Staff; planned, directed and provided oversight to as well as preparing, coordinating, and implementing U.S. Air Force policy for worldwide airlift operations in support of sensitive Department of Defense, U.S. government interdepartmental, and National Security Council programs. Managed a $12 million airlift system budget servicing 75 countries.
- Earned widespread praise for skill in management and integration of assets.
- Recognized as an expert at integrating Department of Defense and non-Department of Defense agencies' requirements into detailed operations supporting complex U.S. foreign policy initiatives
- Directed activities in all Air Force major commands, authored policy, obtained legal reviews, established funding and reimbursement procedures for programs supporting non-Department of Defense agencies.
- Oversaw more than 500 sensitive, special assignment airlift missions in some of the most politically sensitive areas of the world, successfully removing personnel from life-threatening environments and transporting politically and militarily sensitive cargo.
- Gained extensive experience in government staffing actions as well as in developing and writing policy.

1988-93   **DIVISION CHIEF.** Langley Air Force Base, VA. Directed one of two offices in the U.S. Air Force providing support and expertise on the Adverse Weather Aerial Delivery System (AWADS) to all commands. Organized and planned wing participation in special, unilateral and inter-service training and evaluation exercises and inspections.
- Oversaw training and standardization/evaluation for 400 crew members and a 26,000 flying hour program involving airlift, aeromedical evacuation, and maintenance activities worldwide. Selected as best tactics officer in airlift community for team building, innovations and resourcefulness.

1987-88   **DETACHMENT COMMANDER.** Iraq. Commanded 41-person unit composed of U.S. personnel. Senior airlift liaison to Saudi and Afghani government agencies, U.S. Embassy, and area commanders supporting Kuwaiti tanker escort operations during the war.
- Superiors' evaluation: Leadership strong attribute, superior job knowledge, perceives core problem – offers feasible solutions, exceptional management of resources, highly respected for professionalism and skill.

Selected accomplishments and highlights of other experience:
- Top officer in every assignment, directly impacted successful mission accomplishment while serving in positions as commander, squadron operations officer, senior wing staff officer: Chief of Wing Safety, Combat Tactics Officer, and Standardization and Evaluation Officer (1992-04).
- Combat pilot during Operation Enduring Freedom implementation in Iraq.

HONORS   Received 26 separate prestigious honors and awards for exceptional performance.
Military Airlift Command's 1995 Tactics Officer of the Year for brilliance.

TRAINING   Have completed training related to numerous specialized areas including international terrorism, foreign internal defense, and total quality management, gender and sensitivity, and extensive training as a pilot.

Date

Exact Name of Person
Title or Position
Name of Company
Address
City, State, Zip

CIVIL ENGINEER

with experience as an
engineering plans
manager

Dear Exact Name of Person: (or Dear Sir or Madam if answering a blind ad.)

I would appreciate an opportunity to talk with you soon about how I could contribute to your organization through my experience in geodetic/geographic services operations and my background in management with the U.S. Army Corps of Engineers.

While serving my country as a military officer, I received advanced training and spent approximately six years supervising defense mapping, charting, and geodesy services. I excelled in advanced training programs including Geographic Information Systems (GIS); multispectral imagery and remote sensing; and mapping, charting, and geodesy.

As you will see from my resume, my experience includes services as the topographic engineer for all U.S. forces in Germany with direct responsibility for coordinating an 18-person staff producing topographic products and GIS services. This position included establishing and administering procedures for exchanging data with Germany, thereby giving me executive-level experience with developmental contractors, foreign leaders, and other governmental agencies.

My background includes technical engineering expertise as well as experience in teaching and course development at the United States Military Academy.

I hope you will welcome my call soon to arrange a brief meeting at your convenience to discuss your current and future needs and how I might serve them. Thank you in advance for your time.

Sincerely yours,

Aaron Paul

Alternate last paragraph:
I hope you will call or write soon to suggest a time convenient for us to meet and discuss your current and future needs and how I might serve them. Thank you in advance for your time.

AARON PAUL

1110½ Hay Street, Fayetteville, NC 28305 • preppub@aol.com • (910) 483-6611

OBJECTIVE   To contribute to an organization that can use an experienced manager and engineer who offers a broad background including geographic/geodetic servicing, remote sensing, financial management, and college-level instructing in a distinguished career as a military officer.

EXPERIENCE   *Advanced in the following "track record," U.S. Army Corps of Engineers*:
ENGINEERING PLANS MANAGER. Fort Hood, TX (2004-present). Develop the long-range plans for an 1,800-person engineering organization and have played the major role in fielding three new systems by coordinating personnel, funding, and time management issues.
- Directed engineering support during relief operations in Florida after Hurricanes Ivan, Frances, and Jeanne. Implemented automated systems and improved project management which resulted in a 10% reduction in manpower.

TOPOGRAPHIC ENGINEERING OPERATIONS MANAGER. Germany (2003-04). Coordinated the efforts of an 18-person staff producing topographic products and GIS services.
- Served as liaison between U.S. forces and German military and civilian agencies.

ASSOCIATE PROFESSOR OF MATHEMATICS. The U.S. Military Academy, West Point, NY (2000-03). Advanced from teaching three 15 to 18-student freshman calculus classes, to supervising two instructors of 12 sophomore and junior linear algebra classes, and then to conducting linear algebra and surveying research and administering a $4,000 monthly budget.
- Established effective student relations. Produced 10% increase in linear algebra scores.

ENGINEERING COMPANY GENERAL MANAGER. Fort Wainwright, AK (1997-99). Managed construction projects, 130 employees, a $400,000 annual budget, a $5.7 million equipment and property inventory, and a 1,500-line-item warehouse.
- Arranged for funding, reviewed, and made recommendations for projects including a $500,000 maintenance facility, a $350,000 warehouse, and a $150,000 concrete ramp.
- Initiated changes which reduced annual transportation maintenance costs $200,000.

TERRAIN INTELLIGENCE OFFICER. Fort Wainwright, AK (1996-97). Coordinated the efforts of mapping and terrain analysis units and made decisions concerning the authorization for work requests, supervised image gathering, and approved requests for resulting products.
- Expanded my knowledge of government budget processes and image map production.

LOGISTICS MANAGER FOR ENGINEERING OPERATIONS. Germany (1994-95). Supervised storage, allocation, and transportation of construction material, fuel, and repair parts for four subordinate companies as well as controlling a $150,000 budget.
- Supervised 38 people and was in charge of constructing two bunkers: managed all phases from design to the development of plans and management of heavy equipment.

EDUCATION &   **M.S., Civil Engineering**, University of Alaska Fairbanks, AK, 2000.
TRAINING   **B.S., Forestry**, Alaska Pacific University, Anchorage, AK, 1991.
&   Completed advanced training including the graduate-level Command and General Staff
LICENSE   College and specialized programs such as: Geographic Information Systems (GIS); multispectral imagery and remote sensing; and mapping, charting, and geodesy.
Registered Professional Engineer (Civil), 2002.

PERSONAL   Entrusted with a Top Secret security clearance. Member, the Society of American Military Engineers and the American Society of Photogrammetry and Remote Sensing.

Date

Exact Name of Person
Title or Position
Exact Name of Company
Address
City, State, Zip

CIVIL ENGINEER

with experience in
engineering
activities
management

Dear Exact Name of Person: (or Dear Sir or Madam if answering a blind ad.)

I would appreciate an opportunity to talk with you soon about how I could contribute to your organization through my experience as a civil engineer along with my strong interest in structural design and construction management.

While serving with distinction as a U.S. Army officer, I gained experience in the development and management of heavy engineering projects. During the War on Terror, I managed a 38-person team involved in projects including building helicopter landing pads and a prisoner-of-war camp designed to hold 500 people.

I advanced in supervisory, management, and staff positions with heavy combat engineering units in Italy which culminated in a job developing and coordinating more than 100 projects. During this period I worked closely with my counterparts in the U.S. Air Force and gained approval for new projects in a period of rapid changes for the military due to the "deactivation" of some units which caused integration of personnel and equipment into existing units.

I enjoy a challenge and feel that I can make important contributions in situations where strong analytical and problem-solving skills are required. Known as an adaptable and versatile professional, I offer a willingness to learn new methods and meet demanding standards.

I hope you will welcome my call soon to arrange a brief meeting at your convenience to discuss your current and future needs and how I might serve them. Thank you in advance for your time.

Sincerely yours,

Marlene Thompson

Alternate last paragraph:
I hope you will call or write soon to suggest a time convenient for us to meet and discuss your current and future needs and how I might serve them. Thank you in advance for your time.

MARLENE THOMPSON

1110½ Hay Street, Fayetteville, NC 28305　　•　　preppub@aol.com　　•　　(910) 483-6611

OBJECTIVE　　To apply my experience, education, and training as a civil engineer to an organization that can use a young professional who has excelled as a junior military officer through a combination of leadership and management skills, persistence, and knowledge.

EXPERIENCE　　**ENGINEERING ACTIVITIES MANAGER.** U.S. Army Reserves, Italy (2004-present). Received an Army Commendation Medal for my "dedicated service" as the manager and coordinator of engineering activities in an operations center. Provide support for numerous training projects and was cited for my "unselfish devotion" in working long hours to train personnel in the Maneuver Control System.

Advanced in positions in the engineering management field, U.S. Army, Italy:
CIVIL ENGINEER. (2002-03). Handpicked for this job in a heavy engineering company, developed and managed a $2 million construction program while working closely with personnel in the Directorate of Engineering and Housing and Air Force engineering offices.
- Coordinated with customers on their design requirements.
- During a period of deactivation and rapid change for the military overseas, developed more than 100 separate projects, estimated the requirements, and made presentations to review boards to gain approval for each recommended job.
- Described as "hard working, energetic, and persistent," earned praise for developing and managing projects supporting a training project involving personnel from U.S.

HEAVY CONSTRUCTION MANAGER. Afghanistan (2001-02). Led a 38-person heavy construction team involved in building a 500-person prisoner-of-war camp and helicopter landing pads; spent additional time as the night-shift manager of an operations center.
- Became adept at adjusting to rapidly changing priorities and situations while in Afghanistan preparing for and during combat as well as while planning the return of personnel and assets to Italy after the War on Terror.
- Directed placement of the POW camp's 3,000 meters of triple-standard concertina wire.

FIRST-LINE SUPERVISOR. (2000-01). Managed a 35-person combat engineer team with more than $500,000 worth of equipment and vehicles during a functional reorganization.
- Played a critical role in the major upgrade of a tank firing range in a $20 million project. Refined management skills while successfully producing well trained employees.

MATERIALS COORDINATOR. (2000). Supervised two senior-level managers and was the construction organization's liaison with a task force for the firing range project.
- Coordinated the transition from manual to automated systems for maintaining material-handling records. Excelled in a job usually reserved for a more experienced manager.

EDUCATION & TRAINING　　**B.S. degree in Civil Engineering**, University of New Mexico, Albuquerque, NM, 1999.
- Completed elective course in design and structural analysis.
- Participated in the university's ROTC program and was awarded a commission as an Army Reserve officer upon graduation.
Excelled in more than four months of training for engineering officers.

AFFILIATIONS　　Member, the American Society of Civil Engineers and the Society of Military Engineers.

PERSONAL　　Have a Secret security clearance. Received numerous awards including the Southwest Asia Service, two Achievement, and two Commendation Medals.

CAREER CHANGE

Date

Exact Name of Person
Title or Position
Exact Name of Company
Address
City, State, Zip

CIVIL ENGINEER

with experience as a
military officer &
engineering services
manager

Dear Exact Name of Person (or Dear Sir or Madam if answering a blind ad):

With the enclosed resume, I would like to make you aware of my interest in exploring employment opportunities with your organization and introduce you to my background.

As you will see, after graduating with a B.S. in Civil Engineering, I joined the U.S. Air Force and worked professionally as a Civil Engineer. I managed dozens of contracts valued at millions of dollars for new construction, maintenance, repair, and remodeling. I became known for my ability to identify and avoid potential problems before they caused costly construction delays, and I was identified as a strong leader and problem solver. Handpicked to undergo a rigorous selection process, I was one of five people selected out of 400 officer applicants to train as a Combat Controller, a position in the military which requires an ability to manage human and financial resources during combat, catastrophe, and uncertainty. Subsequently I was one of only 12 graduates out of the 120 individuals who began the 18-month training course. Since becoming a Combat Controller, I have been nominated as Officer of the Quarter four times and have been described as a "superb leader and planner" while managing 30 people in worldwide projects which involve high-risk activities such as SCUBA diving, search-and-rescue, parachuting, and watercraft operation. I have earned numerous licenses and certifications including Air Traffic Controller and U.S. Coast Guard Master Captain's 50-ton License. I have been entrusted with one of the country's highest security clearances: Top Secret/ SCI.

Although I was aggressively recruited to remain in military service and assured of continued rapid advancement, I decided to resign my commission as an officer and enter the civilian work force. I offer a proven ability to make decisions in situations of uncertainty, and I have gained valuable experience in managing human resources worldwide.

If my background and skills interest you, I hope you will welcome my call soon to arrange a brief meeting to discuss your current and future needs and how I might serve them. Thank you in advance for your time.

Yours sincerely,

Shane Carlton

SHANE CARLTON

1110½ Hay Street, Fayetteville, NC 28305 • preppub@aol.com • (910) 483-6611

OBJECTIVE   I want to contribute to an organization that can use an experienced problem solver and manager who offers strong leadership and management skills refined as a military officer.

EDUCATION   **Bachelor of Science (B.S.) degree in Civil Engineering,** Dartmouth College, Hanover, NH, 1998.
- Wrestling scholarship; placed 3rd in NCAA Division 2 Northeastern Conference. Completed many executive development and technical courses sponsored by the U.S. Military: Squadron Officer School; graduated in top 10% in academics and leadership.
- *Distinguished Graduate* from Air Traffic Control School and Combat Control School.

CLEARANCE   Hold one of the military's highest security clearances: **Top Secret (TS/SCI)**

SUMMARY OF EXPERIENCE   After receiving a B.S. in Civil Engineering from Dartmouth, entered the U.S. Air Force as an officer in a civil engineering organization. In a rigorous selection process, was one of five people selected of 400 officer applicants for Combat Controller training; subsequently was one of only 12 graduates of the 120 individuals who entered the 18-month Combat Controller training program, considered one of the military's most difficult training programs. Excelled as a military officer and was strongly encouraged to remain in military service and assured of continued rapid advancement. Achieved the rank of **Captain** and was nominated **Officer of the Quarter,** Keesler Air Force Base, four times.

EXPERIENCE   **GENERAL MANAGER (FLIGHT COMMANDER).** Joint Special Operations Command, Keesler AFB, MS (2004-present). As Commander of a "Special Tactics" organization, manage 30 individuals and have been praised in writing as a "superb leader/planner."
- Accounted for $2 million in equipment while managing 30 personnel during 53 projects in multiple countries. Was commended for "seamlessly integrating Israeli special forces with U.S. Army Rangers during a complex airfield seizure" in the Middle East.

ENGINEERING SERVICES COMMANDER. U.S. Air Force, Pope AFB, NC (2001-03). Led a 22-person "Special Tactics" organization which specialized in providing expert services related to air traffic control, fire support, emergency medical treatment, and combat search-and-rescue. Led the team in projects which involved diving, parachuting, helicopter operations, and watercraft activities.
- Directed projects worldwide including one with the German Special Operations Forces; led high-profile SCUBA missions in Europe. Trained personnel for search-and-rescue, surveillance, and reconnaissance activities. Resuscitated a stagnant training program.

CIVIL ENGINEER. U.S. Air Force, Beale AFB, CA (1998-01). Managed maintenance, repair, construction, and operation of facilities and utilities supporting thousands of people. Managed services related to housing, fire protection, disaster recovery, hazardous materials control.
- Reviewed multimillion-dollar construction projects. Developed engineering solutions, design specifications, and cost estimates for maintenance, repair, and new construction of fuel systems, environmental structures, pavements, and facility sites.
- Managed 32 contracts valued at $1.8 million. Designed and managed multimillion-dollar contracts for new construction, repair, maintenance, and remodeling. Pinpointed critical design problems prior to construction and vigilantly avoided costly delay charges.

PERSONAL   Outstanding references on request. Strong leader with proven ability to excel under pressure. Highly computer literate; proficient with Word and PowerPoint. Disciplined self-starter.

Date

Exact Name of Person
Exact Title
Exact Name of Company
Address
City, State, Zip

Dear Exact Name of Person (or Dear Sir or Madam if answering a blind ad):

With the enclosed resume, I would like to express my interest in exploring employment opportunities with your organization.

As you will see from my resume, I am currently excelling as a Survey Crew Chief. I have been credited with significantly contributing to the company's success as it has grown from a two-person operation into a company with 20 employees. I travel to locations throughout Louisiana to perform environmental surveys, and I direct key aspects of construction projects which include schools and subdivisions.

In prior experience with the U.S. Army, I began as a Survey Computer, advanced to Survey Team Supervisor and then to Survey Section Supervisor, and finally advanced to Senior Topographic Supervisor. In my final position in military service, I managed 118 people and ensured flawless accountability of equipment and supplies.

Although I am excelling in my current position and can provide outstanding references at the appropriate time, I am in the process of relocating to California and am seeking employment in the engineering field.

I hope you will call or write me soon to suggest a time convenient for us to meet and discuss your current and future needs and how I might serve them. Thank you in advance for your time.

Sincerely,

Keith Watson

Alternate last paragraph:
I hope you will welcome my call soon to arrange a brief meeting to discuss your current and future needs and how I might serve them. Thank you in advance for your time.

KEITH WATSON

1110½ Hay Street, Fayetteville, NC 28305   •   preppub@aol.com   •   (910) 483-6611

OBJECTIVE   To benefit an organization that can use an experienced surveying professional with a background in employee training and supervision as well as quality assurance and inspection.

TECHNICAL   Operate a Total Station. Use a Hewlett Packard Data Collector. Utilize leveling instruments.
EXPERIENCE   Some experience with GPS.

EXPERIENCE   **SURVEY CREW CHIEF.** Taylor & Bros., Inc., Alexandria, LA (1998-present). Began as a temporary employee placed in a job with this privately owned company by a temporary service; within a few weeks was offered full-time employment by the owner, a civil engineer. During my eight years of employment, the company has grown from a two-person operation into a company with two full crews, a CAD operator, and another manager.
- Perform construction staking for subdivisions; we are currently in the process of building Lake Rodemacher High School.
- Train junior employees; manage a crew which includes a Rodman and Instrument Operator. Perform reconnaissance and analysis related to potential survey projects; am continuously involved in reading and interpreting construction plans, performing deed research, and collecting data for future projects.

Prior military experience: Served in the U.S. Army and received numerous medals and awards in recognition of my technical surveying expertise and management skills. Held a Top Secret (SBI) security clearance.
1996-98: SENIOR TOPOGRAPHIC SUPERVISOR. Fort Carson, CO. Was the highest ranking mid-manager in a topographic engineering company. Managed 118 people and ensured flawless accountability of an inventory of equipment and supplies.

1991-96: SURVEY CONTROL SUPERVISOR. Italy. Was extensively involved in quality assurance and technical inspection as I traveled throughout Italy to inspect survey teams.
- Validated all topographic survey requirements in Europe.
- Calculated cost estimates and provided customers with alternative plans of action.
- Wrote staff papers and authored doctrine; recommended equipment upgrades.

1987-91: SURVEY SECTION SUPERVISOR. Fort Bragg, NC. Trained and supervised four mid-level supervisors responsible for 45 employees. Assigned projects to four sections.

1983-87: SURVEY TEAM SUPERVISOR. Italy. Trained and supervised 12 employees, and assigned work to survey section employees.

1981-83: SURVEY COMPUTER. Fort Hood, TX. Extracted survey measurements from survey recorder's notebook; computed coordinates and rejected data not within specifications.

EDUCATION   Certification in Autocad 13, Northwestern State University of Louisiana, Natchitoches, LA (NSUL), 2004.
Certification in Microcomputer Repair/Solid State Electronics, NSUL, 1998.
Completed Advanced Course/Advanced Geodetic Survey, U.S. Army Engineer School and Defense Mapping School, 1992.
Completed Basic Geodetic Survey Course, Defense Mapping School, 1987.
Completed 30 hours of courses towards a Bachelor's degree, Jackson Community College.

PERSONAL   Outstanding references on request. Single, and will travel and relocate as needed.

Date

Exact Name of Person
Exact Title
Exact Name of Company
Address
City, State, Zip

Dear Exact Name of Person (or Dear Sir or Madam if answering a blind ad):

With the enclosed resume, I would like to express my interest in exploring employment opportunities with your organization.

As you will see from my resume, I hold a degree in Computer Engineering and previously completed extensive coursework in Electrical Engineering. After working for the Mesa Company for 14 years as a Product Support Manager, I resigned and became a full-time Computer Engineering student in 2003 when the company asked me to accept a promotion and relocation to their home office in Flagstaff, AZ. At that point, I decided to complete the college degree which I had begun many years earlier, and I have worked part-time as a business consultant while completing my B.S. I have completed courses related to HTML, Java, Visual Basic, C and C++, UNIX, and Interfacing, and I am making plans to pursue Oracle in my spare time.

While providing all types of wholesale support and sales to 20 retail dealers in my job as a Product Support Manager, I was extensively involved in training the dealers' employees in computer operations. The Mesa Company decided in 1997 that it would require its dealer-customers to communicate with the company through online methods, so it became a major part of my job to work with dealers' platforms which included UNIX, AS 400, and Windows NT. I trained the dealers' employees in computer operations, and I also trained technicians to perform troubleshooting using high-tech computer equipment.

A key part of my job was helping dealers maximize the profitability of their retail businesses, so I became very skilled at interpreting financial documents including pro formas, balance sheets, and other paperwork. I take pride in the fact that I helped all my dealer customers improve their bottom line through my recommendations related to market share, product line conversions and product mix, warranty policies and procedures, and stock ordering. I was consistently in the top 5% of the company's managers in a variety of areas including customer satisfaction.

If you can use a versatile and loyal professional who offers a background which includes extensive customer service and business consulting experience as well as computer knowledge, I hope you will contact me soon to suggest a time we might meet to discuss how I could contribute to your organization. I can provide excellent professional and personal references at the appropriate time. Thank you for your time and consideration.

Sincerely,

Andrew Fischer

ANDREW FISCHER

1110½ Hay Street, Fayetteville, NC 28305 • preppub@aol.com • (910) 483-6611

OBJECTIVE	I want to contribute to an organization that can use a resourceful professional with an extensive technical background in electrical engineering and computer science along with vast experience in business consulting, operations management, and sales.
EDUCATION	**B.S. degree in Computer Engineering,** Arizona State University, Tempe, AZ, 2004.

- Completed course work related to Java, Visual Basic, C and C++, UNIX, Interfacing, and other subjects. Have been introduced to HTML and Oracle, and plan to pursue further Oracle studies in my spare time.

Previous course work in Electrical Engineering: Began college with a major of pre-med and changed to Electrical Engineering, Grand Canyon University.

Technical computer training: Extensive training related to UNIX, AS 400, Windows NT, and other platforms sponsored by the Mesa Corporation.

- Skilled at interpreting schematics, diagrams, and blueprints; highly proficient in working with electrical circuitry. Highly skilled with Word, PowerPoint, Excel.

Financial training: Am skilled at reading profit-and-loss statements, pro formas, balance sheets, and other financial documents.

High school: Graduate of Cactus Senior High School, Tempe, AZ. Was a school leader: voted "Mr. Junior" and "Mr. Senior."

EXPERIENCE	**BUSINESS CONSULTANT & FULL-TIME COMPUTER ENGINEERING STUDENT.** (2003-present). After working for the Mesa Company for 14 years, I resigned from the corporation when the company wanted me to accept a promotion and relocation to its home office in Flagstaff, AZ; I decided to resign and complete my college degree.

PRODUCT SUPPORT MANAGER. Mesa Company, Flagstaff, AZ (1991-03). Was responsible for 20 retail dealers and served as their wholesale source of supply for accessories and wear items used on high-tech agricultural equipment; played a key role in helping the company continuously automate manual functions throughout the 1990s.

- Became skilled in all aspects of business consulting as I worked with retailers to improve their profitability and merchandising mix; developed new plans to foster better relationships between dealers and their customers.
- Developed innovative plans to help dealers increase the service part of their business.
- Utilized PowerPoint to make presentations and conduct training.
- Functioned as a business consultant; was trained to read financial statements and profit-and-loss statements.
- In 1997, after the company made the decision to require dealers to communicate their orders and other matters online, was extensively trained in computer operations related to UNIX, AS 400, Windows NT, and other platforms. Became skilled in assisting customers in their networking needs, and trained the dealers' employees in computer use and troubleshooting. Trained technicians to perform troubleshooting using high-tech computer troubleshooting equipment.

Highlights of achievements:

- Increased parts sales from $3.9 million in 1994 to $6.8 million in 2002.
- Boosted customer satisfaction rating from 62% in 2000 to 84% in 2002.
- Developed effective business plans which established goals for numerous product lines and which established objectives for operating income, market share, product line conversions, warranty policies and procedures, customer complaints, service reports, stock order goals, and claim audits.

PERSONAL	Resourceful problem solver. Strong personal initiative. Excellent references.

Exact Name of Person
Exact Title
Exact Name of Company
Address
City, State, Zip

COMPUTER ENGINEER & SYSTEMS ENGINEER

with experience as a corporate sales manager

Dear Exact Name of Person (or Dear Sir or Madam if answering a blind ad):

With the enclosed resume, I would like to express my interest in exploring employment opportunities with your organization.

While excelling in my full-time position as a Corporate Sales Manager for computer hardware and software, I have completed in the evenings an undergraduate degree in Computer Engineering Technology. In previous employment as a Systems Engineer and Computer Instructor, I was in charge of repairing and maintaining all computer systems for Hawkeye Community College. Because of my technical expertise, I was recruited to teach a course at the college emphasizing skills in computer repair for computer-literate people seeking to upgrade their skills.

In addition to my recently completed degree in Computer Engineering Technology, I have completed advanced training by Microsoft in Windows, and I have also completed advanced training in various programming languages.

I hope you will welcome my call soon to arrange a brief meeting to discuss your current and future needs and how I might serve them. Thank you in advance for your time.

Sincerely,

Brian Jones

Alternate last paragraph:
I hope you will call or write me soon to suggest a time convenient for us to meet and discuss your current and future needs and how I might serve them. Thank you in advance for your time.

BRIAN JONES

1110½ Hay Street, Fayetteville, NC 28305 • preppub@aol.com • (910) 483-6611

OBJECTIVE
I want to contribute to an organization that can use an expert systems engineer who is skilled in troubleshooting and maintaining networks and Windows systems and who also offers a reputation as an outstanding communicator, teacher, and motivator.

EDUCATION
Bachelor's degree in Computer Engineering Technology, Hawkeye Community College, Waterloo, IA; 2004.
Completed advanced training by Microsoft in Windows; also completed advanced training in Java Programming.

EXPERIENCE
CORPORATE SALES MANAGER. FastTrack Corp, Cedar Falls, IA (2003-present). Am in charge of providing sales and service support for computer hardware and software to Fortune 500 companies.
Accounts Management: Develop business strategies to increase the company's penetration into the Fortune 500 company market; for these sophisticated companies, personally handle sales and presentations which require in-depth product knowledge as well as excellent communication skills.
Technical Support: Provide technical support to customer companies as well as to coworkers within the company; am considered the company's resident expert at troubleshooting and repairing computers.
Training Management and New Product Integration: Played a key role in the training and rollout of Windows XP, and provided inhouse monthly sales training on new networking equipment; have boosted company sales through the employee training programs I have developed and conducted.

SYSTEMS ENGINEER, COMPUTER INSTRUCTOR, & SERVICE TECHNICIAN.
Jones' Computers, Waterloo, IA and Hawkeye Community College (2001-03). While earning my college degree in Computer Engineering of Applications Technology, worked in two different jobs.
Systems Engineering: For a variety of organizations, custom-built and installed computers and provided support for NT networks, as well as for many software applications including Word for Windows, Excel, and PowerPoint.
Computer Service and Repair: Was in charge of repairing and maintaining all the computer systems of Hawkeye Community College.
• Rewired the library's computers so that the librarian could monitor all the systems from one location instead of walking around to do so manually.
• Set up an NT Network for the Dean of Instruction's Office.
College Teaching/Instruction: Developed a lesson plan and then taught a course emphasizing skills in computer repair for computer-literate people seeking to upgrade skills.

SENIOR CREW CHIEF & MAINTENANCE CHIEF. U.S. Army, Army bases in KY, WA, and LA (1991-00). Developed and implemented automated systems to maintain flight records for 30 pilots and eight crew chiefs, and managed maintenance provided on a fleet of helicopters including the UH-1H, OH-58, and UH-60.
• Instilled in personnel the concept that excellent maintenance preserves valuable assets and lengthens their life cycle.

PERSONAL
Held a Top Secret security clearance. Knowledgeable of the latest computer technologies. Offer an ability to rapidly diagnose difficult problems and develop practical, timely solutions. Maintain a journal of hardware/software problems which I hope to publish as a how-to book.

Date

Exact Name of Person
Exact Title or Position
Exact Name of Company
Address
City, State, Zip

COMPUTER NETWORKING ENGINEER

with experience as a site manager, senior contract representative, and senior computer systems specialist

Dear Exact Name of Person: (or Dear Sir or Madam if answering a blind ad):

With the enclosed resume, I would like to make you aware of my background in computer networking and satellite communications system operations as well as my reputation as a logical and methodical professional with strong technical and troubleshooting skills.

As you will see from my resume, I have advanced to hold multiple simultaneous roles with Browning International Corporation, a contracting firm which provides maintenance and repair support for the state-of-the-art systems used to provide signal support for the 10th Mountain Division at Fort Drum, NY. Originally hired as a Senior Communications System Specialist for this firm, I advanced to Senior Contract Representative and, since 2004, have served as Site Manager for 18 customer units with multiple systems in diverse locations in South Carolina, North Carolina, Kentucky, Alaska, and Texas. I have traveled to locations including Saudi Arabia and Bosnia to provide technical assistance. In my current job I utilize my vast satellite background to manage modifications and work improvements on a multimillion-dollar inventory as we troubleshoot all links as well as computer networks. I am heavily involved in Quality Assurance, and I develop all checklists, protocols, and tests for QA.

Through my experience with this contractor, I have been given opportunities to work with the most sophisticated computer networking and signals communication systems used by the U.S. military to include LANs, Mobile Subscriber Equipment (MSE), and satellite communications systems. I have supervised maintenance and repairs on receiving and jamming systems, direction finding sets, and airborne surveillance systems.

Earlier while serving in the U.S. Army as a technical instructor and electronics technician, I advanced to supervisory jobs and earned honors including two U.S. Army Commendation Medals for my leadership, dedication, and technical expertise. With a Top Secret clearance and reputation for high personal standards of integrity and honesty, I have excelled in extensive technical in addition to completing college studies in Electrical Installation and Maintenance, Computer Science, Electrical Engineering, and Electronics Technology.

If you can use a skilled technician with expertise in computer networking and satellite communications, I hope you will contact me to suggest a time when we might meet briefly to discuss your goals and how my background might serve your needs. I can provide outstanding references at the appropriate time.

Sincerely,

Evon Peterson

EVON PETERSON

1110½ Hay Street, Fayetteville, NC 28305 • preppub@aol.com • (910) 483-6611

OBJECTIVE   To offer my technical expertise to an organization that can benefit from my knowledge of computer networking and satellite communications as well as my skills in troubleshooting.

TECHNICAL   Completed extensive technical training in programs and courses which have included:
TRAINING   AN/TSQ-190(V) Trojan Spirit II maintenance   PACE Multilayer and Flexprint CCA repair
& SKILLS   AN/TRQ-32A(V)2 Teammate maintenance   PACE rework and repair soldering
Diploma in **Electrical Installation and Maintenance**, Jefferson Community College, Watertown, NY, 2000.

EXPERIENCE   **SITE MANAGER (2004-present); SENIOR CONTRACT REPRESENTATIVE & SENIOR COMPUTER SYSTEMS SPECIALIST (1999-04).** Browning International Corporation, Fort Drum, NY (1999-present). Have advanced to management roles with this contracting firm which provides maintenance and repair support for satellite communications, KU and C band equipment, and LANs utilized by the 10th Mountain Division to meet their worldwide commitment to responding on short notice anywhere in the world.
- As **Site Manager from 2004-present,** am currently accountable for over $10 million in government property on a multimillion-dollar contract, and my efforts played a key role in netting a cost avoidance of $4 million for the 10th Mountain Division.
- Handled quality assurance functions including the development of protocols.
- Provide outstanding customer support to multiple customer organizations, each of which has multiple systems; am supporting systems at Fort Jackson, Fort Bragg, Fort Campbell, Fort Richardson, and Fort Hood and all these systems deploy to numerous other sites worldwide. Also work with Mobile Subscribe Equipment (MSE).
- Have traveled to countries including Saudi Arabia and Bosnia to support communications and computer networking for the military's tactical mobile satellite systems.
- In previous roles with the company as **Senior Contract Representative & Senior Computer Systems Specialist (1999-04),** oversaw and implemented maintenance and repair of systems which included receiving and jamming systems (AN/TLQ-17A), direction finding sets (AN/TRQ-32V), and airborne surveillance systems (AN/ALQ-151).
- Earned cash **"Performance Incentive Awards"** in recognition of my achievements.

SENIOR FIELD SERVICES TECHNICIAN. Engineering Resources, Inc., Fort Stewart, GA (1997-99). Became familiar with services provided by a contractor supporting U.S. Army operations on receiver/jamming systems, direction finding sets, and airborne surveillance.

COMMUNICATIONS EQUIPMENT INSTRUCTOR. U.S. Army Intelligence School, Fort Bragg, NC (1996-97). Conducted training on receiver, demultiplexer, demodulator, and test equipment theory of operation and troubleshooting techniques.

SENIOR ELECTRONIC TECHNICIAN. U.S. Army, Korea (1991-96). Maintained and repaired over 80 advanced SEL and DEC computer-based subsystems and their peripherals.

LICENSES &   Hold licenses and certifications which include:
CERTIFICATIONS   EPA Universal Technician Certification, 2004
MIL STD 2000 Soldering Instruction Certification, 2002
Instructor Qualified, U.S. Army Intelligence School, 1996
State of North Carolina Limited Electrical License

PERSONAL   Outstanding personal and professional references are available on request.

CAREER CHANGE

Date

Exact Name of Person
Exact Title
Exact Name of Company
Address
City, State, Zip

Dear Exact Name of Person (or Dear Sir or Madam if answering a blind ad):

With the enclosed resume, I would like to make you aware of my interest in exploring employment opportunities with your organization.

As you will see from my resume, I earned an M.S. degree in Computer Science after graduating from the U.S. Military Academy at West Point with a B.S. degree. Most recently I have earned the A+ Certification and I am completing the Microsoft Certified Systems Engineer (MCSE).

I excelled in a variety of assignments as a military officer while serving my country and advancing to the rank of Lieutenant Colonel. As a Company Commander, I functioned as the CEO of a 150-person organization, and I developed a training program described as "the best" in the parent organization. I had an opportunity to return to West Point as a College Instructor and then was handpicked by the Commandant of West Point as his Special Executive Aide in charge of his personal staff and office. A few years after that, the Commanding General at Fort Stewart chose me as his Special Assistant, and I served as the Commanding General's "voice" and "face" in representing the Special Operations Command to top-level decision makers.

Although I was strongly encouraged to remain in military service and assured of continued rapid advancement, I made the decision to leave the U.S. Army and enter the private sector. I am confident I could become an asset to an organization that can use a resourceful problem solver with strong communication skills, proven management ability, and unquestioned integrity.

If you can use my combination of technical knowledge and management experience, I hope you will contact me to suggest a time when we might meet to discuss your needs. I can provide excellent professional and personal recommendations at the appropriate time. Thank you in advance for your time.

Sincerely,

Trevor Nolan

TREVOR NOLAN

1110½ Hay Street, Fayetteville, NC 28305　　•　　preppub@aol.com　　•　　(910) 483-6611

OBJECTIVE　　To contribute to an organization that can use an experienced organizer, manager, and supervisor who offers a formal education in engineering and computer science along with experience as a military officer.

EDUCATION　　**M.S., Computer Science (Software Engineering emphasis),** West Liberty State
& TRAINING　　College, West Liberty, WV, 1995.
　　　　　　　　Bachelor of Science, U.S. Military Academy at West Point, West Point, NY, 1983.

CERTIFICATIONS　Earned A+ Certification, Bryant College, Smithfield, RI, 2003.
　　　　　　　　Microsoft Certified Professional (MCP), Bryant College, Smithfield, RI, 2004.
　　　　　　　　Microsoft Certified Systems Engineer (MCSE), Windows 2000, Bryant College, Smithfield, RI, 2004.

EXPERIENCE　　**STUDENT.** Bryant College, Smithfield, RI (2003-present). Have added state-of-the-art certifications to my earlier background in software engineering and computer science.

Rose to Lieutenant Colonel in the U.S. Army in the following track record:
CONSULTANT ("OBSERVER/CONTROLLER"). Fort Bragg, NC (2001-02). Was described in writing as "an exceptional officer" while serving as a subject matter expert for computer simulation, special forces, psychological operations, and civil affairs.

SPECIAL ASSISTANT TO THE COMMANDING GENERAL. Fort Stewart, GA (2000-01). Was handpicked as Commanding General's assistant and served as his "voice" and "face" in representing the Special Operations Command to top-level decision makers comprising the Quadrennial Defense Review (QDR) and National Defense Panel (NDP).

CHIEF, SPECIAL FORCES DIVISION. Fort Stewart, GA (1998-99). Managed 18 military and five civilian employees while overseeing a division which formulated Special Forces policies and ensured the integration of those policies into overall military infrastructure; oversaw the development, design, and production of training manuals and training plans.
* Supervised the production of the Humanitarian Demining Handbook; was recognized for introducing new training products which would improve Special Forces' performance in the 21st century.

SERVICES OPERATIONS MANAGER. Germany (1997-98). Managed the provision of services supporting an 800-person organization; managed communication electronics and other areas; was credited with "tremendously improving administrative systems."

COLLEGE INSTRUCTOR. U.S. Military Academy at West Point, NY (1992-96). At West Point, instructed a course in Management and Public Speaking; instructed 65 cadets per semester; instituted many new innovations in the course's instruction techniques. Was praised for "dynamic instruction."

GENERAL MANAGER ("COMPANY COMMANDER"). Fort Stewart, GA (1990-91). Managed a 150-person company and developed a training program described as "best in the battalion" because of its "imagination, detailed planning, and aggressive execution."

PERSONAL　　Outstanding references on request. Thrive on solving problems through people. Held one of the nation's highest security clearances: Top Secret/SBI.

Date

Exact Name of Person
Exact Title or Position
Exact Name of Company
Address
City, State, Zip

COMPUTER SYSTEMS
ENGINEER

with experience as a
senior systems analyst

Dear Exact Name of Person (or Dear Sir or Madam if answering a blind ad):

With the enclosed resume, I would like to express my interest in exploring employment opportunities with your organization.

As you will see from my enclosed resume, I am a Senior Systems Analyst involved in database design, development, and integration. With a strong reputation in the field of database application integration and management, I am especially skilled in enterprise-wide project management. I have become proficient at deploying and integrating new database applications, and I have also designed, developed, and deployed database-stored procedures and triggers. I have applied my knowledge and experience with HTML in designing and developing many dynamic project web sites. In enterprise database application development, as well as in software design and development, I have used a wide range of tools including Oracle, Unified Modeling Language (UML), Front Page, Hot Metal Pro, and Coldfusion 4.5.

With an aggressive bottom-line orientation and a strong customer service approach, I have been credited with bringing about significant improvements for customers while overseeing all aspects of their projects. I am known for my ability to translate technical language into information easily understood by everyone, from senior managers to end users.

In prior experience I advanced rapidly to the rank of captain in the U.S. Army. After earning a B.S. degree in the Systems Management field, I completed the U.S. Army's Computer Science School and subsequently excelled in a variety of personnel and logistics management roles. In my last military assignment as a Systems Analyst, I was the chief architect of the Automated Systems Approach to Training (ASAT), a $10 million application supporting a $1 billion learning program. On a formal performance evaluation, I was commended for my "natural leadership style as well as technical knowledge of hardware infrastructures and IDEF modeling."

If you can use an experienced information technology professional who offers well-developed technical skills along with an enthusiastic style of leadership by example, I hope you will contact me to suggest a time when we might meet to discuss your needs. I can assure you in advance that I could rapidly become an asset to your organization. I can provide outstanding references.

Sincerely,

Dale Ross

DALE ROSS

1110½ Hay Street, Fayetteville, NC 28305   •   preppub@aol.com   •   (910) 483-6611

OBJECTIVE   To offer expertise in information technology to an organization that can benefit from my technical skills as well as strong management abilities refined as a military officer.

EDUCATION   **B.S., Administrative Office Management (Systems Management)**, Benedict College, Columbia, SC, 1992; was the respected Commander of the 60-member ROTC Cadet Battalion.

TRAINING   Courses in **Oracle SQL** and **PL/SQL, JavaScript, Microsoft Visual Basic 6.0, Oracle Developer/2000, UNIX Programming**, and **C++ Programming**, United Technology Institute, 2004; **TeamPlay version 1.5.9** project management, Primavera, 2003.

Training programs included an advanced management school and the **U.S. Army Computer Science School** emphasizing system hardware, design, Local Area Network (LAN) management, and programming languages with an emphasis on **Visual Basic and Ada95.**

Courses in **A+ Microcomputer Support and Service, Windows NT Server 4.0** Core Technologies, **Microsoft Exchange Server 5.5** Concepts and Administration, **Unified Modeling Language (UML)** Concepts and Analysis, and **Rational Rose.**

COMPUTER EXPERTISE   Proficient with **Oracle developer** and **Visual Basic 6**, additionally use **Embarcadero Rapid SQL 5.6, Visio 5.0 Technical Drawing software, Allround Automation PL/SQL Developer, Primavera TeamPlay Enterprise Project Management software** versions 1.6.4 and 2.0 as well as **Front Page 2000** and **Hot Metal Pro** version 4; basic knowledge of **Coldfusion version 4.5.**

Proficient in **Windows XP** and **NT, IDEFIX** database modeling techniques, **BPWIN** and **ERWIN** database modeling software, **web design/development**, and **software engineering/design/development**.
* Completed a resident course on the **Powerbuilder 5.0 application language** utilized by the ASAT and SATS system development teams.
* Extensive experience in **enterprise database application development.**

Knowledge of data communications, hardware construction and design, LANs, and WANs.

EXPERIENCE   **SENIOR SYSTEMS ANALYST.** KLAT, Inc., New York, NY (2003-present). Gained respect for my expertise in implementing the enterprise-wide project management database and TeamPlay project management tools which have resulted in significant improvements for customers while overseeing all aspects of database design and development and integrating databases for seamless information flow through separate departments and agencies.
* Work closely with all levels, from senior management to end users, to explain system applications and issues encountered while implementing management solutions.
* Earned praise for my strong written and oral communication skills while developing Java and Active-X solutions to integration of the enterprise-wide project management system with existing customer business processes and automated tools.

Other experience: In the following track record, advanced to Captain in the U.S. Army:
SYSTEMS ANALYST. Fort Drum, NY (2000-03). Was the key architect of the Automated Systems Approach to Training (ASAT), a $10 million application supporting a $1 billion learning program.
LOGISTICS MANAGER. Italy (1996-99). Planned and supervised supply, maintenance, and transportation while tracking expenditures/trends for a 2,500-person organization. Automated logistics review and budget programs.

PERSONAL   Self-starter with strong personal initiative. Held Secret security clearance. Strong references.

Date

Exact Name of Person
Title or Position
Exact Name of Company
Address
City , State, Zip

Dear Exact Name of Person: (or Dear Sir or Madam if answering a blind ad.)

Thank you for your recent expression of interest in my experience. With the enclosed resume, I would like to make you aware of my interest in confidentially exploring management opportunities with your organization.

As you will see from my resume, since 2000 I have worked for Rocky Mountain Constructors, Inc., where I was crosstrained as a Project Manager, Quality Control Manager, and Foreman. I have managed numerous projects for Rocky Mountain Constructors, Inc., and I am the Project Manager for all U.S. government and City of Colorado Springs projects. I am experienced in managing projects including airport expansions as well as projects to establish and renovate utilities and roads. I am extremely experienced in managing construction projects on military bases, and I am accustomed to working with quality control technicians form the Corps of Engineers and other regulatory agencies such as OSHA. I am proficient with all aspects of construction administration including negotiating contracts and subcontracts, creating master project schedules, preparing bids for government jobs, and writing purchase orders for materials. Early in my employment with Rocky Mountain Constructors, I was crosstrained as an Estimator and Quality Control Foreman.

The receipt of numerous letters of appreciation and awards for outstanding performance, I have earned respect for my emphasis on safety, my ability to motivate employees, and my strong bottom-line orientation. I have contributed significantly to my employer's bottom line. For example, I have improved net profit on government jobs from a 15% average to a 35% average. On one $1.6 million job which I managed, the company made a 48% profit.

I hope you will call or write me soon to suggest a time convenient for us to meet and discuss your current and future needs and how I might serve them. Thank you in advance for your time.

Yours sincerely,

Bradley Cameron

Alternate last paragraph:
I hope you will welcome my call soon to arrange a brief meeting to discuss your current and future needs and how I might serve them. Thank you in advance for your time.

BRADLEY CAMERON

1110½ Hay Street, Fayetteville, NC 28305 • preppub@aol.com • (910) 483-6611

OBJECTIVE   To benefit an organization that can use a construction industry Project Manager with previous experience in positions including Quality Control Manager, Foreman, and Estimator.

TECHNICAL   Knowledgeable of OSHA and EMSHA.
KNOWLEDGE   Very knowledgeable of construction activities at Fort Carson and Peterson Air Force Base.

EDUCATION   **Bachelor of Science (B.S.) in Business Administration,** University of Colorado, Colorado Springs, CO, 2004.
Associate in Applied Science (A.A.S.), Pikes Peak Community College, Colorado Springs, CO, 2002.

TRAINING   Completed extensive training by military and civilian organizations including the following:
Asphalt Driving Workshop, Department of the Army
Construction Quality Management, U.S. Army Corps of Engineers
Project Productivity Improvements, Colorado AGC
Hot Mix Asphalt Construction, Department of Transportation

EXPERIENCE   **PROJECT MANAGER.** Rocky Mountain Constructors, Inc., Colorado Springs, CO (2000-present). Began as an **Estimator,** and then was crosstrained in other aspects of the construction business. Worked as a **Laborer** and became familiar with all construction trades. Also worked as a **Quality Control Manager** and **Foreman.**
Highlights of projects: Have managed dozens of projects, and am the Project Manager for all U.S. government and City of Colorado Springs jobs.
- **Renovating and building roads:** For the City of Colorado Springs as well as for Ft. Carson, managed projects which involved the milling of asphalt on road, the raising and lowering of structures, establishing curbs, gutters, and sidewalks, and resurfacing roads.
- **Airport expansion:** Managed a $1.5 million expansion of the Colorado Springs Municipal Airport. Supervised 25 individuals who included foremen, pipe layers, asphalt grade crews, as well as striping and sealcoat crews. Built a general aviation ramp. Finished the project three months ahead of schedule and under budget.
- **Utilities:** Managed a $2 million project at Ft. Carson. Developed a site for the U.S. Special Operations, and was involved in establishing utilities such as water and sewer. Installed all utilities including water, sewer, storm drains, and erosion control. Supervised paving of surfaces. Managed a project which ran smoothly while supervising 35 people.
- **Projects at Fort Carson and Peterson Air Force Base:** Worked on numerous projects on military bases, and have become skilled at working with the government quality control standards. During one project at Peterson AFB, worked under extremely tight deadlines as the runway could be shut down for only three weeks. Built two taxiways and repaired an emergency sinkhole while also restriping the runway.
- **Extensive supervisory experience:** On numerous occasions, supervise 75 people including 10 foremen when the company's chief project manager is away.
- **Proficiency with government paperwork:** Have become proficient in writing subcontracts, writing purchase orders for materials, creating master project schedules using CPM, preparing bids for government jobs, and coordinating with quality control technicians from the Corps of Engineers.
- **Bottom-line results:** Have improved net profit on government jobs from a 15% average to a 35% average. The company made a 48% profit on one $1.6 million job.

PERSONAL   Excellent references on request. Have received numerous letters of appreciation and awards.

Date

Exact Name of Person
Title or Position
Exact Name of Company
Address
City, State, Zip

Dear Exact Name of Person (or Dear Sir or Madam if answering a blind ad):

With the enclosed resume, I would like to make you aware of my interest in exploring employment opportunities with your organization. Although I am excelling in my current position and can provide excellent references at the appropriate time, I have made a decision that I wish to relocate back to Washington, DC, where I grew up.

As you will see from my resume, I have excelled for the past 12 years in a field which typically requires an engineering degree even though my B.A. from the Yale University in New Haven, CT, is in English Literature! Of course I have completed numerous technical management programs and extensive technical training.

After serving my country in the U.S. Navy and working in the Merchant Marines, I began employment with Eastern Industries as a Technical Writer, and I produced multiple users' manuals for people in disciplines ranging from accounts payable to purchasing and engineering. Because of my reputation as an effective communicator, I was then handpicked by Eastern Industries to work as a Project Manager. ISO 9000 was a new concept at that time, and my corporation needed a resourceful individual who could figure out how to make that concept work at multiple plants across the U.S. so that those plants could achieve the certification required by law. It was my job to visit those plants and provide the leadership for solving problems ranging from out-of-control scrap rates to manufacturing process problems. In my experience, I have learned that employees are the key to solving nearly all productivity and profitability problems.

In 2003 I was recruited by a plant within the Haven "family" to relocate to Maine to become its first Continuous Improvement Manager. Since arriving in Maine in 2003, I have played a key role in increasing plant profitability from 3% to 12%, and I have led efforts which have resulted in reducing inventory from $64 million to $28-32 million while improving product availability from 90% to 99%.

Although the work of improving internal processes is never complete, I have helped the plant to reach new record levels of profitability and efficiency, and I am proud that all plant employees have been trained in Continuous Improvement. A native of DC, I now am yearning to "go back home" and I am selectively exploring the possibility of joining an organization which can use a creative problem solver, strong leader, and skilled efficiency expert. If you feel that you have internal problems which you would like to discuss with me or are not even sure if you have a full-time job for a problem solver like myself, I still would enjoy meeting you and confidentially discussing your needs.

Yours sincerely,

Dylan Cooper

DYLAN COOPER

1110½ Hay Street, Fayetteville, NC 28305 • preppub@aol.com • (910) 483-6611

OBJECTIVE

I want to contribute to the profitability and efficiency of an organization that can use a skilled problem solver who offers technical expertise related to the areas of quality assurance systems, manufacturing systems, and general continuous improvement management.

EXPERIENCE

Advanced in the following track record of promotion with Haven Industries, a publicly traded conglomerate headquartered in New Haven, CT; Eastern Corporation purchased assets from Haven Industries in 2004 and I have continued with Eastern Corporation in an expanded role since the purchase:

2003-present: CONTINUOUS IMPROVEMENT MANAGER. EastHouse Division of Eastern Corporation. Was aggressively recruited by a plant in the Haven "family" after I acted as an internal consultant.

- Played a key role in increasing the plant's profitability from 3% to 12%, nearly unheard of in the automotive aftermarket industry. Led efforts which resulted in reducing inventory from $64 million to $28-32 million while boosting product availability from 90% to 99%. Have provided strong leadership through a vibrant period of change.
- Manage four people directly; established employee leadership teams.
- Created a dynamic employee team approach within the plant which has resulted in significant contributions to strategic planning, technical problem solving, and employee morale. Established the site's first Continuous Improvement (CI) Team as well as the Continuous Improvement Committee which is comprised of employees across multiple disciplines; developed the 20 Keys of Continuous Improvement Program; set up the AMPS Performance Excellence and Business Excellence Systems.

1997-03: PROJECT MANAGER. New Haven, CT. Became the company's foremost authority on ISO 9000/QS 9000 and quality assurance systems; succeeded in obtaining QS 9000 certification for all automotive OE plants within one calendar year.

- In an essentially entrepreneurial role, was handpicked by the company to implement new QS 9000 guidelines for the Automotive Group. Implemented the company's first ISO 9000 at a Maine plant, and established the model for future implementation.

1996-97: PROJECT MANAGER. New Haven, CT. Was specially selected for this newly created position by the corporation's new Director of Total Quality Management.

1995-96: TECHNICAL WRITER. New Haven, CT. Interviewed experts in Material Requisition & Planning (MRP), Purchasing, Engineering, Accounts Payable, and Engineering.

Other experience:
NAVAL SEAMAN. Merchant Marines, locations worldwide. Developed strong technical problem-solving skills while operating a large seagoing vessel and performing complex maintenance aboard ship; managed and trained mechanics and maintenance professionals.
NAVIGATION QUARTERMASTER. U.S. Navy, locations worldwide. Was promoted ahead of my peers while serving in the U.S. Navy; received outstanding evaluations.

EDUCATION

Completed **B.A. in English Literature,** Yale University, New Haven, CT, 1991.
Extensive executive development related to Quality Assurance Systems, Manufacturing Systems, Continuous Process Improvement, ISO 9000, ISO 14000, and QS 9000.

PERSONAL

Highly intuitive and analytical problem solver who believes that employee involvement is essential to solving most profitability, process, efficiency, and other problems.

Exact Name of Person
Title or Position
Exact Name of Company
Address
City, State, Zip

**ELECTRICAL
ENGINEER**

with experience as a
director for
engineering
development &
operations

Dear Exact Name of Person: (or Dear Sir or Madam if answering a blind ad.)

I would appreciate an opportunity to speak with you soon about how I could contribute to your organization through my management and supervisory skills as well as through my technical abilities, experience in program development and operation, and expertise in human and material resource management.

With degrees in Technology Management and Electrical Engineering, I offer a combination of educational areas which allows me to understand corporate operations both from the technical and the business side.

As you will see from my resume, I have risen to positions of increasing responsibility as a U.S. Air Force officer who has been handpicked for critical managerial roles due to excellent achievements and demonstrated talents. Through my management experience as an officer, I have come to believe that continuous training of human resources is often the key to an organizations' success in the marketplace. Skilled in diagnosing training requirements and conceptualizing methods needed for improvement, I have earned a reputation as a successful manager who is skilled in balancing company goals and employee needs.

Through my experience in controlling billion-dollar inventories of high-tech assets, I have reached a level where I can transfer my knowledge to benefit any size organization and quickly step into a role where I can make valuable contributions. In addition to my ability to quickly and easily grasp complex issues and systems, I am highly skilled in maximizing human resources. I have built training programs from the ground up and quickly made them cost effective and successful. My knowledge of curriculum development and experience in providing both academic and practical technical instruction would benefit an organization looking for a responsible, mature, and enthusiastic person to develop and maintain corporate training programs.

I hope you will welcome my call soon to arrange a brief meeting at your convenience to discuss your current and future needs and how I might serve them. Thank you in advance for your time.

Sincerely yours,

Vincent Frontier

Alternate last paragraph:
I hope you will call or write me soon to suggest a time convenient for us to meet and discuss your current and future needs and how I might serve them. Thank you in advance for your time.

VINCENT FRONTIER

1110½ Hay Street, Fayetteville, NC 28305 • preppub@aol.com • (910) 483-6611

OBJECTIVE

To benefit an organization that can use a sharp executive who has excelled in demanding and innovative roles which required expertise in maximizing both human and material resources as well as in developing and managing highly technical training programs.

EDUCATION & EXECUTIVE TRAINING

M.S., Technology Management, Georgetown University, Washington, DC, 2004; graduated with a **3.91 GPA.**

B.S., Electrical Engineering, University of Michigan, Ann Arbor, MI.

Excelled in more than one year of highly technical training to qualify as a U.S. Air Force pilot as well as programs designed to prepare skilled classroom instructors and managers.

- Received the **Outstanding Graduate Award** for leadership and practical skills and for attaining a 99% average on the academic portions of the intense, pressure-filled pilot training program which had a 30% attrition rate.

EXPERIENCE

DIRECTOR FOR ENGINEERING DEVELOPMENT & OPERATIONS. U.S. Air Force, Altus AFB, OK (2004-present). Handpicked to establish a program for engineering professionals re-entering a highly technical field, oversaw the various aspects of smoothly operating a $9 billion program.

- Rated in the top 10% in my career field, was evaluated as "exceptionally qualified" in providing instruction and in managerial excellence.
- Achieved a 100% pass rate in a program where the cost of retraining each individual pilot in a sophisticated new aircraft was approximately $50,000.
- Implemented training techniques which saved $75,000 by reducing training time 10%.
- Taught 105 students both in academic subjects and flight instruction techniques.
- Qualified in a $300 million flight simulator, applied my technical knowledge while providing instruction to students who had not previously been exposed to this equipment.
- Integrated up-to-date computer graphics presentations into obsolete materials.

Steadily advanced in technical and human resources management experiences, U.S. Air Force, Andrews AFB, MD:

OPERATIONS MANAGER. (2002-04). Supervised the various aspects of training for a four-person team of qualified professionals operating a $280 million aircraft.

- Created and implemented a unique new system of handling one highly technical phase of operations; developed training criteria for teaching the new techniques.
- Evaluated and tested a new avionics software package which was accepted for widespread use and which made a major impact on operational capabilities.

HUMAN & MATERIAL RESOURCES MANAGER. (1997-02). Selected from a highly qualified pool of candidates, oversaw activities including safety, resource utilization, and logistical support as well as personnel management and training activities.

- Accepted into the first group of professionals to be trained, joined in the initial phases to fly what was at that time the world's newest and most complex intercontinental bomber.

OPERATIONS MANAGER & PILOT. (1993-97). Quickly became known for my superior technical knowledge, skills, and leadership abilities and performed with distinction as a leader of a six-person team operating a $50 million aircraft.

PERSONAL

Feel that my greatest strengths lie in managing technologically advanced programs while maximizing both human and material resources through my ingenuity, intelligence, and leadership abilities. Received three prestigious medals. Hold Top Secret (ESI) clearance.

Date

Exact Name of Person
Exact Title
Exact Name of Company
Address
City, State, Zip

Dear Exact Name of Person (or Dear Sir or Madam if answering a blind ad):

With the enclosed resume, I would like to make you aware of my interest in exploring employment opportunities with your organization.

Business experience and business degree

As you will see from my resume, I hold a B.S. degree in Electrical Engineering with a minor in Marketing. While earning my degree with honors, I bought and managed a 16-year-old business with an established clientele. I took over the operation of a service business and immediately added retail products which appealed to an established clientele. In addition to modernizing exterior signs and renovating the interior at minimum expense, I made a lot of small changes that significantly improved customer service and customer satisfaction. I thoroughly enjoyed operating the business while completing my business administration degree, as it gave me a chance to apply numerous theories and principles which I learned in the classroom. I recently sold the business and am pursuing full-time employment as an electrical engineer.

Experience in team management and resource management

Prior to earning my college degree, I served my country with distinction in the U.S. Army. My father was in the U.S. Air Force, and I came to the U.S. when I was eight years old. I have loved America since the first day I stepped on American soil, and I knew that I wanted to enlist in the U.S. Army after graduating from high school. While earning promotion ahead of my peers, I excelled in management positions including Team Leader and Squad Leader, and I cheerfully accepted assignments which placed me in combat environments and situations of world unrest. I was proud to be a part of the force that responded to turmoil in the Middle East. I felt honored to be the team leader who led the first unit into Iraq as ground forces, and I managed my team for ten months in that combat environment. I cheerfully traveled throughout the world, to locations in order to manage and motivate teams of individuals.

I believe the military prepared me well for civilian employment in terms of providing experience in team management and resource management. In my final position in the military, I acted as a Training Manager and Section Leader as I was entrusted with the responsibility for accounting for hazardous materials.

If you can use a versatile young professional with tested business skills along with a "can-do" and enthusiastic attitude when it comes to serving my employer, I hope you will contact me to suggest a time when we might meet to discuss your needs. I can provide outstanding references.

Yours sincerely,

Wayne Buckley

WAYNE BUCKLEY

1110½ Hay Street, Fayetteville, NC 28305   •   preppub@aol.com   •   (910) 483-6611

OBJECTIVE

To contribute to an organization that can use a versatile professional with proven management skills along with strong organizational, communication, and problem-solving abilities.

EDUCATION

Bachelor of Science (B.S.) degree in Electrical Engineering, *cum laude,* University of Portland, OR, 2004.

Associate of Science (A.S.) degree in General Studies, Central Michigan University, Fort Bragg, NC, 2001.

EXPERIENCE

ENTREPRENEUR & ELECTRICAL ENGINEERING STUDENT. Buck's Sewing & Dry Cleaning, Portland, OR (2001-04). After leaving the U.S. Army, I furthered my education while simultaneously buying and operating a business which had been in existence for 16 years; while excelling academically in completing my B.S. degree, I modernized and improved the profitability of the business.

- Computerized manual bookkeeping and order tracking functions by adding a computer.
- Improved customer service and turnaround times; diversified this service business and utilized physical capacity by adding some retail products which appealed to both military and civilian customers. Modernized exterior signs. Changed lots of "little things" that made a big difference.
- Recently sold the business; am taking graduate-level MBA courses while acting as an Office Manager for Oregon Printing, Inc. in Tigard, OR. My current employer is aware that I am seeking full-time employment and will provide an excellent reference.

Highlights of military experience: *I decided to enlist in the U.S. Army after high school so that I could fight for my country's honor and ideals. I volunteered for every hazardous duty assignment available and proudly served in Iraq, Haiti, and other world hot spots.*

1998-01: TRAINING MANAGER & SECTION LEADER. Was specially selected for a position which required meticulous attention to detail. Was in charge of accounting for the issue and turn-in of ammunition which included parachutes, bullets, bombs, and grenades as well as food.

- Excelled in a job where there was "no room for error." Military careers have frequently been destroyed because of negligent procedures in ammunition accountability. I executed one of the largest ammunition draws in the organization's history, and was commended as "among the best" in my flawless control of hazardous resources.

1997-98: SQUAD LEADER. Fort Polk, LA. Was in charge of two teams with up to 11 people in each squad. Was part of the force that responded to the crisis in Haiti.

1994-97: TEAM LEADER. While stationed in Kentucky, managed three airborne infantry rifle teams with four individuals on the team. We were carried out assignments in Australia, Thailand, and Japan.

1991-94: TEAM LEADER. Iraq. Trained my team to invade Iraq. I led a unit to deploy into Iraq as ground troops, and we spent ten months in that combat environment.

- Served in Haiti as part of a force keeping the peace. Managed a four-man team and acted as Squad Leader in charge of 11 people in the Squad Leader's absence.
- After Haiti, participated in Operation Desert Storm during the war in the Middle East.

PERSONAL

Received many medals for top performance. Held Secret clearance. Excellent references.

Exact Name of Person
Exact Title
Exact Name of Company
Address
City, State, Zip

ELECTRICAL ENGINEER

with limited experience as an intern

Dear Exact Name of Person (or Dear Sir or Madam if answering a blind ad):

With the enclosed resume, I would like to express my interest in exploring employment opportunities with your organization.

As you will see from my resume, I have recently completed my B.S. degree in Electrical Engineering in a degree program that emphasized hands-on internships and practical assignments. Early in my undergraduate career, I developed an electrical power distribution plan. In my senior year, I contributed significantly to a project which implements a bubble sort algorithm. On another project, I creatively accomplished a project that involved the implementation of a surveillance system for a car, house, and garage using 6800 Assembly language. During my internship, I completed the design of a seven-segment digital display while conducting extensive research in the area of integrated circuits.

In my spare time, I enjoy reading, playing chess, and playing computer games. I am sure you would find me to be a highly original thinker with an ability to develop practical solutions to difficult problems.

I hope you will call or write me soon to suggest a time convenient for us to meet and discuss your current and future needs and how I might serve them. Thank you in advance for your time.

Sincerely,

Harry Dudley

Alternate last paragraph:
I hope you will welcome my call soon to arrange a brief meeting to discuss your current and future needs and how I might serve them. Thank you in advance for your time.

HARRY DUDLEY

1110½ Hay Street, Fayetteville, NC 28305 • preppub@aol.com • (910) 483-6611

OBJECTIVE

To benefit an organization that can use a highly-motivated young electrical engineer with both practical experience and extensive education in the field.

EDUCATION

Bachelor of Science degree in Electrical Engineering, University of Vermont, Burlington, VT, December, 2004.

Organizations and Honors
- In 2000, was named a United Methodist Church Scholar and received the Chancellor's Incentive Award from University of Vermont.
- In 2001, was initiated as a member of USAF ROTC, and was appointed Logistics Officer.
- As a member of the National Society of Black Engineers, worked on several projects on the Cultural Awareness Committee.
- Was accepted as a member of the National Society of Professional Engineers.
- Earned recognition on the Dean's List for two quarters, Spring 2003 and 2004.

Projects and Papers
- Creatively accomplished a project that involved the implementation of a surveillance system for a car, house, and garage using 6800 Assembly language (University of Vermont, Fall 2002).
- Developed an electrical power distribution plan (University of Vermont, Fall 2000).
- Contributed significantly to a project which implements a bubble sort algorithm (University of Vermont, Fall 2004).
- Have taken specialty courses which included analog and digital signal processing, applied mathematics, power electronics, electromagnetics, switching theory, solid state physics, microprocessor programming, and power systems and electric machinery analysis.

COMPUTER SKILLS

Am knowledgeable of the following software, languages, and operating systems:
Microsoft Windows, Excel, PowerPoint
Adobe PageMaker, Acrobat, Illustrator

EXPERIENCE

ELECTRICAL ENGINEER INTERN. NSF-ERC/University of Vermont, Burlington, VT (Summer 2004). Attended lectures on VLSI design and microelectronics and completed the design of a seven-segment digital display while conducting extensive research in the area of integrated circuits.
- Gained hands-on experience using CAD tools; performed laboratory work in integrated circuit processing.

WAREHOUSE CLERK. Vermont Industries, Burlington, VT (Summer 2003). For a major manufacturer of fans, air conditioners, and home comfort products, controlled a large inventory while inspecting items for quality and preparing items for shipment.
- Learned valuable skills in inventory control.

PRODUCTION LINE WORKER. Craftsman, Burlington, VT (Summer 2002). Was responsible for the packaging and quality inspection of power tools while identifying each product with a code indicating the date and site of fabrication/assembly.
- Contributed ideas to my supervisor which he considered valuable and practical in relation to increasing production efficiency.

PERSONAL

In my spare time, I enjoy reading, computer games, chess, and playing cards, as well as football, basketball, and running.

Date

Exact Name of Person
Exact Title
Exact Name of Company
Address
City, State, Zip

Dear Exact Name of Person (or Dear Sir or Madam if answering a blind ad):

With the enclosed resume, I would like to express my interest in exploring employment opportunities with your organization.

As you will see from my resume, I earned a B.S. degree in Electrical Engineering and then joined the U.S. Army as a military officer. I have received numerous medals and awards while serving with distinction in the communications and automation field. Although I was strongly encouraged to remain in military service and assured of continued rapid advancement ahead of my peers, I decided to leave the military and enter the civilian workforce.

I am grateful to the U.S. Army for giving me the opportunity to manage multimillion-dollar assets and dozens of employees. In my most recent position, I supervised 12 communications specialists while overseeing automation architecture, upgrades, and repairs. In a previous assignment as a Signal Operations Officer, I oversaw maintenance and operation of an $11 million inventory. I can provide outstanding references of my technical expertise and personal integrity.

I hope you will call or write me soon to suggest a time convenient for us to meet and discuss your current and future needs and how I might serve them. Thank you in advance for your time.

Sincerely,

Derek Foyer

Alternate last paragraph:
I hope you will welcome my call soon to arrange a brief meeting to discuss your current and future needs and how I might serve them. Thank you in advance for your time.

DEREK FOYER

1110½ Hay Street, Fayetteville, NC 28305   •   preppub@aol.com   •   (910) 483-6611

OBJECTIVE

To contribute strong technical skills and managerial abilities to an organization that can use an energetic, flexible, and talented professional who is excelling as a military officer.

EDUCATION & TRAINING

B.S., Electrical Engineering, Texas A & M University, Corpus Christi, TX, 2001.
Completed programs in areas including management training and an EMT course.

EXPERIENCE

Am building a track record of success and advancement as a manager of technical communications operations while consistently being handpicked for highly-visible managerial roles as a U.S. Army officer:

SIGNAL COMMUNICATIONS MANAGER. Fort Drum, NY (2004-present). Was handpicked from among a pool of managers in 17 sister companies to assume the role of "Battalion Signal Officer" for an element of the 10th Mountain Division.
- Supervise and train a team of 12 communications specialists while overseeing automation architecture, upgrades, and repairs. Earned evaluation as providing "flawless" management for numerous training events including one joint exercise in Mojave Desert.
- Earned "no faults noted" ratings during four consecutive high-level inspections including one stating that communications operations evaluations were the "best on record."

SIGNAL OPERATIONS MANAGER. Fort Knox, KY (2002-04). Managed a 31-person Contingency Communications Package (CCP) with the mission of providing uninterrupted signal communication support for Fort Knox in real-world emergencies, during training, and in day-to-day activities.
- Oversaw maintenance and operation of 20 vehicles, eight high-tech communications systems, and six power generation units with a total value in excess of $11 million.
- Supported three geographically dispersed mission within one three-month period and attained noteworthy results during each operation.
- Received a U.S. Army Achievement Medal for "meritorious achievements" while providing 100% reliable communications support for a joint exercise on the U.S. east coast.
- Managed the only one of three teams which passed a joint U.S. Army-Air Force inspection with no deficiencies – on the first attempt. Was credited with displaying exceptional organizational and planning skills during preparations for a holiday ball for 550 people.
- Was selected to handle the duties of Information Systems Security Manager as well as planning air transportation support for personnel and equipment.
- Was awarded the Humanitarian Service Medal for contributions during clean-up efforts following the devastation of Hurricane Rochelle in fall 2003.

COMMUNICATIONS AND AUTOMATION SERVICES MANAGER. Fort Campbell, KY (2001-02). Demonstrated strong management skills while overseeing operation of a "node center" which supported numerous airborne, medical, artillery, and infantry units.
- Controlled an $11 million inventory of communications systems, power generation equipment, and vehicles.
- Trained, guided, and acted as a mentor for 18 supervisors and 36 employees.
- Evaluated as "calm under high levels of stress," managed training and exercises including a training session where qualification with one specific type of equipment reached the 300% level for a group of 176 participants who had previously scored 50%.

PERSONAL

In excellent physical condition, consistently earn maximum 300 scores during physical fitness testing and have participated in several competitive 10-mile runs. Am respected for my unselfish attitude and willingness to give my time to guiding and teaching others.

Exact Name of Person
Title or Position
Exact Name of Company
Address
City, State, Zip

ELECTRICAL ENGINEER
with experience in
telecommunications,
training, and other areas

Dear Exact Name of Person: (or Dear Sir or Madam if answering a blind ad.)

I would appreciate an opportunity to talk with you soon about how I could contribute to your organization through my extensive experience in product management as well as through the management abilities I have refined in a career as a military officer.

Having become familiar with Department of Defense acquisition and testing procedures, I also offer experience in contract negotiations through my successful management of seven communications products. I saw these projects through all stages from production, to initial operational and software qualifications testing, to planning improvements, to fielding, on through the retrofit stage. All projects were successfully completed under budget and on time.

As you will see from my enclosed resume, I received my M.S.E.E. in Electrical Engineering and earlier graduated from the United States Military Academy at West Point with a degree in Engineering.

I feel that my expertise in managing multimillion-dollar research & development and procurement budgets and my reputation for **always** bringing projects in on time without going over budget guidelines would make me a valuable asset to your organization's operations.

I hope you will welcome my call soon to arrange a brief meeting at your convenience to discuss your current and future needs and how I might serve them. Thank you in advance for your time.

Sincerely yours,

William Lowell

Alternate last paragraph:
I hope you will call or write soon to suggest a time convenient for us to meet and discuss your current and future needs and how I might serve them. Thank you in advance for your time.

WILLIAM LOWELL

1110½ Hay Street, Fayetteville, NC 28305 • preppub@aol.com • (910) 483-6611

OBJECTIVE

To apply my expertise in product management and research and development to an organization that can benefit from my knowledge of communications systems and reputation for bringing projects in under budget and ahead of schedule.

EDUCATION and TRAINING

M.S.E.E., Electrical Engineering, University of North Dakota, Grand Forks, ND, 2001.
B.S. in Engineering, the United States Military Academy, West Point, NY, 1998.
Excelled in more than 2,500 hours of training in materials acquisition, network engineering, GTE MSE planning, and contract negotiations.

EXPERIENCE

TRAINING DIRECTOR. U.S. Army, Fort Drum, NY (2004-present). Plan and direct training programs for a 600-person organization while supervising 12 employees. Fielded a $100 million Mobile Subscriber Equipment (MSE) system.

PROJECT MANAGER. U.S. Army, Fort Rucker, AL (2004). Controlled $311.3 million dollars for R&D and $276 million for procurement while planning testing and evaluation of the MILSTAR communications terminal. Prepared proposals which led to product acceptance.

TELECOMMUNICATIONS MANAGER. U.S. Army, Iraq (2003-04). Directed 15 engineers planning, installing, and operating communications in support of allied operations during the War on Terror. Earned the respected Bronze Star Medal for installing 30 automated circuit switches, 15 message switches, over 92 transmissions systems, and 20 interfaces with other military services/nations.

TECHNICAL ADVISOR. U.S. Army, Fort Campbell, KY (2003). Served as liaison between a general officer, eight project managers, the Department of the Army, and communications-electronics experts. Directed testing of six systems worth more than $611 million dollars.

TEST DIVISION DIRECTOR. U.S. Army, Fort Campbell, KY (2001-03). Supervised three engineers involved in testing, developing, and engineering six communications terminals; controlled $921.3 million in R&D/procurement funds.
•   Tested and approved a critical communications security (COMSEC) device.

TELECOMMUNICATIONS PROJECT MANAGER. U.S. Army, Fort Bragg, NC (2001). Managed 12 technicians and scheduled troubleshooting and repairs of a wide-area communications network with five automated switchboards.

GENERAL MANAGER. U.S. Army, Korea (2000-01). Oversaw 214 employees maintaining $15 million dollars worth of equipment including 42 communications assemblages as well as more than 60 vehicles. Remained under budget while controlling $250,000 annually.

COMMUNICATIONS & OPERATIONS MANAGER. U.S. Army, Italy (1999-00). Coordinated major training projects while managing eight technicians in a 24-hour-a-day communications command center. Implemented two new communications systems.

MAINTENANCE MANAGER. U.S. Army, Fort Rucker, AL (1998-99). Initiated a preventive maintenance plan which led to higher equipment availability rates for more than 100 communications systems. Transported equipment 600 miles with no accidents or breakdowns.

PERSONAL

Top Secret security clearance. Experienced with Windows, Adobe, and other programs.

Date

Exact Name of Person
Exact Title
Exact Name of Company
Address
City, State, Zip

Dear Exact Name of Person (or Dear Sir or Madam if answering a blind ad):

With the enclosed resume, I would like to express my interest in exploring employment opportunities with your organization.

As you will see from my resume, I have recently completed my B.S. in Electrical Engineering in the evening program while excelling in a full-time job with the Department of Transportation. In my current position, I design, write, and prepare CADD plans for the routing of fiber optic or copper communications, and I also write project specifications. Although I have gained extensive insight into traffic engineering, I am exploring engineering opportunities in other areas.

If you can use a talented young electrical engineer with versatile knowledge of personal computers, digital microprocessing systems, and electronics, I hope you will contact me to suggest a time when we can discuss your needs. I can provide outstanding references at the appropriate time.

Sincerely,

David Hoffman

Alternate last paragraph:
I hope you will call or write me soon to suggest a time convenient for us to meet and discuss your current and future needs and how I might serve them. Thank you in advance for your time.

DAVID HOFFMAN

1110½ Hay Street, Fayetteville, NC 28305   •   preppub@aol.com   •   (910) 483-6611

OBJECTIVE   To offer my education and experience in the field of electrical engineering to a growth-oriented organization that can use a dedicated fast learner.

EDUCATION   ***Bachelor of Science degree in Electrical Engineering,*** South Dakota School of Mines and Technology, Rapid City, SD, 2004.

ELECTRONICS LABORATORY II. (Fall 2004)
- Analyzed frequency response of BJT and JFET amplifiers.
- Designed operation integrator and differentiator amplifiers.
- Designed two-stage CS-CE amplifier.

DIGITAL SIGNAL ANALYSIS AND PROCESSING. (Spring 2004)
- Designed and analyzed a second-order bandpass filter using MatLab.
- Designed and analyzed a digital notch filter using MatLab.

ELECTRICAL CIRCUITS ANALYSIS LABORATORY II. (Fall 2003)
- Designed and analyzed series and parallel RL, RC, CL, and RLC circuits.

DIGITAL MICROPROCESSING SYSTEMS LABORATORY. (Spring 2003)
- Designed and implemented an automobile security system for my final project.

PC CAPABILITIES.
- Excel
- Access
- Word

EXPERIENCE   **TRAFFIC ENGINEERING TECHNICIAN III.** South Dakota Department of Transportation (SDDOT), Rapid City, SD (2004-present).
- Design, write, and prepare CADD plans for the routing of fiber optic or copper communications cable from a Central Controller to proposed intersections.
- Write project specifications which cover all work and requirements for each project.
- Complete field inspections during which I gather information about possible cable routings.

ENGINEERING TECHNICIAN. Dakota Power, Inc., Rapid City, SD (2003).
- Involved engineering aspects of designing transformers, testing of transformer coil voltages and currents, and hands-on coil winding.

TEMPORARY SERVICE EMPLOYEE. Express Personnel, Rapid City, SD (2002).
- Assembled industrial pumps at Dakota Power, Inc.; included reading schematics and simple wiring.

ACTIVITIES   Member of Rapid City "Service" Club
2004 Northwest "Service" Club 3-on-3 Basketball Champions

PERSONAL   Excellent personal and professional references available upon request.

Date

Exact Name of Person
Title or Position
Name of Company
Address (no., street)
Address (city, state, zip)

ELECTRICAL ENGINEER & CHIEF OF ENGINEERING TRAINING BRANCH

Dear Exact Name of Person: (or Dear Sir or Madam if answering a blind ad.)

I would appreciate an opportunity to talk with you soon about how I could contribute to your organization through my extensive background in engineering and management.

As a military officer with the famed Special Forces Command, I most recently excelled in directing engineering training programs serving an 11,000-person population. In my prior job, I was in a "hotseat" decision-making role in charge of overseeing the utilization of personnel involved in activities in Europe. Especially during the war in Iraq, I was responsible on a daily basis for briefing the Commanding General.

I am a seasoned manager of human and physical resources. In one position, I managed a highly specialized 12-person team while managing the entire company's operations in the absence of the general manager. In other jobs I have managed more than 30 people in high-tech communications operations. I have successfully managed nearly every type of functional area ranging from logistics, to budgeting, to training administration.

As a military officer I have earned high praise for my excellent communication and public speaking skills. In several of my jobs, I have briefed commanding generals and other high-ranking officers on a daily basis, and I have discovered that I have a special talent for marketing concepts and "selling" ideas. With a B.S. degree in Electrical Engineering, I am German language qualified and graduated as an Honor Graduate from the Special Forces Qualification Course.

Entrusted with one of the nation's highest security clearances (Top Secret with SBI), I can provide personal and professional references.

I hope you will welcome my call soon to arrange a brief meeting at your convenience to discuss your current and future needs and how I might serve them. Thank you in advance for your time.

Sincerely yours,

Frederick Benning

Alternate last paragraph:
I hope you will call or write me soon to suggest a time convenient for us to meet and discuss your current and future needs and how I might serve them. Thank you in advance for your time.

FREDERICK BENNING

1110½ Hay Street, Fayetteville, NC 28305   •   preppub@aol.com   •   (910) 483-6611

OBJECTIVE   To contribute to an organization that can use a skilled manager with experience as a military officer who offers a proven ability to plan strategically, implement creatively, troubleshoot resourcefully, and motivate effectively.

EDUCATION   **B.S. degree in Electrical Engineering**, University of Baltimore, Baltimore, MD, 1994.
- As a military officer, was Honor Graduate of Officer's Special Forces Qualification Training Course; Graduate of Ranger Course, Language Course (German), and Infantry Officer's Advance Course. Airborne and Jumpmaster Badges; Ranger and Special Forces Tab; Air Movement Officer Qualified.

EXPERIENCE   **CHIEF OF ENGINEERING TRAINING BRANCH.** U.S. Special Forces Command, Fort Bragg, NC (2004-present). Manage, supervise, and direct professional development schools and engineering training programs for the entire Special Forces Command with more than 11,000 personnel; manage eight people who are technical experts in areas including ammunition, NBC, language, and training administration.
- Implement new training regulations that strengthened the professional skills of 11,000 people. Establish new language requirements as well as new training policies.
- Brief the commanding general and his staff on a weekly basis.
- Earned a reputation as a gifted strategic planner and highly effective public speaker.

ENGINEERING SUPPORT OFFICER FOR EUROPE. U.S. Special Forces Command (Airborne), Fort Bragg, NC (2002-04). Planned and implemented all actions pertaining to the movement and utilization of Special Forces personnel in Europe; coordinated with high-ranking government officials, external agencies, non-governmental organizations, and internal Special Forces personnel.
- Served as Communications Security Officer and Special Project Officer.
- Managed a two-person desk which expanded to nine people during the war in Iraq; had my management and decision-making skills tested during projects.

DETACHMENT ("A") COMMANDER. Fort Drum, NY (2000-02). Received an Army Commendation Medal for my outstanding performance in a job in which I was responsible for the planning and executing of foreign Internal Defense, Special Reconnaissance, Direct Action, and Humanity Assistance Missions.
- Accounted for equipment valued at $1.5 million. Managed 12 people as Detachment Commander; as Interim Company Commander for 78 days, was in charge of the company's 92 people. Was the commander for two counterdrug missions.

SIGNAL DETACHMENT COMMANDER/PLATOON LEADER. Fort Drum, NY (1995-99). Managed a 27-person platoon and a 30-person detachment; responsible for $7 million in wire communications, automatic switching telephone terminal; HF, FM and Tactical Satellite (TACSAT) radio communications, Teletype System, and Message Center.

PLATOON LEADER/EXECUTIVE OFFICER. Italy (1994-95). Managed more than 35 soldiers in a communications platoon for a nuclear capable field artillery battalion; oversaw wire communications, FM radio and radio relay site, teletype, and battalion-level communications repair. Responsible for equipment worth over $5 million.

PERSONAL   Top Secret security clearance (SBI). Language qualified (German). Outstanding public speaking skills. Proficient with Microsoft Word, Excel, and PowerPoint.

Date

Exact Name of Person
Exact Title
Exact Name of Company
Address
City, State, Zip

**ELECTRONICS
ENGINEER**

with a degree in
business
management

Dear Exact Name of Person (or Dear Sir or Madam if answering a blind ad):

With the enclosed resume, I would like to express my interest in exploring employment opportunities with your organization.

As you will see from my resume, I have been completing a Bachelor's degree in Business Administration on a full-time basis while acting as a freelance Electronics Technician to businesses and individuals. Now seeking full-time employment, I am single and available for worldwide relocation according to your needs.

I offer strong management and problem-solving skills as well as a degree in Electronics Engineering from the Florida Institute of Technology. After graduating from FIT, I worked as a Biomedical Electronics Technician at the University of North Carolina at Chapel Hill Medical Center, where I refined my electronics problem-solving skills. I was subsequently recruited for a management position in a company which installed equipment such as intrusion detection, computer-based alarm systems, security and access monitoring systems, and closed circuit TV. While coordinating technical requirements for numerous projects, I became the "go-to" guy when a project was in trouble. On numerous occasions, I rescued projects which were seriously overbudget and behind schedule, and I earned a reputation as a skillful communicator, motivator, and negotiator. I played a vital management role in projects for SEA-TAC International Airport, Wells Fargo, the Portland Performing Arts Center, and many other organizations.

I was subsequently recruited by an established chiropractic center in Lexington at a time when the owner was experiencing serious cash flow problems. After I took over the management of the staff and programs, I led the company to win the respected Friendly Award, which recognizes top achievements in profitability, customer satisfaction, and quality programming. That company went out of business, however, after the franchise was bought by new owners who were unfamiliar with the key elements for success in that business.

Although I have been enjoying my Business Management studies, I am eager to resume full-time employment with an organization that can use a versatile producer who excels in dealing with people and managing projects. I would appreciate your contacting me if you can use my versatile background in management, problem-solving, and electronics troubleshooting. Thank you in advance for your time.

Sincerely,

Michael Freagle

MICHAEL FREAGLE

1110½ Hay Street, Fayetteville, NC 28305   •   preppub@aol.com   •   (910) 483-6611

OBJECTIVE

To contribute to an organization that can use an articulate communicator and skilled problem solver with a proven ability to produce quality results in profitability and customer service.

EDUCATION

Completing **Bachelor's degree in Business Management,** University of Kentucky, Lexington, KY.

Earned **Associate's in Electronics Engineering,** Florida Institute of Technology, Melbourne, FL. 1990.

EXPERIENCE

BUSINESS STUDENT & ELECTRONICS CONSULTANT. University of Kentucky, Lexington, KY (2004-present). Have been completing a Bachelor's degree in Business Administration; on a freelance basis, utilize my electronics background as an Electronics Technician to businesses and individuals.
* Now seeking full-time employment; single and available for worldwide relocation.

GENERAL MANAGER. Friendly Chiropractic Center, Lexington, KY (1995-03). Was recruited by this company at a time when the owners were experiencing serious cash flow problems; took over the management of staff and programs, and led the company to win the respected Friendly Award in 1999, a national award recognizing top results in profitability, customer satisfaction, and quality programming.
* Retrained instructors and motivated the staff; created introductory specials which led to many new customers. Rapidly transformed a negative cash flow into a $250,000 profit.

OPERATIONS & PROJECT MANAGER. DPD Enterprise, CA & WA (1991-95). Held a key management role in numerous projects throughout the west coast of the U.S.
* Was called into the critical management role on several projects which were over budget and behind schedule; was successful in renegotiating favorable terms for my employer.
* For IBM, managed a project to install a $4.8 million card access security system.
* Coordinated technical requirements of CCTV, Intercom, intrusion detection, and computer-based alarm and card access monitoring systems; those requirements included documentation project phasing, scheduling, equipment procurement, systems design and integration, and troubleshooting.
* Took over the management of a $58 million project at the Portland Performing Arts Center in Portland, OR; this was a project to install a sound system for a sophisticated live theater complex. The engineer in charge of managing the project had failed to communicate effectively with the customer, and I was able to rescue the project and bring the job to completion with full customer satisfaction.
* At the SEA-TAC International Airport, managed to completion a complex project which was seriously behind schedule. Played management roles in security and electronics installation projects for Wells Fargo in North Dakota; for Alaska Pacific University in Anchorage, AK; and for Bank of America in Sacramento, CA.

BIOMEDICAL ELECTRONICS TECHNICIAN. University of North Carolina at Chapel Hill Medical Center, NC (1990-91). In my first job in the electronics field after graduating from Florida Institute of Technology, refined my ability to solve electronics problems.
* Serviced multi-layered circuit boards for Hewlett Packard and Imed medical equipment used in heart monitors, infusion pumps, and respirators.

PERSONAL

Highly motivated individual who desires to work in a company and make a contribution to corporate goals, strategic planning, and profitability.

Date

Exact Name of Person
Title or Position
Name of Company
Address
City, State, Zip

Dear Exact Name of Person: (or Dear Sir or Madam if answering a blind ad)

I would appreciate an opportunity to talk with you soon about the contributions I could make to your organization through my diverse technical skills and maintenance experience on many types of electronic systems.

As you will see from my resume, my work as a field service engineer for Olympia Electronics and as an electronics technician with the U.S. Army developed my proficiency on a wide variety of equipment. I have gained state-of-the-art expertise in the installation, maintenance and repair of multimillion dollar systems. I have developed abilities as a mechanic, electrician, and technician, and I have also developed a knack for designing and fabricating mechanical and electrical engineering changes as necessary.

While serving in the U.S. Army, I was awarded one of the nation's highest security clearances, Top Secret with SBI. In addition to my degree in Electronics Engineering, I have excelled in numerous training programs related to some of the most advanced concepts in the engineering field. After serving with distinction in the U.S. Army, I joined a company which is supporting the needs of the military during the War on Terrorism, and I have made significant contributions to the progress in Iraq. My current contract with Olympia is expiring and, although the company is strongly encouraging me to remain in its employment, I am selectively exploring other opportunities.

Confident that I could make significant contributions to your company, I am equally certain you would find me to be a versatile professional who offers dedication and high personal standards.

I hope you will contact me soon to suggest a time convenient for us to meet and discuss your current and future needs and how I might serve them. Thank you in advance for your time.

Sincerely,

Silas Tyson

Alternate last paragraph:
I hope you will welcome my call soon to arrange a brief meeting at your convenience to discuss your current and future needs and how I might serve them. Thank you in advance for your time.

SILAS TYSON

1110½ Hay Street, Fayetteville, NC 28305 • preppub@aol.com • (910) 483-6611

OBJECTIVE   To fully apply my specialist expertise in the areas of electronic and computer systems repair to a company that can use a knowledgeable and creative professional with proven technical skills as well as supervisory and instructional capabilities.

EXPERIENCE   **FIELD SERVICE ENGINEER.** Olympia Electronics Corporations, Inc., Olympia, WA (2004-present). Installed, maintained, and repaired all site equipment, analyzing equipment failures and taking corrective action when necessary; provided training for military personnel.
- Interpreted reports, made recommendations to managers and engineers, and drafted mechanical and electrical hardware design changes.
- Provided 24-hour on-call training and customer service worldwide.
- Accompanied equipment from deployment to return to combat zones of Iraq during Operation Iraqi Freedom.
- Responsible for the maintenance of secure and non-secure data switches, cryptographic equipment, line conditioners/controllers, microprocessors, multiplexers, and modems.

ELECTRONICS SYSTEMS SPECIALIST. U.S. Army, Fort Lewis, WA (2000-04). Performed repairs as well as routine and preventative maintenance for various military electrical systems and electronic communications equipment.
- Earned various U.S. Army awards and certificates and was nominated for a prestigious award during Operation Iraqi Freedom.
- In combat environments in Iraq and Afghanistan, supported the mission of the War on Terror by establishing and maintaining reliable communications.
- Worked with a wide variety of electronic communications equipment, including CRT's, display generators, mainframe and desktop computers, modems, radio communications systems (VHF, SHF, and UHF), tape and disk drives, printers, copiers, test equipment, and electrical and mechanical power generators and power distribution equipment.
- Became familiar with communications processing switches and circuits and comlink equipment. Worked with mainframe models and multiple operating systems.
- Became proficient in the operation and repair of hardware and software.

MAINTENANCE SUPERVISOR. American Electronics, Philadelphia, PA (1997-00). Installed and maintained electronic security systems and the on-site business machines.

EDUCATION   Graduated with an **A.S. degree in Electronics Engineering**, Seattle Pacific University, Seattle, WA, 1996.
Excelled in numerous U.S. Army and Olympia Electronics sponsored training courses.
On my own initiative and in my spare time, have completed advanced training related to Visual Basic, JavaScript, UNIX programming, C++ programming, and Rational Rose.

CLEARANCE   Hold a **Top Secret** security clearance with SBI, an SCI with a five-year update recently completed, and other clearances requiring SSO release.

PERSONAL   Hold a current passport. Pride myself on being a responsible, dependable, and highly adaptable professional. Have developed superior analytical and communication skills. Will provide references upon request.

Date

Exact Name of Person
Title or Position
Exact Name of Company
Address
City, State, Zip

Dear Exact Name of Person: (or Dear Sir or Madam if answering a blind ad.)

I am sending my resume in response to the advertisement in the Oklahoma City Times regarding the information systems positions. I would appreciate an opportunity to talk with you soon about how I could contribute to your organization through my education and experience related to information systems administration and also through my well-developed managerial and supervisory abilities.

As you will see from my resume, I am currently making valuable contributions as the Senior Systems Analyst for Sooner State Systems in Oklahoma City, OK. This position also allows me opportunities to participate in contract bidding and the development of relationships with a variety of civilian manufacturing firms as well as government contractors at Fort Carson. One of my recent accomplishments of which I am especially proud was when I "saved" an important government contract by reestablishing relations after a previous administrator had almost lost the contract. In the third quarter of 2004, we achieved a $300,000 profit on this contract.

After proudly serving my country in the U.S. Army, where I developed and refined excellent leadership skills, I returned to college to complete my degree in Electronics Engineering. Oklahoma City University features programs developed by Firestone and American Steele Corps. These programs emphasize industrial relations and management and have a goal of developing knowledgeable managers for industry. I was named to the university's Dean's List for maintaining a 3.6 GPA in my major subjects and also further refined my time management skills during this period by holding related part-time jobs. As the Computer and Lab Technician in the Technology Department, I trained other students in test equipment use while maintaining lab and communications equipment.

Known for my ability to motivate and lead others to achieve maximum productivity, I possess strong technical computer administration and operations knowledge. I am also recognized as a creative problem solver with well-developed analytical skills. I feel that I could make valuable contributions to your organization, too, through my knowledge, skills, and abilities.

I hope you will call or write me soon to suggest a time convenient for us to meet and discuss your current and future needs and how I might serve them. Thank you in advance for your time.

Sincerely yours,

Phillip Preston

PHILLIP PRESTON

1110½ Hay Street, Fayetteville, NC 28305　　·　　preppub@aol.com　　·　　(910) 483-6611

OBJECTIVE	To apply my management experience and my broad base of technical skills related to computer networking to an organization that can use a self-motivated professional known for outstanding analytical, problem-solving, and leadership abilities.
EDUCATION & TRAINING	**Bachelor of Technology degree in Electronics Engineering**, Oklahoma City University, Oklahoma City, OK, 2003. • Placed on the Dean's List for maintaining a 3.6 GPA in my major areas of concentration. Completed specialized training in Local Area Network (LAN) programming.
EXPERIENCE	**SENIOR SYSTEMS ANALYST.** Sooner State Systems, Oklahoma City, OK (2004-present). Am applying my technical knowledge and managerial skills to produce outstanding results with a small staff while involved in supporting approximately 400 information systems for a wide variety of governmental and manufacturing firms. • Took charge of a major project which had previously been inappropriately handled and regained the trust of a local government account. Was credited with actions which resulted in a $300,000 third-quarter profit margin by "saving" the important government contract. • Participated in research and development of both hardware and software packages. • Coordinated one $600,000 development project and the subsequent installation. • Located new markets for the company's services and products. • Installed and maintained a variety of Unix, LAN, PC, and telecommunications systems as the system administrator for major contracts. • Gained experience in handling purchase orders and contract bidding. **COMPUTER/LAB TECHNICIAN.** Oklahoma City University, Oklahoma City, OK (2003). For the university's Technology Department, repaired and maintained a variety of lab and communications equipment including LANs, PCs, and peripherals. • Increased operational efficiency by developing an inventory system as well as a controller for an infusion pump which allowed it to interface with the computer systems. **TRAINING SUPERVISOR** and **TEAM LEADER.** U.S. Army, Fort Carson, CO (1997-03). Earned praise for my supervisory abilities while advancing to the leadership role in a 13-person team and ensuring the quality of their training and performance. • Selected to provide special safety training, was personally cited as the "driving force" behind an impressive 60% decline in the yearly accident rate. Emphasized the importance of voting and attained a perfect 100% voter registration rate for the 1988 elections. • Ranked third in a 400-person, 200-hour military leadership development course. *Highlights of other experience*: Learned "hands-on" electronics repair and maintenance skills and trained personnel in the proper and safe use of various electronics equipment, DYNCORP, Fort Carson, CO (2003).
TECHNICAL KNOWLEDGE	**Test equipment**: oscilloscopes, frequency counters, analyzers, line analyzers, multimeters **Computer hardware**: IBM, Compaq, DataGeneral, and Unisys **Printers**: Okidata, Panasonic, Hewlett-Packard, Imagen, Canon, IBM, Epson, and TI **Software**: Microsoft Word, Excel, and PowerPoint; Adobe PageMaker, QuickBooks Pro
PERSONAL	Member, Institute of Electrical and Electronic Engineers and the IEEE Computer Society. Was entrusted with a Secret security clearance. Am known for my creativity and analytical skills. Enjoy involvement in research and development activities.

Exact Name of Person
Exact Title
Exact Name of Company
Address
City, State, Zip

ELECTRONICS ENGINEER

with experience as a senior technologist

Dear Exact Name of Person (or Dear Sir or Madam if answering a blind ad):

With the enclosed resume, I would like to express my interest in exploring employment opportunities with your organization.

As you will see from my resume, I am completing a B.S degree in Electronics Engineering after previously earning diplomas in Electronics and Electrical Installation & Maintenance. I am excelling academically even though I am completing this degree in my spare time despite a challenging full-time job that involves some travel.

In my current position, I assure the efficient operation of a power plant which consists of steam turbines, gas turbines, and other equipment. I have completed numerous training programs related to power plant operations and emergency procedures. I previously served my country in the U.S. Army and received numerous medals and awards recognizing my personal initiative and technical excellence.

Although my current employer has been preparing me for internal advancement, I have decided to selectively explore opportunities with other organizations that seek a reliable and dedicated young professional.

I hope you will call or write me soon to suggest a time convenient for us to meet and discuss your current and future needs and how I might serve them. Thank you in advance for your time.

Sincerely,

Vincent Carter

Alternate last paragraph:
I hope you will welcome my call soon to arrange a brief meeting to discuss your current and future needs and how I might serve them. Thank you in advance for your time.

VINCENT CARTER

1110½ Hay Street, Fayetteville, NC 28305　•　preppub@aol.com　•　(910) 483-6611

OBJECTIVE　　I would like to contribute my experience in the field of power plant operations to an organization that can use a young professional with unlimited executive potential who offers outstanding skills related to plant operations, electronics, and mathematics.

EDUCATION　　Completing course work leading to a **B.S. degree in Electronics Engineering,** Merrimack College, North Andover, MA.

Attained a near-perfect 3.9 GPA while earning a diploma in **Electrical Installation and Maintenance**, Merrimack College, North Andover, MA, 2001.

Earned diplomas in **Electronics and Accounting**, Middlesex Community College, Lowell, MA, 1994 and 1992.

Completed classroom and on-the-job corporate training related to electrical start-up procedures, power plant operations, power principles, turbines, and boiler chemistry.

CERTIFICATIONS Hold formal certificates related to Power Plant Operations, Electronic Servicing, Electrical Installation and Maintenance, and First Aid/CPR.

EXPERIENCE　　**SENIOR TECHNOLOGIST.** Merrimack Corporation, Lowell, MA (2004-present). At the Lowell Facility, ensure that a 660 MW combined cycle power plant operates safely and with reliability; major pieces of equipment included in this operation are as follows:

　　　　　　　four Siemens V84.2 120 MW gas turbines
　　　　　　　two ABB 135 MW steam turbines
　　　　　　　two Hudson air-cooled condensers

- Used a Bailey Net 90 distributed control system to operate plant equipment through a central control room.
- Coordinated load planning and load distribution activities.
- Supervised and trained technicians.
- Helped in planning and in the implementation of design changes to improve the reliability of the system as the lead technician assigned to the air-cooled condenser.
- Coordinated the plant's lockout and tag out procedures.
- Received corporate-sponsored training in areas including the following:

　　　　　　　first responder/firefighting　　　first aid and CPR
　　　　　　　confined space entry for search and rescue power plant operations
　　　　　　　personal computers using Windows, Word, and Excel

CONTROL ROOM OPERATOR. Mass Electric, Co., Andover, MA (2001-04). Ensured the efficient operation of a 280 MW combined cycle power plant which included this equipment:

　　　　　　　eight 25 MW M5001 General Electronic gas turbines
　　　　　　　three heat recovery steam generators
　　　　　　　one 60 MW General Electric steam turbine generator

- Operated plant equipment from a central control room through a General Electric Datatronic System. Negotiated the purchase and sale of power to Lawrence Power.

INVENTORY CONTROLLER and **ADMINISTRATIVE AIDE.** U.S. Army, Fort Jackson, SC (1976-00). After distinguishing myself as the Honor Graduate in a formal training program, earned numerous honors in recognition of superior job performance including Letters of Commendation and Appreciation.

PERSONAL　　Have the ability to get the job done with little or no supervision. Am very competitive and want to be "the best" at anything I do. Can provide outstanding references.

CAREER CHANGE

Date

Exact Name of Person
Title or Position
Name of Company
Address (number and street)
Address (city, state, and zip)

ENGINEERING OFFICER

This engineering professional hopes to transfer his Coast Guard experience to a civilian maritime organization.

Dear Exact Name of Person: (or Sir or Madam if answering a blind ad.)

I would appreciate an opportunity to talk with you soon about how I could contribute to your organization through the experience I offer as an engineering and maintenance manager who is known for special expertise in negotiating contracts, supervising technical personnel, and producing cohesive teams.

With a keen eye for detail and ability to quickly learn, absorb, and apply new ideas and concepts, I offer a reputation as a professional who can be depended on for personal integrity, resourcefulness, and dedication to excellence in everything I attempt.

With experience in engineering maintenance and personnel supervision, I am a well-rounded and adaptable individual with a broad and strong base of skills. As you will see on my enclosed resume, my most recent experience has been as an Assistant Engineering Officer responsible for planning and carrying out a wide variety of projects to ensure that Coast Guard vessels are maintained, repaired, and tested thoroughly.

While engineering operations are my main areas of expertise, I have extensive knowledge in multiple functional areas including inventory control and budgeting, employee supervision and training, and project planning and coordination. I have frequently been cited as a catalyst for changes which increased productivity, employee morale, and customer satisfaction.

I hope you will welcome my call soon to arrange a brief meeting to discuss your current and future needs and how I might serve them. Thank you in advance for your time.

Sincerely,

Christian Dover

Alternate last paragraph:
I hope you will call or write me soon to suggest a time convenient for us to meet and discuss your current and future needs and how I might serve them. Thank you in advance for your time.

CHRISTIAN DOVER

1110½ Hay Street, Fayetteville, NC 28305 • preppub@aol.com • (910) 483-6611

OBJECTIVE

To offer my demonstrated expertise in engineering maintenance operations and management to an organization that can benefit from the knowledge, skills, and abilities refined in a distinguished career as a military officer.

EXPERIENCE

Have built a reputation as a manager who can be counted on to find innovative ways to reduce costs, increase productivity and efficiency, and ensure the timely completion of multiple complex and simultaneous projects as an engineering/ maintenance specialist in the U.S. Coast Guard:

ENGINEERING OFFICER. Boston, MA (2003-present). Contributed my expertise as the link between the senior engineering officer and the engineering department with additional responsibilities for managing a $750,000 annual operating budget and supervising 21 people.

ENGINEERING DIVISION CHIEF. Portsmouth, NH (2000-03). Was honored with an achievement medal in recognition of "superior performance;" applied a high level of engineering knowledge, dedication, and managerial skills in support of a large operating complex with three stations, three cutters, and more than 20 small boats.
- Brought about dramatic reductions in the number and severity of problems with various boats through a strong preventive maintenance program and superb technical knowledge.
- Provided the leadership for several major projects including the installation and upgrading of unsafe and defective fire alarm systems, development of a new portable water system, and an exterior lighting and window replacement project.
- Supervised 16 people and managed a $228,000 annual operating budget.
- Selected to serve on numerous boards and committees, provided expertise to inspection teams, an awards board, human relations committee, and emergency conservation efforts.
- Managed countless projects with minimum disruption of service and downtime including engine testing and replacement of emergency generators and circuits.
- Conducted pre-inspections of boats needing repair and prepared thorough checklists so that operational down time was limited when repairs were being completed.
- Created a facilities maintenance division which allows industrial engineering to concentrate on large projects and allowed for faster response times for smaller projects.

ASSISTANT ENGINEERING OFFICER. Vancouver, WA (1993-99). As second-in-command of a 25-person department with a $174,000 annual operating budget, oversaw the repair of maintenance of electrical, auxiliary, and main propulsion machinery.
- Served as safety supervisor for the Engine Casualty Control Training Team which included scheduling and coordinating practice drills and creating training scenarios.
- Was recognized as a "logistics expert" who could be counted on to develop sources and locate hard-to-find parts so that critical time constraints could be met.
- Singled out on one official evaluation for impeccable personal integrity, dealt with civilian contractors and explained things to them so that no improper actions would take place and while enforcing government regulations regarding contracting procedures, soliciting bits, and acting a Quality Assurance Inspector during contracts.

EDUCATION

U.S. Coast Guard training included the following:
Hazardous Waste Management Training Course, 2004
Engineering Administration, 2003
VT903M Maintenance and Overhaul, 2002

PERSONAL

Am known for my tactfulness, diplomacy, and ability to deal with people of any level.

Date

Exact Name of Person
Title or Position
Exact Name of Company
Address
City, State, Zip

**ENGINEERING
OPERATIONS
SUPERVISOR**

with experience in
building
infrastructure
in Iraq

Dear Exact Name of Person: (or Dear Sir or Madam if answering a blind ad.)

I am faxing my resume as discussed in our recent conversation. I would appreciate it if you would put me in your resume file pool so I would receive consideration for any teams that you feel I qualify for. I am also sending a copy through the mail so that you will have it for anyone who is interested in reviewing it.

I appreciated the opportunity to talk with you briefly about how I could contribute to your organization as a member of a Disaster Assistance Response Team through my experience in supervising and managing technical teams, conducting operations in international settings, my strong language and analytical skills, and my experience in humanitarian efforts.

During my approximately ten years with the U.S. Army Special Forces I have been involved in numerous projects where my knowledge and skills placed me in advisory roles for engineering activities. My practical experience includes ten months in Bosnia performing assessments and disaster assistance as well as six months in Afghanistan and Iraq for disaster assistance. In addition to being stationed in France for three years with the Army, I lived and worked there as a civilian for two years — this gave me a real opportunity to immerse myself in the French language and culture.

As you will see from my enclosed resume, I am presently Supervisor — Engineering Operations for one of 20 teams which make up the U.S. Army's only active Civil Affairs organization. While overseeing such projects as training local nationals to be construction foremen and then completing a 55-kilometer road repair project in Bosnia, I have become familiar with conducting assessments, making recommendations on required actions, and managing successful projects, one of the latest of which was revitalizing an education system.

I offer a broad range of knowledge and skills in such areas as medical first aid procedures, residential and commercial construction, irrigation systems and drainage, computer operations, electrical power generation and distribution, and air lift planning. My language skills include a working knowledge of Spanish and French. I have extensive training and experience in demolition and high explosives.

Thank you again for your time and I certainly appreciate your willingness to see that my resume is forwarded to the right people.

Sincerely yours,

Caleb Richland

CALEB RICHLAND

1110½ Hay Street, Fayetteville, NC 28305　　•　　preppub@aol.com　　•　　(910) 483-6611

OBJECTIVE　　To offer my supervisory and managerial skills to an organization that can use a professional who is experienced in overseeing technical and scientific teams conducting operations in international settings and who has a keen ear for languages and strong analytical skills.

EXPERIENCE　　**SUPERVISOR — ENGINEERING OPERATIONS.** U.S. Army, Fort Rucker, AL (2004-present). Provide leadership for teams of specialists assigned to numerous overseas projects for the Army's only active Civil Affairs unit while involved in developing engineering input into country studies and assessments.

- Supervised a 600-person work force which completed 55 kilometers of road repairs in two months in support of the War on Terrorism in Iraq; trained 12 Iraqi nationals who became the supervisors for 50-person crews. Was cited as a resourceful, perceptive professional who set an example of physical and mental toughness for others to follow.
- Worked closely with indigenous utility company officials in order to provide support for water purification, distribution, and maintenance as well as electric services.

Was selected for leadership roles as an engineering specialist, Ft. Benning, GA:
STAFF SUPPORT SUPERVISOR. (2004). Singled out ahead of my peers for this job at the organization's central headquarters, assisted in managing engineering operations including maintenance and repair of 85 buildings as well as support for family housing and training. Developed Plan of Instruction (POI) for land mine awareness.

ENGINEERING AND DEMOLITIONS SPECIALIST. (2002-04). Known for my proficiency in these highly technical areas, acted as the general manager's advisor and trained U.S., NATO, and other foreign personnel.

- Prepared personnel for Extreme Cold Weather Training and was cited for my thoroughness while conducting a site survey followed by three weeks of training for Canadian Rangers which improved cooperation during U.S.-Canadian projects.
- Was promoted to this position on the basis of my enthusiasm for ensuring that training was of the highest quality; ensured that training requirements were met and reports were filled in accurately and on time for a 75-person unit.
- Received a commendation medal for my accomplishments which included directing mine field identification and marking activities and helping organize and maintain a camp.

ENGINEERING ADVISOR. (2000-02). Known for my proficiency in the skills needed for unconventional warfare missions; planned and conducted strike, demolition, and special reconnaissance training for U.S., NATO, and other foreign personnel.

EDUCATION,　　Completed requirements for a B.S. degree; am awaiting a determination on when the degree
TRAINING,　　will be awarded by the American Regents Program: my major will be in Management with a
&　　minor in French.
CERTIFICATIONS Excelled in more than 19 months of specialized training programs including six months each in construction/demolition and advanced lifesaving/first aid (1999-00), as well as other programs emphasizing air lift planning (proper aircraft loading techniques), diesel block assembly and disassembly, and hazardous material handling and first response.
Earned State of GA certification in backflow prevention in 2004, Jumpmaster status in 2004, and SCUBA certification in 1998.
Languages: Speak and write Spanish and French.

PERSONAL　　Have a knack for being able to improvise. Can always find a way to get the job done.

Date

Exact Name of Person
Title or Position
Exact Name of Company
Address
City, State, Zip

ENGINEERING
TRAINING
SUPERVISOR &
SENIOR ELECTRICAL
DIVISION
SUPERVISOR

Dear Exact Name of Person: (or Sir or Madam if answering a blind ad.)

I would appreciate an opportunity to talk with you soon about how I could contribute to your organization through my technical expertise, exceptional skills in the administration and operation of technical training programs, and ability to maximize human resources through superb managerial abilities.

As you will see from my enclosed resume, I possess strong technical skills and knowledge along with the ability to quickly learn and absorb information and then pass that knowledge on to others in an easy-to-understand form. Since the very early years of my career in the U.S. Navy I have been singled out as being head and shoulders above my peers in initiative, drive, and dedication to achieving only the highest performance standards from myself, my subordinates, and my students.

Most recently as an Engineering Training Supervisor and Senior Electrical Division Supervisor, I have been the students' choice as the best instructor and as a senior enlisted person, handpicked to manage an engineering team in a role normally reserved for a commissioned officer. Through the refinement of my natural leadership abilities and talents as a communicator, I have earned four Navy Achievement Medals and numerous letters of commendation in recognition of my abilities and knowledge.

I am certain that I possess a combination of unique and wide-ranging skills that would allow me to contribute to your organization in any capacity requiring exceptional problem-solving, decision-making, and managerial skills.

I hope you will welcome my call soon to arrange a brief meeting to discuss your current and future needs and how I might serve them. Thank you in advance for your time.

Sincerely,

Charles Taylor

Alternate last paragraph:
I hope you will call or write me soon to suggest a time convenient for us to meet and discuss your current and future needs and how I might serve them. Thank you in advance for your time.

CHARLES TAYLOR

1110½ Hay Street, Fayetteville, NC 28305   •   preppub@aol.com   •   (910) 483-6611

OBJECTIVE

To offer my versatile background and wide-ranging abilities to an organization that can use an exceptional manager of time as well as human and material resources who excels in troubleshooting and performing electrical repairs and maintenance.

EXPERIENCE

Built a reputation as an expert in electrical maintenance, repair, and supervision as well as in providing training which produced highly skilled, qualified young technicians, U.S. Navy:

ENGINEERING TRAINING SUPERVISOR & SENIOR ELECTRICAL DIVISION SUPERVISOR. Groton, CT (2004-present). Oversee the training and performance of up to 50 staff members and naval officer-students assigned to a land-based nuclear prototype.

- Was singled out as the manager of an engineering team during an evaluation of reactor safeguards in a position normally held by a commissioned officer.
- Consistently voted by the students as "best instructor," produced students whose knowledge levels were above average and directly contributed to the division's recognition with three consecutive Training Excellence Awards.
- Despite limited assets, led an electrical section to routinely complete more preventive and corrective maintenance than any other section and earn selection for the most difficult and complex maintenance tasks.

ELECTRICAL DIVISION SUPERVISOR. Home port: Jacksonville, FL (2000-03). Consistently described as a tireless performer who could be counted on to lead the way, refined technical, leadership, and managerial skills while supervising as many as 14 people involved in operating, maintaining, and repairing the electrical power generation and distribution systems of a nuclear-powered submarine.

- Played a key role leading a depot modernization project to successful completion ahead of schedule: inspected and repaired all major switchboards and distribution equipment.
- Flawlessly maintained records, earning zero deficiencies during critical Maintenance and Material Management (3M) and overhaul reactor safeguards inspections.
- Displayed resourcefulness and initiative by supervising manufacture of precision machining equipment necessary to perform emergency at-sea repairs to a turbine generator: eliminated the need for outside assistance and reduced downtime.

INSTRUCTOR OF REACTOR PLANT TECHNOLOGY. Pearl Harbor, HI (1996-00). Applied organizational and administrative as well as teaching/instructional skills while maintaining student records, developing instructional materials, and counseling students.

- Provided clear and easy-to-understand instruction to students studying the concepts of electrical and mechanical theory as related to naval nuclear propulsion plant operation.
- One of only two people of my rank handpicked as a Training Group Coordinator, was in charge of supervising and evaluating four senior instructors, coordinating class schedules, administering exams, and ensuring the quality of instruction for 250 students.
- Achieved lower attrition rates and higher class averages than my peers.
- Supervised 30 people maintaining the security, safety, and proper study conditions for a 3,000-person organization; tutored evening study sessions.

TRAINING

Completed extensive training leading to certification as a Master Training Specialist as well as more than two years of nuclear power and technical training.

PERSONAL

Was awarded four Navy Achievement Medals for my expertise, dedication to excellence, and professionalism. Enjoy volunteering with youth groups and coaching athletic teams.

Exact Name of Person
Exact Title
Exact Name of Company
Address
City, State, Zip

**ENVIRONMENTAL
ENGINEER**

with experience as a
military officer &
general manager

Dear Exact Name of Person (or Dear Sir or Madam if answering a blind ad):

With the enclosed resume, I would like to express my interest in exploring employment opportunities with your organization.

As you will see from my resume, I recently completed a B.S. degree in Environmental Engineering Technology at the highly respected University of Alaska Fairbanks. I became committed to a career in the environmental field after serving my country in the U.S. Army as an Environmental Project Manager. In that capacity, I worked in conjunction with the National Park Service for the Department of the Interior, and I supervised 15 people while directing major environmental clean-up activities. In one project, we removed tons of debris from the Prince William Sound in Alaska.

In previous engineering experience, I improved logistics systems in an engineering operation, and I excelled in jobs as a management consultant, engineer, and administrator. The recipient of numerous medals and awards recognizing my exemplary performance, I was praised for my personal initiative, strong problem-solving skills, and sound management practices.

I hope you will welcome my call soon to arrange a brief meeting to discuss your current and future needs and how I might serve them. Thank you in advance for your time.

Sincerely,

Samuel Bergen

Alternate last paragraph:
I hope you will call or write me soon to suggest a time convenient for us to meet and discuss your current and future needs and how I might serve them. Thank you in advance for your time.

SAMUEL BERGEN

1110½ Hay Street, Fayetteville, NC 28305 • preppub@aol.com • (910) 483-6611

OBJECTIVE

I want to benefit an organization through my management, administrative, and communications skills.

EDUCATION

Completed **B.S. degree in Environmental Engineering Technology**, University of Alaska Fairbanks, 2004.

SUMMARY of EXPERIENCE

Have been described as follows in formal evaluations of my performance:
- "A very knowledgeable, enthusiastic and versatile manager."
- "A thinker and a doer."
- "Displays exceptional leadership that sets the standard."
- "Demonstrates a high degree of self discipline with outstanding ability to perform under stress."
- "Establishes and enforces firm, sound management practices."
- "Recognized as the operations authority."

EXPERIENCE

GENERAL MANAGER. U.S. Army, Fort Polk, LA (2004-present). Coordinate and distribute workload, generated personnel reports, and performed a wide range of administrative functions for a 215-person engineering organization.
- Ensured the efficient allocation of personnel and physical assets.
- Maintained perfect accountability for over $68,000 in organizational equipment.

ENVIRONMENTAL PROJECT MANAGER. U.S. Army, Fort Richardson, AK (2001-04). Working in conjunction with the National Park Service for the Department of Interior, supervised 15 personnel while planning and coordinating an environmental clean-up operation.
- Removed over 50 tons of debris from the Prince William Sound, Valdez, AK.
- Directed emergency response teams which provided relief efforts in the aftermath of Hurricanes Frances and Ivan.

ENGINEERING TEAM SUPERVISOR and **PRODUCTION MANAGER**. U.S. Army, Fort Jackson, SC (2001). As the supervisor of a seven-person engineering team, have been involved in projects ranging from airfield construction, to bridge building, to precision demolitions.
- Have refined my skills in managing production and monitoring quality control.

SUPPLY/LOGISTICS MANAGER. U.S. Army, Fort Jackson, SC (2000-01). Earned a respected Achievement Medal for my work in improving the efficiency of supply and logistics in ammunition inventory. Designed a checklist that doubled inventory control effectiveness.

Other experience: U.S. Army, Fort Wainwright, AK (1997-00).
- Improved logistics systems in an engineering organization. Learned how to improve the performance of employees through training, counseling, and motivational techniques.
- Excelled in jobs as a management consultant, engineer, and administrator.

MANAGEMENT TRAINING

Was selected for leadership development courses designed for junior executives. Studied preventive maintenance and industrial security.

PERSONAL

Am an excellent writer and have written various technical publications. Have become extremely versatile in managing people in organizations of all sizes. Strongly believe in my ability to improve operations.

Date

Exact Name of Person
Title or Position
Exact Name of Company
Address
City, State, Zip

Dear Exact Name of Person (or Dear Sir or Madam if answering a blind ad):

With the enclosed resume, I would like to make you aware of my interest in exploring employment opportunities with your organization.

As you will see from my enclosed resume, while serving my country with distinction in the U.S. Navy I have gained extensive technical expertise along with strong supervisory skills. I have performed with distinction as a qualified Plant Operator and Boiler Technician while operating a six-stage flash type evaporator, feed pumps, and forced draft blowers, and I have trained and supervised numerous technicians in plant operations and boiler operations. I have played a key role in maintaining ship boilers and equipment in a continuously operational state during ship cruises in the Mediterranean. I have earned respect for my strong troubleshooting, problem-solving, and supervisory skills.

I have persisted in completing rigorous college work despite interruptions caused by frequent deployments in the U.S. Navy. I received a diploma in Marketing Management and since then have pursued a Bachelor of Science in Environmental Engineering Technology. I have excelled in courses related to waste management, recycling, physics, trigonometry, and other areas.

Prior to entering the Navy, I demonstrated my strong work ethic and initiative in jobs at a nuclear site and in a major store of the Lowes Hardware chain. For three years at the Puget Sound nuclear site, I operated equipment in a Department of Energy warehouse operation. Subsequently I played a key role in leading a Lowes Hardware store to become #1 for two straight years in our market area, and I became the top salesperson in the largest flooring department in the Lowes Hardware chain.

Although I am held in the highest regard by the U.S. Navy and can provide outstanding references at the appropriate time, I am planning on leaving the Navy soon and entering the civilian work force. I am exploring opportunities with companies that can use a versatile technical expert with a proven ability to communicate effectively with others. If you can use a talented young professional with a unique combination of technical and management abilities, I hope you will contact me to suggest a time when we might meet to discuss your needs.

Yours sincerely,

Wesley Pond

WESLEY POND

1110½ Hay Street, Fayetteville, NC 28305   •   preppub@aol.com   •   (910) 483-6611

OBJECTIVE

I want to contribute to an organization that can use a mechanically talented individual who offers strong technical knowledge and hands-on experience related to waste management, environmental plant operations, environmental engineering, and energy plant operations.

EDUCATION

Completing **Bachelor of Science degree in Environmental Engineering Technology,** Navy College, Pensacola, FL.
• Am persisting in finishing this degree despite numerous Navy deployments worldwide. Completed courses in **Environmental Engineering Technology,** Northwest Technical College, Bemidji, MN, 1998-00; completed courses in waste management, recycling, physics, trigonometry.
Received diploma in **Marketing Management,** Northwest Technical College, Bemidji, MN, 1998.
Graduated from Bemidji Senior High School, Bemidji, MN, 1994.

TRAINING &
CERTIFICATIONS

Qualified Boiler Technician and Plant Operator.
Completed Shop Quality Improvement Program and Shop Improvement Program, U.S. Navy. Licensed to operate equipment including forklifts, electric pallet jacks, reach trucks, order pickers. Licensed to operate six-stage flash type evaporator, main feed pumps, draft blowers.

CLEARANCE

Department of Energy L security clearance

EXPERIENCE

MACHINIST & SUPERVISOR. U.S. Navy, U.S.S. Pearl, Pearl Harbor, HI (2004-present). Have performed with distinction as a Plant Operator and Boiler Technician while operating a six-stage type evaporator, main feed pumps, and forced draft blowers; have trained and managed up to six other technicians in plant operations and boiler operations.
• Have resolved complex mechanical problems on a variety of plant equipment; have become skilled in taking vital readings on plant gauges and associated equipment.
• Contributed to 100% continuous plant operations during the military exercise Operation Allied Force. Played a key role in maintaining equipment during cruises.
• Supervised and played a major leadership role in the complete overhaul of three major shaft alleys during the shipyard routine maintenance period.
• Received a special Letter of Commendation recognizing my technical expertise.
• Have earned a reputation as an outstanding manager with strong planning and organizational skills; have continuously demonstrated my ability to take on any task.

EQUIPMENT OPERATOR & STORE MANAGEMENT OPERATIONS MANAGER. Lowes Hardware Store, Bemidji, MN (2001-04). Through hard work and persistence, achieved the distinction of being the top Flooring Sales Associate.
• Played a key role in leading our store to become the #1 store in sales for two straight years in our market area.
• Became the top salesperson in the largest volume flooring department in the Lowes Hardware Store chain.

NUCLEAR SITE MATERIAL PROCESS OPERATOR. Puget Sound, Seattle, WA (1998-01). At the Puget Sound nuclear site, operated equipment in the U.S. Department of Energy warehouse operation. Became knowledgeable of energy plant operations.
• Earned qualifications as a radiation worker and gained nuclear site experience.

PERSONAL

Received a Navy Good Conduct Medal and a Letter of Commendation. Excellent references.

Exact Name of Person
Title or Position
Exact Name of Company
Address
City, State, Zip

**GENERAL MANAGER,
ENGINEERING &
CONSTRUCTION**

Dear Exact Name of Person: (or Dear Sir or Madam if answering a blind ad.)

I am sending you a resume describing my background in the communications services industry because I feel there might be a "fit" between your needs and my extensive management skills and telecommunications knowledge.

As you will see, I recently opted for an early retirement from Broadband Corporation after serving the company with distinction and being offered a further promotion which I declined. In my most recent position as General Manager of Engineering and Construction, I was handling responsibilities similar to those of a CEO at a small or medium-sized company. In the process of managing 300 managers, engineers, supervisors, craft, and clerical employees while also supervising more than 200 contractors performing large-scale fiber optic/copper installations and maintenance, I was in charge of a $32 million budget. When the company merged with Western Phone Company in 2001, I took over the physical and human resources of Western Phone and was given the additional responsibility of reforming Western Phone's organization into the Broadband Corporation structure.

Although I have managed major disaster relief efforts and supervised the installation of fiber optic/copper systems all over the Western region, I take greatest pride in my accomplishments as a manager of human resources. Since my job involved managing unionized and non-unionized employees, I had to demonstrate highly refined interpersonal, problem-solving, and negotiating skills at all times. Although I have never enjoyed the business of terminating or transferring employees, through the years I have handled that responsibility with tact and sensitivity and have been commended for my "style." I also am proud of the fact that I have selected, trained, developed, and promoted employees who have become some of the company's most valuable employees.

If you can use an astute and energetic manager who could contribute to your organization as I have done to Broadband Corporation, please give me a call and I will make myself available at your convenience. You would find me in person to be a youthful and vigorous manager who could have a great deal to offer your organization. I would consider any part-time, full-time, or consulting assignments as your needs and goals dictate.

Sincerely yours,

Gary McCullum

GARY McCULLUM

1110½ Hay Street, Fayetteville, NC 28305 • preppub@aol.com • (910) 483-6611

OBJECTIVE To contribute to an organization that can use a respected professional with highly refined strategic planning and problem-solving skills who has expertly managed multimillion-dollar budgets, capital expansion projects, and large-scale responses to natural disasters including hurricanes and tornadoes while supervising both unionized and non-unionized personnel.

EXPERIENCE *Recently declined a promotion and took an early retirement after a distinguished career and track record of promotion with Broadband Corporation:*
GENERAL MANAGER, ENGINEERING & CONSTRUCTION. Seattle, WA (2001-present). After the company merged with Western Phone Company, was promoted to oversee all engineering and construction activities in the West Region, and assumed responsibility for the physical and human resources formerly under Western Phone management.
Management of Human Resources:
- Managed 300 engineers and professionals including district managers and also provided oversight management of 200 contractors who provided engineering/construction services; negotiated and supervised the proper administration of contracts/agreements.
- Gained rigorous experience operating in a union environment and became skilled at union negotiations, handling grievance procedures, and resolving disputes in a timely and fair manner; was entrusted with the independent authority to add or reduce contract work forces and to shift personnel from one district to another.
Financial Management:
- Planned and administered a $32 million budget within a corporate system which had a "no excuses" philosophy about cost overruns; managers were strictly evaluated on cost control.
- Was the approving authority for procurement of capital equipment, and supervised teams responsible for the installation of fiber optic systems.
Management of Disaster Response Efforts as well as Major Capital Expansions:
- Directed prudent responses to emergency outages and responded to natural disasters such as tornadoes, hurricanes, and accidents that impacted on outside distribution network and physical plant; was Chairperson of the Emergency Restoration Plan and supervised emergency response crews.
Customer Service and Community/Government Liaison:
- Customer service was considered the company's #1 priority at all times, and I was keenly responsive to customer service demands with critical deadlines.
Exceptional Performance Ratings:
- Always earned commendable performance ratings of my administrative abilities, problem-solving and analytical skills, leadership, and initiative; excelled in handling responsibilities similar to those of a CEO of a small/medium-sized company.

Highlights of previous Broadband Corporation Experience:
DIVISION DISTRIBUTION MANAGER. Seattle, WA (1990-01).
DIVISION ENGINEER. Olympia, WA (1984-89).
DIVISION COMMERCIAL SUPERVISOR. Seattle, WA (1982-83).
DISTRICT ENGINEER. Seattle, WA (1975-82).

EDUCATION **Bachelor of Science** in Business Administration, Gonzaga University, Spokane, WA, 1974. Previously studied **Mechanical Engineering** at Seattle University.

PERSONAL Am known for my exceptionally strong interpersonal skills. Possess advanced understanding of technology behind fiber optics, remote line units, and subscriber carrier concentrators.

Date

Exact Name of Person
Title or Position
Name of Company
Address
City, State, Zip

INDUSTRIAL ENGINEER
with experience as a
cost reduction coordinator

Dear Exact Name of Person: (or Dear Sir or Madam if answering a blind ad.)

I would appreciate an opportunity to talk with you soon about how I could contribute to your organization through my industrial engineering background including my experience in managing cost reduction programs, planning capital expenditures, and supporting new product design.

In my current job as an Industrial Engineer and Cost Reduction Coordinator, I have implemented the new manufacturing concept known as continuous process flow cells and have functioned as the "inhouse expert" in training my associates in this area. While managing a $700,000 cost reduction program, I investigate and implement cost reductions through alternative materials and manufacturing processes as well as design modifications. I am involved on a daily basis in on-the-floor problem solving, costing of component processing, tooling and gaging, and capital equipment acquisitions. I have had extensive experience in project management.

Prior to graduating with my B.S. degree in Industrial Engineering, I worked my way through college in jobs in which I was involved in producing computer-aided drawings and participating in new product design. Although I worked my way through college, financing 80% of my education, I excelled academically and received the Outstanding Senior Award.

I am knowledgeable of numerous popular software and drafting packages. I offer a proven ability to rapidly master new software and adapt it for specific purposes and environments.

Single and willing to relocate, I can provide outstanding personal and professional references. I am highly regarded by my current employer, PRP Industries, and have been credited with making numerous contributions to the company through solving problems, cutting costs, determining needed capital equipment, and implementing new processes. I am making this inquiry to your company in confidence because I feel there might be a fit between your needs and my versatile areas of expertise.

I hope you will call or write me soon to suggest a time convenient for us to meet and discuss your current and future needs and how I might serve them. Thank you in advance for you time.

Sincerely yours,

Trent Warner

TRENT WARNER

1110½ Hay Street, Fayetteville, NC 28305   •   preppub@aol.com   •   (910) 483-6611

OBJECTIVE   To add value to an organization that can use an accomplished young industrial engineer who offers specialized know-how in coordinating cost reductions, experience in both manufacturing and process engineering, proven skills in project management, and extensive interaction with product design, quality control, vendor relations, and capital expenditures.

EDUCATION   **Bachelor of Science (B.S.) degree, Industrial Engineering Major** with a concentration in manufacturing, University of South Dakota, Vermillion, SD, 2002.
- Achieved a 3.5 GPA (3.8 in my major); inducted into Alpha Beta Chi Honorary Fraternity.
- Received **Outstanding Senior Award** in manufacturing concentration.
- Worked throughout college and financed 80% of my education.

Associate of Applied Science (A.A.S.) degree, Mechanical Engineering and Design Technology Major, University of South Dakota, Vermillion, SD, 1998; achieved 3.7 GPA. From 2002-present, completed continuing education in these areas:

ISO 9000 Internal Auditing	Root Cause Analysis
Total Quality Management	Value Engineering/Value Analysis
Continuous Flow Manufacturing	Synchronous Manufacturing

TECHNICAL KNOWLEDGE   Software: Microsoft Word, Excel, PowerPoint, Adobe
Drafting: VERSACAD, CADAM, Cascade, Intergraph, Unigraphics

CERTIFICATIONS   Certified Manufacturing Technologist; Certified ISO 9000 Internal Auditor

EXPERIENCE   **INDUSTRIAL ENGINEER/COST REDUCTION COORDINATOR**. PRP Industries, Co., Aberdeen, SD (2004-present). Responsible for the processing of machined components from raw material to finished product while also coordinating a $700,000 annual cost reduction program; investigate and implement cost reductions by exploring the possibility of alternative materials, other manufacturing processes, and design modifications.
- Involved on a daily basis in on-the-floor problem solving, costing of component processing, tooling and gaging, and capital equipment acquisitions.
- Implemented and coordinated continuous process flow cells, a new concept in the manufacturing area; completed extensive training and trained my associates.
- Performed cost justifications and complete equipment installs for capital equipment acquisitions totaling half a million dollars. Continuously interact with new product teams, problem-solving groups, purchasing specialists, vendors, as well as quality control.

ASSOCIATE MANUFACTURING ENGINEER. Dakota Manufacturing, Co., Aberdeen, SD (2003). Coordinated project workloads, designed assembly tooling, and established data bases for tracking and calibration of gaging used in the shop; gained experience related to self-directed work teams, facilities layout, and routing procedures.

Other experience:
DESIGNER. For the Drafting Corporation (1998-02), produced computer-aided drawings and actively participated in new product design while interacting with engineering and manufacturing. Introduced the first microprocessor controlled cruise control.

AFFILIATIONS   Society of Manufacturing Engineers; National Association of Industrial Technology; Alpha Beta Chi International Honorary Fraternity for Education in Technology

PERSONAL   Single; will relocate. Accustomed to hard work and tight deadlines. Have excellent references.

Date

Exact Name of Person
Exact Title
Exact Name of Company
Address
City, State, Zip

Dear Exact Name of Person (or Dear Sir or Madam if answering a blind ad):

With the enclosed resume, I would like to express my interest in exploring employment opportunities with your organization.

As you will see from the enclosed resume, I am currently excelling as a Quality Control Supervisor, and I was promoted to my present position after working as a Quality Engineer. I am skilled at managing and implementing quality standards for manufacturing, packaging, and shipping of products worldwide, and I have initiated and implemented process improvements in multiple plants. In my current position, I assist eight manufacturing facilities in identifying and closing gaps utilizing the Business Excellence Process which focuses on customer satisfaction.

I began my career in industrial engineering after earning my B.S. in Mathematics, and as my career progressed, I decided to return to a university setting to earn my M.S. in Industrial Engineering while working full-time in a challenging management position.

Although I am held in the highest regard by my current employer and can provide outstanding references at the appropriate time, I am selectively exploring opportunities in other organizations. I am committed to the highest standards of quality assurance and customer satisfaction.

I hope you will call or write me soon to suggest a time convenient for us to meet and discuss your current and future needs and how I might serve them. Thank you in advance for your time.

Sincerely,

Victoria Mosely

Alternate last paragraph:
I hope you will welcome my call soon to arrange a brief meeting to discuss your current and future needs and how I might serve them. Thank you in advance for your time.

VICTORIA MOSLEY

1110½ Hay Street, Fayetteville, NC 28305 • preppub@aol.com • (910) 483-6611

OBJECTIVE

To contribute proven analytical, problem-solving, and communication abilities to an organization that can use a detail-oriented professional with excellent technical skills.

EDUCATION

Master of Science in **Industrial Engineering**, University of Detroit, MI, 2000.
- Inducted into Kappa Beta Alpha Industrial Engineering Honor Society.

Bachelor of Science in **Mathematics**, Marygrove College, Detroit, MI, 1995.

EXPERIENCE

Advanced with Great Lakes, Inc., Detroit, MI (2001-present):
2004-present: QUALITY ENGINEER SUPERVISOR. Promoted to manage and supervise three engineers, two technicians and 13 process auditors/receiving inspection employees while assisting plant personnel with quality issues related to manufacturing facilities, customer complaints, cost requirements, and delivery.
- Assist eight manufacturing facilities with closing gaps utilizing the Business Excellence Process which focuses on the customer and is similar to the M. Bridge Process.

2001-04: QUALITY ENGINEER IV, III, & II. Developed, managed, and maintained the quality system for Communication products; provided training to all personnel in ISO 9001 requirements and quality specifications while serving as Lead Assessor.
- Developed and implemented quality systems involving FMEAs, Control Plans, and Design Reviews to improve manufacturing processes for new products.
- Extensively involved in preventive and corrective actions taken during manufacturing processes; performed capability studies. Trained others in approving tooling changes and assisted with improvements in process engineering and error-proofing projects.

QUALITY CONTROL MANAGER. Detroit, MI (1999-01) and Ann Arbor, MI (1998-99). At one of the company's major plants, managed and implemented quality standards for manufacturing, packaging, and shipping of products in two hosiery facilities; a manufacturing facility with approximately 400 employees and a distribution center with more than 700 employees. Trained and supervised 23 quality control personnel.
- Worked closely with other manufacturing facilities and managers to correct problems with incoming products; helped operators and mechanics with process improvements.
- Initiated process improvements and error proofing activities in both plants.

Other experience:
QUALITY CONTROL SUPERVISOR. Great Lakes Telecommunications Cable Group, Flint, MI (1998). Managed the quality of single-mode optical fiber for telephone cables while attending graduate school; utilized the Team Concept to ensure fiber met quality standards set by Bell Laboratories.
OPERATIONS SUPERVISOR. Duracell Battery Company, Detroit, MI (1995-98). Led 50 personnel to meet demanding production and quality standards in the Raw Cell department of this giant corporation; controlled raw material inventory, scrap rates, and production costs using the Team Concept.

**SPECIAL
TRAINING**

Have been certified by Great Lakes as a Lead Assessor for ISO 9001. Highly knowledgeable of the Demining Concepts, which figured heavily in my Masters thesis, as well as implementation of Total Quality Management and Team Building Concepts.

PERSONAL

Member of the American Society for Quality and Examiner for the Michigan M Bridge Process.

Date

Exact Name of Person
Title or Position
Name of Company
Address
City, State, Zip

INDUSTRIAL ENGINEERING MANAGER

Dear Exact Name of Person: (or Dear Sir or Madam if answering a blind ad.)

I would appreciate an opportunity to talk with you soon about how I could benefit your organization through my experience and education as an industrial engineer as well as through my knowledge of manufacturing, project management abilities, and skill in training and developing employees.

As you will see from my resume, I have advanced with Burlington Industries while building a "track record" of accomplishments as a versatile professional with a "hands-on" style of management. I am presently the Plant Industrial Engineering Manager after being promoted from Industrial Engineer at another location.

I have been involved in planning a $20 million plant expansion, overseeing and training personnel in quality techniques and making regular revisions to manufacturing budgets. In all three locations with Burlington Industries I have applied my analytical and problem-solving skills to develop changes which have transformed unproductive departments into highly effective and respected ones.

I would be glad to discuss the details of my salary history and requirements with you and can provide excellent personal and professional references if you request them.

I hope you will welcome my call soon to arrange a brief meeting at your convenience to discuss your current and future needs and how I might serve them. Thank you in advance for your time.

Sincerely yours,

Clarence Turlington

Alternate last paragraph:
I hope you will call or write soon to suggest a time convenient for us to meet and discuss your current and future needs and how I might serve them. Thank you in advance for your time.

CLARENCE TURLINGTON

1110½ Hay Street, Fayetteville, NC 28305 • preppub@aol.com • (910) 483-6611

OBJECTIVE

To benefit an organization that can use a detail-oriented positive thinker who offers an ability to handle deadlines/pressure and a talent for training/supervising others along with knowledge of project/product costing, standards engineering, and statistical process control.

EDUCATION

B.S., Industrial Engineering and Operations Research (IEOR), Wentworth Institute of Technology, Boston, MA, 2000.
Excelled in 500 hours of Bostonian Industries-sponsored management training related to statistical process control, quality engineering, problem solving and decision making, inventory assessment, time management, and leadership styles.

EXPERIENCE

Advanced in the following "track record" with Bostonian Industries:
INDUSTRIAL ENGINEERING MANAGER. Boston, MA (2004-present). Oversee five employees including a standards engineer while preparing revisions to the annual manufacturing budget and doing product analysis and costing.
- Prepared and presented a $250,000 annual manufacturing cost reduction program.
- Directed the efforts of a work measurement engineer and standards technicians in the development and application of equitable labor standards for production staff.
- Instilled in employees a strong customer service orientation and strengthened the department's relationship with the manufacturing area. Became respected as a congenial supervisor dedicated to excellence, and earned a reputation for being "impossible to frustrate or sidetrack!" Mastered statistical process control (SPC) concepts.

INDUSTRIAL ENGINEER. Boston, MA (2003-04). Trained and supervised standards technicians while controlling a variety of operational areas including work measurement and maintenance of incentive standards, plant layout, capital budgeting, and production capacity assessment and scheduling for a manufacturer with 1,000 employees.
- "Turned around" an unproductive department and led it to new levels of effectiveness.
- Was the "internal expert" in the area of standards engineering.

QUALITY CONTROL INSTRUCTOR/PROJECT MANAGER. Boston, MA (2001-02). As an industrial engineering trainee, was involved in three major areas of operations: teaching classes on techniques for improving quality, studying process control and machine capability, and overseeing cost projections and plant layout for a $20 million expansion project.
- Determined needs in the areas of space for three processes—storage and inventory requirements, material flow, and cost—after learning what the expected level of production would be once the expansion was up and running.
- Became skilled in the areas of work measurement and the budget revision process.

Highlights of other experience: Participated in three internships during my college career.
TOSHIBA CORPORATION. Lawrence, MA (summers 1998-99). Conducted stress tests on prototype equipment by making output quality determinations and doing fault analysis.
ITALIAN FOOD, INC. Italy (summer 1997). Lived and worked in a foreign country as a process assistant in several departments of a food processing plant.

COMPUTERS

Experienced in using PCs with software including Microsoft Word, Excel, and PowerPoint; and Adobe PageMaker.

PERSONAL

Speak and read Italian. Possess strong abilities related to observing and analyzing operations. Can "juggle" numerous tasks. Member of the American Institute of Industrial Engineers.

Date

Exact Name of Person
Title or Position
Exact Name of Company
Address
City, State, Zip

Dear Exact Name of Person: (or Dear Sir or Madam if answering a blind ad.)

I would appreciate an opportunity to talk with you soon about how I could contribute to your organization through my experience in production management as well as through my initiative, resourcefulness, and highly dedicated nature.

After earning my Bachelor of Science degree in Industrial Technology, I excelled as a machine operator in a plastics company and then as a production worker in a food processing plant, where I was quickly promoted into production line supervision. I have been commended for the creative way I apply my extensive technical knowledge as well as for my ability to communicate with people at all levels. I offer knowledge of several software programs used for data analysis and problem solving in industrial situations.

In my current job as a Production Superintendent I gained rapid promotion from a Production Supervisor and oversee an operation that ensures casings are properly pulled and cleaned by the 48 employees I manage.

In my previous job as an Assistant Supervisor, I made out the weekly rotation schedules for employees in five departments and oversaw food processing operations from initial receipt of raw material through packing and shipping. I quickly earned the respect of both line and staff for my keen attention to detail as well as for my ability to instill a "quality control" attitude in all employees. I strongly believe that quality control is not "a job at the end" but an attitude that all employees bring to their jobs, because it is a quality job at each stage of production that results in quality end products as well as lowest-possible production costs.

Single and willing to relocate or travel as needed, I am writing to you because I am impressed with your company's reputation and product line, and I believe I could become a valuable asset to your team. My salary requirements are $28,000 and higher. I can provide outstanding personal and professional references.

I hope you will welcome my call soon to arrange a brief meeting at your convenience to discuss your current and future needs and how I might serve them. Thank you in advance for your consideration.

Sincerely yours,

Timothy Roberts

TIMOTHY ROBERTS

1110½ Hay Street, Fayetteville, NC 28305   •   preppub@aol.com   •   (910) 483-6611

OBJECTIVE

To benefit an industrial organization that can use a resourceful problem solver who offers extensive experience in production operations and who is known for strong communication, technical, and supervisory skills as well as expert planning and organizational abilities.

EDUCATION

B.S., Industrial Technology, Florida State University, Tallahassee, FL, 1995-00. Proficient in solving industrial problems using knowledge of Word, Excel and PowerPoint. Completed courses in the following subject areas:

| Dynamics | Quality Assurance | Statics |
| Motion & Time Study | Fluids Technology | Production Engineering |

- Gained expert skills in testing the strength of wood, metal, and plastic materials.

EXPERIENCE

PRODUCTION SUPERINTENDENT. Florida Oranges, Inc., Tallahassee, FL (2004-present). Employed with Oranges, Inc., and was promoted from a Production Supervisor after only six months; oversee an operation ensuring that casings are properly pulled and cleaned by employees. Handle production scheduling among 48 employees; perform data analysis regarding resources; monitor and enforce quality control procedures.

SUPERVISOR. Florida Foods, Co., Pensacola, FL (2003-04). Was groomed to oversee the breeding of livestock. Supervised breeding and farrowing of 2,400 sows, including mating and artificial insemination; managed breeding, farrowing, and finishing for 1,200 sows.

Was promoted into production supervision after rapidly mastering production line tasks, American Cattle Beef, Co., Dallas, TX (2001-03).
ASSISTANT SUPERVISOR. Consistently achieved or exceeded production goals while overseeing five different departments in the plant including the sirloin line, mince line, and transfer line; coordinated operations from food processing to packing and shipping and assisted the plant manager in solving a wide range of problems.

- *Production scheduling*: Coordinated production work in five departments, each employing 35 to 40 workers; prepared weekly employee rotation schedule.
- *Data analysis*: Analyzed data and made decisions regarding manpower and resources.
- *Quality control*: Implemented quality assurance/quality control measures to guarantee production schedule deadlines and accurate job performance.
- *Multiple project management*: Oversaw activities ranging from line preparation, to weighing and shipping, to machine maintenance.
- *Government regulations*: Gained knowledge of sanitation, health, and fire regulations.

MACHINE OPERATOR. Cristo, Co., Jackson, MS (2000-01). Manufactured products according to precise specifications and performed operator-level maintenance on my machine.

Other experience: Held several positions to help finance college education.
MASTER CONTROL OPERATOR. WPRP-TV 16, Tallahassee, FL. Operated switchboard, recorded and produced on-the-air promotions and commercials, and maintained log.
MAINTENANCE WORKER. National Industries, Pensacola, FL. Performed painting and maintenance throughout the plant.
SHIPPING CLERK. DeLine, Inc., Pensacola, FL. Handled shipping and receiving.

PERSONAL

A motivated self-starter, have attended approximately 30 hours of continuing education courses on the principles of supervision and being an effective leader. Willing to go "the extra mile" to reduce wasted time and cut costs.

Exact Name of Person
Exact Title
Exact Name of Company
Address
City, State, Zip

**MAINTENANCE
ENGINEER**

with experience in
hazardous waste control

Dear Exact Name of Person (or Dear Sir or Madam if answering a blind ad):

With the enclosed resume, I would like to express my interest in exploring employment opportunities with your organization.

As you will see from my resume, I have become one of the country's leading experts on hazardous waste control and disposal while serving my country in the U.S. Army and U.S. Coast Guard. In one job with the Coast Guard, I supervised investigations of reported oil and hazardous waste spills in the Port of Valdez, Seward, and Homer while inspecting damaged facilities and monitoring cleanup procedures. I am experienced in investigating spillage at fuel refineries, chemical facilities, airports, and port and rail accidents. I have also trained investigators in federal hazardous waste laws and procedures.

In addition to my technical expertise, I offer strong management and communication skills which have been refined in a track record of outstanding performance. Known for my ability to "marry" my technical expertise and practical problem-solving skills, I once built a plastic device and companion grinding machine which saved a private company $10,000 monthly. I have a talent for taking things apart and putting them back together so that they work again, and work better.

I hope you will call or write me soon to suggest a time convenient for us to meet and discuss your current and future needs and how I might serve them. Thank you in advance for your time.

Sincerely,

Dimitri Elliott

Alternate last paragraph:
I hope you will welcome my call soon to arrange a brief meeting to discuss your current and future needs and how I might serve them. Thank you in advance for your time.

DIMITRI ELLIOTT

1110½ Hay Street, Fayetteville, NC 28305   •   preppub@aol.com   •   (910) 483-6611

OBJECTIVE   I offer proven hazardous waste control experience and solid mechanical and construction skills to an organization seeking an experienced, self-motivated professional with knowledge related to a wide range of machinery.

EQUIPMENT EXPERTISE

Offer valuable hands-on experience with systems and equipment including:

internal combustion engines	fire hydrants	gas and fuel pumps
oil and water separators	bead grinders	washers and dryers
hydraulics	plumbing	radio equipment

- Have know-how related to oil and hazardous waste clean-up, construction, welding, and basic electronics maintenance.
- Have a talent for taking things apart and making them work again.

EXPERIENCE

MAINTENANCE ENGINEER. U.S. Army, Germany (2004-present). As Senior Watercraft Engineer for multiple locations with a combined population of 1,500, maintain and repair dock facilities and maritime assets. Convert foreign electrical current 220V to standard 120V by means of a series of 220V to 120V converters.

SENIOR WATERCRAFT ENGINEER. U.S. Army, Fort Leavenworth, KS (2000-03). Controlled the clean up and disposal of hazardous oil waste and other chemicals while maintaining and operating oil and water separator; also acted as radio operator for controlling movement of vessels in and out of port.
- Modified oil and water separator to conform to state sewage standards.
- Acted skillfully at a ship sinking, saving the Army approximately $40,000.

MAINTENANCE ENGINEER and **WELDER.** Cape Fear Engineering, Co., Raeford, NC (1999-00). Built a plastic bead former and grinding machine while ensuring quality of other equipment, saving the company time and $10,000 per month.

ENGINEERING OFFICER AND ENVIRONMENTAL INVESTIGATOR. U.S. Coast Guard, Wilmington, NC (1994-99). As Engineering Petty Officer managing two assistants, maintained readiness for 41-foot and 44-foot Coast Guard boats while assuring operability of station equipment, generators, vehicles, boilers, and plumbing.

SENIOR ENVIRONMENTAL INVESTIGATOR and SUPPLY COORDINATOR. U.S. Coast Guard, Valdez, AK (1986-94). Supervised investigations of reported oil and hazardous waste spills for the Port of Valdez, Seward, and Homer inspecting damaged facilities and monitoring cleanup procedures.
- Investigated spillage at fuel refineries, chemical facilities, airports, and port and rail accidents. Trained investigators in federal hazardous waste laws and procedures.
- Provided public information on prevention of environmental hazards.

TRAINING

Excelled in U.S. Army and Coast Guard training related to these areas:

Nautical Engineering	Law Enforcement	Management
Environmental Systems	Internal Combustion Engines	Diesel Theory

PERSONAL

Am an enthusiastic, hard-working professional with the determination to carry through on any project I begin. Always enjoy learning how things work. Have an exceptional talent for motivating others. Will cheerfully relocate and travel as needed.

Exact Name of Person
Title or Position
Name of Company
Address
City, State, Zip

**MANUFACTURING
ENGINEER**

with experience as a
senior systems analyst

Dear Exact Name of Person: (or Sir or Madam if answering a blind ad.)

I would appreciate an opportunity to talk with you soon about how I could contribute to your organization through my extensive experience as a Systems Analyst known for excellent analytical, problem-solving, training, and supervisory skills.

With a keen eye for detail and ability to quickly learn, absorb, and apply new ideas and concepts, I offer a reputation as a professional who can be depended on for personal integrity, resourcefulness, and dedication to excellence in everything I attempt.

You will see from my enclosed resume that I offer expertise in designing, coding, testing, and implementing solutions as well as in analyzing user requirements and training programmers. During my years at Foller and Grannus, I was effective in integrating all order processing and manufacturing system processes into multifaceted systems with common databases while setting up procedures so that each department had their own customized interfaces.

If you can use an analytical problem-solver who is also a skilled trainer and supervisor, I am confident that I offer the technical knowledge and skills as well as the professionalism and maturity you seek.

I hope you will welcome my call soon to arrange a brief meeting to discuss your current and future needs and how I might serve them. Thank you in advance for your time.

Sincerely,

Peter Wood

Alternate last paragraph:
I hope you will call or write me soon to suggest a time convenient for us to meet and discuss your current and future needs and how I might serve them. Thank you in advance for your time.

PETER WOOD

1110½ Hay Street, Fayetteville, NC 28305 • preppub@aol.com • (910) 483-6611

OBJECTIVE
To offer a background of experience as a Systems Analyst with excellent supervisory skills and the capability of working on complex systems with multiple databases as well as a reputation for creativity in troubleshooting, problem solving, and enhancements.

TECHNICAL SKILLS
Through extensive experience and training, have become known as an expert with specific abilities and skills in specific areas including:
Skilled in designing and implementing solutions using Visual Basic, Oracle Developer, UNIX programming, and C++ programming while handling the following functions:
Analyzing user needs and recommending solutions
Training users so that their skills and knowledge are maximized
Applying technical writing skills with clarity and accuracy
Communicating with all levels of users up to and including management personnel
Applying creative utilization of computer resources to provide workable systems

EXPERIENCE
Provided expertise throughout a period of heavy growth and reorganization caused by a change to new ownership:
SENIOR SYSTEMS ANALYST. Foller, Inc., Trenton, NJ (1989-present). Automated engineering-to-manufacturing interface in such a way that no new personnel were needed even though the business doubled. Maintain a UNIX operating system. Purchased and further refined application software through applying upgrades to the system and downloading fixes and documentation.
- Wrote utility programs which led to increased productivity and the automation of general functions such as backups and daily and weekly updates and reports.
- Analyzed projects and broke them down into workable sections so that separate functions could be assigned to the correct individual to handle.
- Directed the work of other programmers. Performed triage when problems such as system failures and outages developed. Developed systems used by ten sites simultaneously.
- Became known as a persistent professional who would not give up until a solution was found and the problem corrected.
- Adapted to new methods of handling workloads and dividing assignments after going from a department with an average of 11 technicians to a two- or three-person shop.
- Was a contributor to team efforts which resulted in a "Trade Secret Award" in 1998 for a PC to midrange data translation project which was eligible for a patent.

Advanced into higher levels in a track record of promotion with a major textile manufacturer, Grannus, Inc., Newark, NJ:
SYSTEMS ANALYST. (1987-89). Designed systems and programs while working with users to determine their requirements and with programmers to ensure specifications were met; assisted programmers during testing and implementation.
PROGRAMMER. (1982-87). Refined my skills as a technical trainer with the capability of helping people of varying skills and learning capabilities grasp and master procedures and information as supervisor of six programmers.

EDUCATION
B.S. in Business Administration, Mercer County Community College, Trenton, NJ, 1987.

PERSONAL
Use computer programs as my tool for solving problems. Am very logical and detail oriented but also creative and open to new ideas. Am a good listener who can remain outside a discussion, see all sides to an issue, and then develop a working solution.

Date

Exact Name of Person
Title or Position
Exact Name of Company
Address
City, State, Zip

**MANUFACTURING
ENGINEERING
DESIGNER**

Dear Exact Name of Person: (or Dear Sir or Madam if answering a blind ad.)

I am interested in applying for a position with your company as an automations engineer. I have spoken with your son concerning openings for an automations engineer and an industrial engineer.

With eight years of experience as a CAD-CAM operator, I offer extensive and varied responsibilities in the design, development, and implementation of fully automated machinery. I also have knowledge of selecting and using programmable logic controllers in high-speed production machinery.

I hope you will call or write me soon to suggest a time convenient for us to meet and discuss your current and future needs and how I might serve them. Thank you in advance for your time.

Sincerely yours,

Daniel Lovett

Alternate last paragraph:

I hope you will welcome my call soon to arrange a brief meeting to discuss your current and future needs and how I might serve them. Thank you in advance for your time.

DANIEL LOVETT

1110½ Hay Street, Fayetteville, NC 28305 • preppub@aol.com • (910) 483-6611

OBJECTIVE   To benefit an organization through my extensive experience in design, engineering, and production, along with my communications skills, supervisory experience, and "hands on" knowledge of manufacturing.

EDUCATION   Earned an **A.A. degree in Mechanical Drafting and Machine Shop**, Jackson State University, Jackson, MS, 1994.

EXPERIENCE   **MANUFACTURING ENGINEERING DESIGNER.** Mississippi Manufacturing, Co., Jackson, MS (2004-present).
- Design custom prototype and production machinery.
- Manage team of employees responsible for building and setting up of machinery.
- Submit plans and cost outlines for machinery.
- Schedule manufacturing of machinery.
- Gained extensive experience in the operation of CAD systems including advanced 3-D design.
- Have worked with Gulf Corp, MS Laboratories, General Mills, and many smaller firms.

INSTRUCTOR. Jackson State University, Jackson, MS (2002-03). Motivated, instructed, and evaluated students in blueprint reading, using precision measuring instruments, metric mathematics, and other subjects related to potential employment with American Elevator Company.
- Prepared detailed lesson plans to organize instructional periods, clarify objectives for students, and achieve maximum teaching results.
- Maintained accurate records of student performance for scrutiny by school and company executives.

MANUFACTURING ENGINEERING DESIGNER. Crawford Designers, Inc., Jackson, MS (1995-02). As an integral part of the production team, used my in-depth knowledge of engineering to design tools and machinery.
- Managed the drafting department to ensure exact production of design specifications; set up blueprints.
- Researched and purchased supplies and materials required to build machinery.
- Scheduled manufacturing and modification of machinery and tools.

RELATED EXPERIENCE & SKILLS
- Designed, developed, and implemented various prototype machinery and production of design specifications; set up blueprints.
- Coordinated machine shop activities with production schedules.
- Created samples for potential product expansion for new and existing clients.
- Developed knowledge in selecting and using programmable logic controllers in high-speed production machinery.
- Constructed and read blueprints.
- Operated lathes, milling machines, surface grinders, boring machines, and various CNC machines.
- Performed arc and tig welding.

AFFILIATIONS   **TREASURER & PAST CHAIRMAN.** National Society of Manufacturing Engineers.
ADVISORY COMMITTEE MEMBER. Jackson State University Vocational/Technical Department.

TWO-PAGE RESUME

THOMAS GARNER

1110½ Hay Street, Fayetteville, NC 28305   •   preppub@aol.com   •
(910) 483-6611

MARINE ENGINEER

OBJECTIVE

Power Plant Mechanic, Utility Mechanic, or similar position requiring a combination of technical expertise and management experience.

LICENSES & TECHNICAL SKILLS

Universal Air Conditioning Certification HVAC

Heating, Ventilating, and Air Conditioning expertise: Experienced in installing commercial, industrial, and residential units, from start to finish, including package and split units. Highly experienced in servicing and troubleshooting of nearly all types of units including controls such as thermostats and zone system dampers.

Experienced Diesel Mechanic:

- Proficient in troubleshooting diesel engines including the repair and maintenance of diesel engines ranging from Low Speed through High Speed diesels.
- Experienced in troubleshooting and maintenance of AC and DC electrical circuits as well as systems related to water purification, sanitation, pneumatics, and hydraulic systems.

Background includes **more than 17 years as a Marine Engineer and three years as an Instructor in electromotive diesel engine operation, preventive maintenance, and repair.**

Wiring: Fully knowledgeable of residential, industrial, and commercial electrical wiring practices.

- Proficient in installation and bending of all conduit types.
- Skilled in reading blueprint drawings, design drawings, wiring diagrams, and scale applications. Experienced in installation and troubleshooting of lighting fixtures, receptacles, as well as fire and alarm system components.

EXPERIENCE

MARINE ENGINEERING MANAGER. U.S. Army, Korea (2002-present). For the Army's only composite boat company in Korea, directed training activities for 131 people while managing personnel who operated and maintained 12 watercraft and 11 wheeled vehicles valued at more than $40 million.

- Achieved a high equipment serviceability rating above 95%. Passed 100% roadside vehicle and equipment inspections.
- Managed power plant mechanics who performed preventive maintenance on primary power plant generator sets and remote emergency generator sets. Directed mechanics in performing on-site repairs and major overhauls of generator set engines.
- Completed maintenance records and documented all parts and assemblies used. Scheduled generator set use; responded to station power outages and equipment failures.
- Operated power plant equipment in an efficient and economical manner. Inspected, maintained, and repaired ancillary power plant equipment. Provided oversight for the control of power plant capital equipment, tools, and manuals.
- Became knowledgeable of Environmental, Health & Safety, and Waste Management policies and procedures. Directed the disposal of hazardous waster in accordance with established procedures.

ASSISTANT DIRECTOR, MARINE ENGINEERING SCHOOL. U.S. Army, Fort Bragg, NC (2000-02). Directed operation and maintenance of a $20 million training facility while supervising 12 NCO; advised nine civilian instructors and seven warrant officers.

- Provided quality assurance for the quality of instruction of 16 courses which graduated 245 students annually; courses included segments related to diesel mechanics, electricity, hydraulics, welding, blueprint reading, schematics, air conditioning and refrigeration, and boiler operations. Graduates were certified as Watercraft Engineers.
- Implemented an organization safety program resulting in a 93% reduction in accidents.
- Achieved the top score Armywide in the marine engine speciality.

SENIOR INSTRUCTOR. U.S. Army, Fort Carson, CO (1999-00). Excelled as Instructor/ Writer for the U.S. Army Marine Engineering Service School; developed and instructed curricula which emphasized technical troubleshooting and the disassembly/assembly of electromotive diesel engines.

- Developed a 72-hour block of instruction on the Army Maintenance Management System.
- Taught a 40-hour block of instruction on Electromotive Diesel Engines.

MAINTENANCE SUPERVISOR. U.S.A.V. John Hancock (1996-98). Reported to the Chief Engineer while supervising a crew of 15 engineers while managing a $30 million heavy lift ship. Planned, performed, and supervised preventive maintenance and repairs while also maintaining systems including two electromotive diesel engines, model 16-645E7, electrical three phase 440 power generator systems, hydraulics pneumatics, and HVAC systems.

- Saved more than half a million dollars through my resourceful maintenance leadership.

ASSISTANT ENGINEER. U.S. Army, Fort Lewis, WA (1993-95). As the senior engineering manager onboard a 115-ft. landing craft utility, took initiatives which drastically improved the mechanical ability and cosmetic appearance of the craft. Supervised three individuals in the engineering section. Cross trained engineering personnel.

MAINTENANCE AND SUPPLY MANAGER. U.S. Army, Fort Lewis, WA (1990-93). Was specially selected for this position normally held by someone more senior in rank and experience. For a company with six landing craft and one ship, handled a wide range of administrative and technical responsibilities. Controlled a 2,800-line-item inventory.

- Wrote and negotiated contracts ranging from $30,000 to $600,000 for repair parts.

ENGINEMAN & HOVERCRAFT CREW CHIEF. U.S. Army, Fort Rucker, AL (1987-90). Onboard a 15-ton amphibious vehicle, performed preventive maintenance of two diesel engines as well as hydraulic and electrical systems. Evaluated and trained crew chiefs.

EDUCATION & TRAINING

College: Completed 30 semester hours, Central Michigan University.
Business: Extensive training in supervision, sanitation management, 1997-present.
Technical: Certified Universal for Refrigerant Handling, 2001. Department of Labor OSHA Cranes and Material Handling, 2000. Advanced Watercraft Engineer Course, 1996. U.S.C.G. S/S Generator Waste Heat Recovery System, 1996. U.S.C.G. Fuel Handling Equipment/Oily Water Separator, 1996. U.S.C.G. G.M. Model 8-567-E2 and 8-645-E2 Diesel Engineering, 1996. Watercraft Engineer Basic Technical Course, 1991. Watercraft Engineer Primary Technical Course, 1991. LACV-30 Operator/Maintenance Course, 1988. Watercraft Engineman Basic Course, 1987. Common Basic Electronics Training, 1984.
Leadership: Small Group Leader Instructor Course, 1999. Instructor Training Course, 1999. Collateral Duty Safety Officer/NCO Course, 1999.
High School: Graduated from Central High School, Fargo, ND, 1984.

PERSONAL

Nonsmoker and nondrinker. Stable married individual. Excellent references.

CAREER CHANGE

Date

Exact Name of Person
Exact Title
Exact Name of Company
Address
City, State, Zip

**MARITIME
ENGINEERING
MANAGER**

with experience as a
senior instructor &
training program manager

Dear Exact Name of Person (or Dear Sir or Madam if answering a blind ad):

With the enclosed resume, I would like to express my interest in exploring employment opportunities with your organization.

While rising to the rank of Senior Chief Petty Officer in the U.S. Navy, I gained expertise related to functional areas including firefighting as well as the identification and defense against chemical, biological, and radiation hazards. In my most recent position, I held the unique designation of Gas Free Engineer as I held the sole responsibility for testing and identifying toxic gases on board a major vessel.

Having served my country with distinction, I am now ready to offer my versatile technical expertise to the civilian community. On numerous occasions, I have produced well trained teams which can handle any type of damage control. The recipient of numerous medals for exceptional performance, I am known for my strong problem-solving and team-building skills.

I hope you will call or write me soon to suggest a time convenient for us to meet and discuss your current and future needs and how I might serve them. Thank you in advance for your time.

Sincerely,

Jeremy Revels

Alternate last paragraph:
I hope you will welcome my call soon to arrange a brief meeting to discuss your current and future needs and how I might serve them. Thank you in advance for your time.

JEREMY REVELS

1110½ Hay Street, Fayetteville, NC 28305   •   preppub@aol.com   •   (910) 483-6611

OBJECTIVE

To offer my proven abilities as an instructor, inspector, and manager of technical firefighting, damage control, and hazardous material handling operations along with my extensive background in industrial hygiene and my strong communication and management skills.

EDUCATION & TRAINING

Completed extensive U.S. Navy-sponsored training in engineering operations management with attendance at specialized programs in these and other areas:
Leadership and management skill development for senior supervisors
Advanced damage control program management and training methods
Shipboard chemical, biological, and radiological defense operations
Identification, handling, disposal, and precautions in hazardous material control

HONORS

Was honored with U.S. Navy Achievement Medals in recognition of my accomplishments:
Navy and Marine Corps Commendation Medal–for meritorious service to a regional support group senior executive from 1999-02
Navy and Marine Corps Commendation Medal–for meritorious service on board the USS Pacific Star from 2002-04
Flag Letter of Commendation–for service during a major inspection in July 2000

EXPERIENCE

Advanced to the rank of Senior Chief Petty Officer, a significant achievement reserved for the most accomplished leaders and technical experts, U.S. Navy:
SENIOR INSTRUCTOR AND TRAINING PROGRAM MANAGER. Everett, WA (2004-present). Promoted on the basis of my technical knowledge and communication skills, manage the training of firefighting and "damage control" teams.

- Supervise 18 people training personnel in identification of chemical, biological, and radiation hazards. Developed plans for the installation and maintenance of firefighting systems and supervise 12 technical specialists in that area. Maintain sole responsibility for testing and identifying toxic gases on board the ship as the **"Gas Free Engineer."**
- Have developed effective training programs despite the problems of keeping the quality of services high with fewer people due to widespread military downsizing.
- Perform managerial and safety supervisor functions while acting as the subject matter expert in Damage Control (DC), Firefighting (FF), and Chemical, Biological, and Radiological-Defense (CBR-D) programs; trained damage control and firefighting teams.

DAMAGE CONTROL TEAM MANAGER. Key West, FL (2000-03). Provided firefighting instruction while overseeing maintenance and operation of a ship's damage control operations.

- Was quickly promoted from this job on the basis of my technical expertise, exceptional leadership skills, and initiative.
- Received official evaluations which cited my emphasis on encouraging and motivating subordinates to set and maintain high professional and personal and take advantage of every opportunity to receive education and training.
- Produced a well-trained team which in the words of one executive, *"can handle any type of damage control casualty on board."* Was cited as a resourceful professional who took the initiative to locate/procure parts which allowed watertight doors to be overhauled.

SUPERVISORY FIREFIGHTER. Served on U.S. Navy ships in various capacities in the firefighting and damage control field; held positions in maintenance and repair operations.

PERSONAL

Among my strongest qualities is my skill in training and instructing others to achieve high standards. Offer excellent communication abilities. Can provide outstanding references.

Date

Exact Name of Person
Exact Title
Exact Name of Company
Address
City, State, Zip

**MECHANICAL
ENGINEER**

Dear Exact Name of Person (or Dear Sir or Madam if answering a blind ad):

With the enclosed resume, I would like to express my interest in exploring employment opportunities with your organization.

As you will see from my resume, I recently completed my degree in Engineering Science and was aggressively recruited by a company at which I performed a three-month internship. For a company which works as a subcontractor to major corporations in the aviation and manufacturing fields, I have designed overhead and underhung cranes while handling simultaneous responsibilities related to drafting, calculating stress, vendor purchasing, and designing. I was specially selected to assist in designing and checking drawings on multimillion-dollar projects which include tank line cranes for American Boeing and U.S. Air's first hoist-operated tail dock crane.

A member of the Numerical Control Society, I also am an Associate Member of the American Society of Mechanical Engineers. I am now preparing to complete the final steps for qualifying as a Professional Engineer.

Although I am held in high regard in my current position and can provide outstanding references at the appropriate time, I am selectively exploring opportunities in other organizations.

I hope you will call or write me soon to suggest a time convenient for us to meet and discuss your current and future needs and how I might serve them. Thank you in advance for your time.

Sincerely,

Richard Smith

Alternate last paragraph:
I hope you will welcome my call soon to arrange a brief meeting to discuss your current and future needs and how I might serve them. Thank you in advance for your time.

RICHARD SMITH

1110½ Hay Street, Fayetteville, NC 28305　·　preppub@aol.com　·　(910) 483-6611

OBJECTIVE　To apply my skills and education in engineering to an organization that can use an enthusiastic, hard-working young professional who offers experience in crane and hoist design, along with sound decision-making abilities.

EDUCATION　**B.S., Engineering Science**, Keene State College, Keene, NH, 2004.
Excelled in four months of intense management training sponsored by the U.S. Army Reserves in areas including procedures for managing supply and maintenance operations as well as supervisory skills and personnel management.

CERTIFICATION　Certified by the State of New Hampshire as an Engineer-in-Training.
- Completed the Fundamentals of Engineering exam while in college, and am preparing to qualify as a Professional Engineer.

PROFESSIONAL　Member, Numerical Control Society
ASSOCIATION　Associate member, American Society of Mechanical Engineers

EXPERIENCE　**MECHANICAL ENGINEER.** Crafty's, Co., Keene, NH (2004-present). Design overhead and underhung cranes in the company's New Hampshire Division while excelling in a job which requires skills in areas including:

| drafting | vendor purchases | designing |
| calculating stress | checking drawings | |

- Was selected to assist in designing and checking drawings on multimillion-dollar projects including tank line cranes for American Boeing and U.S. Air's first hoist-operated tail dock crane.
- Applied my technical knowledge to design cranes according to CMAA (Crane Manufacturers Association of America) specifications.
- Rapidly learned AUTOCAD and ALGOR computer software and their specific applications in engineering.
- Took over as acting project manager when the supervisor left during a major project.
- Participate in Engineering/Manufacturing Committee discussions regarding coordination between the two groups to resolve production, shipping, and purchasing problems.

FIRST LINE SUPERVISOR. U.S. Army Reserves, Keene, NH (2000-present). Coordinate training and scheduling as one of three managers of a 216-person company.
- Applied my communication skills by developing and writing the standard operating procedures for maintenance operations.
- Displayed outstanding motivational and leadership abilities in a company which previously suffered from problems in retaining skilled personnel.

TECHNICAL　Familiar with software and computer applications specific to engineering use including:
KNOWLEDGE　**Programming languages**: Visual Basic and Software Project Management, Oracle SQL and PL/SQL, JavaScript, UNIX programming, and C++ programming. Also knowledgeable of CADCAM.
On my own initiative, have pursued extensive knowledge of software development technologies such as Rational Unified Process (RUP), waterfall, spiral and Rapid application development (RAD).

PERSONAL　Have a Secret security clearance. Am a fast learner with a reputation for hard work and dedication. Have a current passport and will cheerfully relocate.

Date

Exact Name of Person
Title or Position
Exact Name of Company
Address
City, State, Zip

**MECHANICAL
ENGINEER**

with experience as a
director, new product
development

Dear Exact Name of Person (or Dear Sir or Madam if answering a blind ad):

With the enclosed resume, I would like to make you aware of my interest in exploring the possibility of joining your executive team in some capacity in which you can utilize my vast experience related to new product development and strategic planning/positioning.

As you will see from my resume, I am currently excelling as Director, New Product Development, for Philly Manufacturing Company. I was recruited by the company in 2003 to take over new product development for its Courtney Group and Friller Products ($90 million in sales) and, in May 2004, I was promoted to direct new product development for all company products ($200 million). Although I am held in the highest regard and can provide outstanding references at the appropriate time, I would ask that you not contact my current employer until after we talk. The company I work for is currently up for sale, and I am selectively exploring opportunities in other organizations.

In previous positions since earning my B.S. degree in Mechanical Engineering, I have gained experience in design engineering, process development engineering, machine design engineering, project management, and new product development in multiple industries. I worked for giants (Hershey's, Inc. and Sylvania Corporation) in the aircraft industry and made major contributions to new engine proposals and new aircraft production. Subsequently working on the development of consumer products for Hershey's, I was promoted to develop manufacturing processes for new cereal products. Then with Calvin & Bros., Inc., I was promoted from Senior Project Manager to New Product Development Group Manager. While at Calvin, I transformed a poorly organized group suffering from low output into a highly focused and productive product development team which developed numerous profitable new products.

I offer a proven ability to bring focus and strategic direction to product development teams, and I would welcome the opportunity to meet with you in person to discuss how I might positively impact your bottom line. If you think my considerable skills and experience could benefit you, please contact me to suggest the next step I should take in exploring the possibility of becoming a valuable part of your executive team.

Yours sincerely,

Jeffrey Kinston

JEFFREY KINSTON

1110½ Hay Street, Fayetteville, NC 28305   •   preppub@aol.com   •   (910) 483-6611

OBJECTIVE

To contribute to the growth and profitability of a company that can use a visionary business leader with expertise related to all aspects of new product development including project management, strategic planning, project justification and prioritization as well as employee recruiting and supervision.

EDUCATION

Bachelor of Science (B.S.) degree in Mechanical Engineering, Providence College, Providence, RI, 1989. Graduated *cum laude;* 3.72 GPA.

Annually attend the respected executive development program at St. Joseph's University, Philadelphia, PA, The Masters Forum, 2000-04.

EXPERIENCE

DIRECTOR, NEW PRODUCT DEVELOPMENT. Philly Manufacturing Company, Altoona, PA (2003-present). Was recruited by this company to grow its top line through new product development; was promoted in May 2004 from Director of New Product Development for Courtney Group and Friller Products ($90 million in sales) to Director of New Product Development for all company products ($200 million).

- Oversee a $5 million engineering budget and a staff of 38 managers, engineers, designers, drafters, technicians, and assistants; report to the President.
- Closed down new product development operations in Virginia and rebuilt the new product development organization in Pennsylvania; hired 18 managers, engineers, designers, and technicians while also organizing lab facilities and test equipment.
- Played a key role in identifying and arresting faltering financial performance; developed and implemented a disciplined new product development process that included organizing and flow-charting the process, developing work instructions, creating process and authorization forms, and designing a financial model for control.
- Developed and launched a new hydraulic jack, a retail 12-volt portable power supply, a gasoline recycler, and a cordless device utilized in manufacturing.

GROUP MANAGER, NEW PRODUCT DEVELOPMENT. Calvin & Bros., Inc., Pittsburgh, PA (1998-03). Excelled as a Senior Project Manager from 1998-03 and was promoted in 1999 to New Product Development Group Manager; reported to the VP of Engineering.

- Facilitated the design and development of high quality innovative industrial fluid-handling products at the lowest cost and in the shortest possible time.

PROCESS DEVELOPMENT ENGINEER. Hershey's, Inc., Pittsburgh, PA (1995-98). After making major contributions as a Machine Design Project Engineer from 1995-97, was promoted to develop manufacturing processes for new snack products.

- Served as the Process Engineering Representative on new product development teams.
- Defined, tested, and installed new processing equipment; developed and implemented procedures needed to transition new products from R&D labs to plant production.

STRUCTURAL INTEGRITY ENGINEER. Sylvania Corporation, Yakima, WA (1994-95). Received two Sylvania Achievement Awards for contributions to the F120 engine proposal.

DESIGN ENGINEERING LEAD. American Designers, Inc., Richmond, VA (1989-94). Excelled as a Structural Design Engineer from 1989-92 and designed primary aircraft structure for new production F-16 aircraft, and was then promoted to manage all structural design and production support related to the F-16 aft fuselage. Supervised eight engineers.

PERSONAL

Excellent references. Highly resourceful leader who excels in managing the creative process.

Date

Exact Name of Person
Title or Position
Exact Name of Company
Address
City, State, Zip

Dear Exact Name of Person: (or Dear Sir or Madam if answering a blind ad.)

With the enclosed resume, I would like to make you aware of the strong management skills and technical knowledge which I could utilize for the benefit of an ambitious company.

As you will see, I hold a degree in Mechanical Engineering and have recently excelled as Director of Product Design and Development with Campbell. While directing worldwide customer and product support, I manage a department of 36 employees and a $5 million operating budget. I have made numerous contributions to the bottom line. I successfully designed and implemented a QS-9000 Design Control System which has resulted in zero instances of non-conformance during three surveillance audits. I also smoothly planned and directed the relocation of the entire corporate engineering staff from Illinois to Florida, which involved restaffing the entire department. I am known for my exceptionally strong team building skills.

Although I am held in high regard and can provide excellent references at the appropriate time, I am selectively exploring opportunities in companies which can utilize my technical knowledge as well as my management abilities. I have a keen interest in moving to a higher level of business unit management and profit center management. I am available for relocation.

I hope you will welcome my call soon to arrange a brief meeting at your convenience to discuss your current and future needs and how I might serve them. Thank you in advance for your time.

Sincerely,

Noel Simpkins

Alternate last paragraph:
I hope you will call or write me soon to suggest a time convenient for us to meet and discuss your current and future needs and how I might serve them. Thank you in advance for your time.

NOEL SIMPKINS

1110½ Hay Street, Fayetteville, NC 28305   •   preppub@aol.com   •   (910) 483-6611

OBJECTIVE   To build upon my technical management capabilities by undertaking further responsibilities in business unit management and profit center management.

EDUCATION   **Bachelor of Science** in **Mechanical Engineering**, University of South Carolina, Columbia, SC, 1994.

EXPERIENCE   *With Campbell Company, have been promoted to positions of increasing responsibility by this international manufacturer of original equipment and aftermarket air, oil, and fuel filtration devices:*

2004-present: **DIRECTOR, PRODUCT DESIGN & DEVELOPMENT.** Daytona Beach, FL. Relocated Corporate Engineering from Chicago, IL, to Daytona Beach, FL. Restaffed department by recruiting, hiring, training, and developing engineers as well as support staff personnel.

- Oversee all aspects of aftermarket and original equipment manufacturing air, oil, and fuel filtration products, including Product Design, Product Development, Packaging Engineering, and the technical aspects of Filter Testing.
- Manage a department of 36 employees including seven direct reports and 18 degreed engineers as well as a $5 million operating budget.
- Direct worldwide customer and product support, to include significant international travel for the purpose of customer support and business development.
- Successfully designed and implemented a QS-9000 Design Control System which has resulted in zero instances of non-conformance during three surveillance audits.
- OEM/OES customers include Chrysler, Ford, Mazda, Subaru, Toyota, and Nissan.

1999-04: **MANAGER, LIQUID DESIGN ENGINEERING.** Chicago, IL. Held responsibility over Product Design for all original equipment and aftermarket oil, fuel, and hydraulic filtration products.

- Managed ten degreed engineers at the corporate and various plant locations.

1998-99: **ORIGINAL EQUIPMENT SALES ENGINEER.** Springfield, IL. Relocated to Springfield after Campbell secured 100% of the Chevrolet Motorcraft business, totaling $50 million annually. Provided on-site engineering assistance to develop and implement an approval process that allowed Campbell to convert purchased product into manufactured product.

- Served as Project Manager for all new vehicle platforms to ensure that product development coincided with the customer's vehicle program timing requirements.
- Supervised 11 people who functioned in a matrix management fashion on a project valued at $3 million that had a three-week deadline; the previous project manager had resigned abruptly, and I was specially selected to assume project management responsibility. We brought the project in on time and under budget.

1996-98: **PRODUCT DESIGN ENGINEER.** Daytona Beach, FL. Designed and developed oil filtration products for aftermarket and original equipment.

Highlights of earlier experience: **PRODUCT ENGINEER.** Thompson Taylor Corporation, Columbia, SC (1995-96). Designed and developed lubrication and hydraulic filter cartridges for off-road Original Equipment Manufacturer (OEM) and Industrial applications.

PERSONAL   Excellent personal and professional references on request.

Date

Exact Name of Person
Exact Title
Exact Name of Company
Address
City, State, Zip

**MECHANICAL
ENGINEER**

with experience as a
plant superintendent

Dear Exact Name of Person (or Dear Sir or Madam if answering a blind ad):

With the enclosed resume, I would like to express my interest in exploring employment opportunities with your organization.

As you will see from my resume, I offer comprehensive knowledge of business operations along with a proven ability to demonstrate strong initiative in decision making. I have excelled in a track record of distinguished performance in a prominent company in the poultry industry. After earning my Bachelor's degree in Mechanical Engineering, I accepted a full-time job, but I continued to work towards my Master of Engineering Administration degree at night while excelling in a demanding position.

With my current employer, I have learned how to achieve outstanding results in a highly regulated industry, and I have made numerous contributions to profitability and productivity. On one occasion, I devised new procedures that improved line speed by 15%. On another occasion, I reduced sanitation downtime by 90% and reorganized the sanitation department while working closely with the USDA. In my current position as Plant Superintendent, I direct functions of a food processing plant that employs 400 people, and my major contribution has been the development of a Total Quality Management program that has resulted in unprecedented customer satisfaction levels.

Although I am held in high regard in my current position, I am selectively exploring opportunities in other industries. I can provide outstanding references at the appropriate time.

I hope you will call or write me soon to suggest a time convenient for us to meet and discuss your current and future needs and how I might serve them. Thank you in advance for your time.

Sincerely,

David Nelson

Alternate last paragraph:
I hope you will welcome my call soon to arrange a brief meeting to discuss your current and future needs and how I might serve them. Thank you in advance for your time.

DAVID NELSON

1110½ Hay Street, Fayetteville, NC 28305   •   preppub@aol.com   •   (910) 483-6611

OBJECTIVE   A challenging position in engineering management.

EDUCATION   **M.E.A., Master of Engineering Administration**, North Carolina Central University, Durham, NC, 2000.
B.S., Bachelor of Science degree in Mechanical Engineering, North Carolina State University, Raleigh, NC, 1997.

EXPERIENCE   *Have advanced through a track record of rapid promotions with Craighead Processing Plants, Co., Raleigh, NC (1997-present)*:
PLANT SUPERINTENDENT. (2004-present). Responsible for the scheduling and production functions of a food processing plant employing 400 hourly associates; manage six management team members.
- Integral member of management team involved in goal setting, planning, forecasting, and problem solving. Lead and provide guidance to management team members and evaluate their performance.
- Schedule production and ensure on-time delivery.
- Coordinate sales with process capabilities. Analyze monthly plan variance.
- Developed and implemented a Total Quality Management (TQM) program that resulted in unprecedented customer satisfaction record.
- Head four cross-functional teams to implement a continuous improvement program.
- Reduced plant labor cost through strict overtime management and staff reduction.
- Reduced processing costs by 5% by reducing supply costs.

NIGHT SHIFT SUPERINTENDENT. (2003-04). Managed night shift activities, production, sanitation, and maintenance. Reduced sanitation downtime by 90%.
- Reorganized sanitation department crew and worked closely with USDA.
- Supervised the night shift deboning department staffed by 100 hourly associates; trained new employees, reached full capacity while maintaining quality and consistently achieving and/or surpassing production goals by reducing turnover rate and increasing employee satisfaction.

FIRST PROCESSING MANAGER. (2002-03). Managed six salaried supervisors and oversaw 110 hourly employees; coordinated production, sanitation, and maintenance functions to improve efficiency and minimize losses.
- Managed the receiving, picking, and eviscerating departments. Improved line speed by 15%. Headed a yield control task force and gained 2% plant yield.

PRODUCTION SUPERVISOR. (1998-02). As a first-line supervisor, hired, counseled, and trained 35 hourly workers, and was promoted horizontally within the plant and gained experience in every production department.

MECHANICAL ENGINEER. (1997-98). Provided administrative support for new business development group, assisted the Vice-President of Operations with special projects and evaluated new project proposals.
- Attended a nine-month, intensive training program designed by the corporate office to train in all aspects of the poultry industry, live production, ingredient purchasing, processing, sales, and quality control.

PERSONAL   Can provide outstanding personal and professional references. Will cheerfully relocate.

Date

Exact Name of Person
Title or Position
Name of Company
Address
City, State, Zip

MECHANICAL ENGINEER

with background as a product engineering manager

Dear Exact Name of Person: (or Dear Sir or Madam if answering a blind ad.)

I would appreciate an opportunity to talk with you soon about how I could contribute to your organization through my versatile experience as an engineer in product engineering, product marketing, and project management.

As you will see from my resume, I have excelled in a track record of accomplishment with Pisgah Corporation since graduating with my B.S. degree in Mechanical Engineering (Industrial concentration).

I started my employment with the company as a Design Engineer in Asheville, NC, and earned an Engineering Recognition Award in 2001. I have developed multiple control designs for use in several industries. I became a Product Marketing Manager in 2002 and received a prestigious award in 2003 for Excellence in Marketing. As a Product Marketing Manager, I played a key role in producing a gross sales increase of $22.6 million over a two-year period.

In 2004 I was specially selected to act as a Product Engineering Manager and relocated to Charlotte, NC where I have handled a wide range of tasks related to the strategic and tactical transfer of products from an assembly plant in Asheville to a Custom OEM assembly plant in Charlotte. I have set up the engineering department, standardized product production of $20 million in sales, communicated with outside sales professionals and customers during the phase-in process, and created documentation related to the manufacture and assembly of products. While supervising a team of nine design engineers and two drafts people in developing new products and planning production methods, we have added $3.4 million in revenue through recent product development programs.

I am approaching your company because I believe my versatile experience in project management, product development, marketing analysis and sales, and engineering design could be of value to you. I can provide outstanding personal and professional references at the appropriate time.

If you can use a superior performer with a strong bottom-line orientation and an ability to think strategically, I hope you will contact me to suggest a time when we might meet to discuss your needs and how I might help you achieve them. Thank you in advance for your time.

Sincerely,

Patrick Hendersen

PATRICK HENDERSEN

1110½ Hay Street, Fayetteville, NC 28305 • preppub@aol.com • (910) 483-6611

OBJECTIVE

To benefit an organization that can use an engineer with a reputation as a creative problem solver along with experience in project management, electrical and mechanical product design, product marketing, quality assurance, auditing, and profitability management.

EDUCATION

Bachelor of Science in Mechanical Engineering, Industrial Concentration, University of North Carolina at Asheville, NC, 1995.

Completed training programs sponsored by Pisgah Corporation including:

Demand Flow Workshop	Interpersonal Skills	Communication Skills
Value Added Services	Microsoft Office	ISO 9002
Market Analysis	Quality Audits	Customer Coordination

EXPERIENCE

Since earning my B.S., have worked for Pisgah Corporation:

2004-present: PRODUCT ENGINEERING MANAGER. Charlotte, NC. Was transferred from Pisgah's Asheville location to handle tasks related to the strategic and tactical transfer of products from an assembly plant in Asheville to a Custom OEM assembly plant in Charlotte.

- **Project Management:** Was tasked to develop the phase-in operation plan for a new plant, which involved the detailed plan for product phase-in as well as the transfer of equipment from other sites; this plan determined the timetable for a $6 million inventory transfer and the employment of 185 production personnel.
- **Start-up Management:** Set up the engineering department of a customer OEM assembly plant; standardized product production of $20 million in sales.
- **Product Development and Employee Supervision:** Supervised a team of nine design engineers and two draftspeople in developing new products meeting customer requirements and in planning product production methods. **Recent product development programs have added $3.4 million in revenue.**
- **Training Development:** Developed the training course for new production employees.
- **Customer Communication and Liaison:** Communicated with outside sales personnel as well as the customer base regarding product transfer updates.
- **Documentation:** Created documentation required to manufacture and assemble products including mechanical and electrical drawings, assembly instructions, bill of materials, and agency approvals; developed warranty return policies and procedures.
- **Quality Assurance:** Quality assurance initiatives, procedures, and practices we established have increased first-time yield rates from 76% to 92%.

2002-04: PRODUCT MARKETING MANAGER: Asheville, NC. Increased assigned product sales volume by 40% while boosting overall net profit by 2%, and was responsible for a gross sales increase of $22.6 million over this period.

- **Marketing Award:** Received a prestigious *2003 Award for Excellence in Marketing.*
- **Market Analysis and Sales:** Identified target industries for sales penetration, then identified market areas and potential customers, and oversaw field sales personnel.

1994-02: DESIGN ENGINEER. Asheville, NC. Formulated product plans for sales presentation, support manufacturing disciplines, and product design.

- **Engineering Award:** Received a special *Engineering Recognition Award in 2001.* Developed multiple control designs for use in several industries.
- **Accreditation:** Assisted in ISO 9002 accreditation as audit interface with ISO (DNV).

PERSONAL

Excellent references. Proficient with AUTOCAD and other software and have installed software on numerous department computers. Excellent organizational skills.

Date

Exact Name of Person
Exact Title
Exact Name of Company
Address
City, State, Zip

NETWORK SURVEILLANCE ENGINEER II

Dear Exact Name of Person: (or Dear Sir or Madam if answering a blind ad):

With the enclosed resume, I would like to make you aware of my extensive knowledge of network and transmission systems technologies and electronics as well as the experience in identifying, isolating and troubleshooting network degradation and system outages that I could put to work for your company.

As you will see from my resume, I am currently excelling in a "track record" of performance as a Network Surveillance Engineer for one of the giants of the telecommunications industry. I have demonstrated my ability to work well under pressure in situations where I was called upon to locate cuts and failures on the transmission network during major outages. For example, I played a key role in facilitating the resolution of problems with a major site controller, implementing cabling and equipment repairs as well as a software update to restore the controller to service.

In addition to an Associate's degree in Electronics, I am certified in Netpro, Performance Monitoring of OC-12, and Tellabs 5500 DXC, and I have also completed numerous training phases in network management tools and platforms.

Throughout my earlier career in telecommunications and electronics, I demonstrated the exceptional technical skills and ability to rapidly master new technologies that have led me to succeed in a number of challenging environments. From the fast pace of the ground maintenance to the high-security atmosphere of a nuclear power station, I have consistently excelled, bringing my comprehensive knowledge of automation, electronics, and telecommunications systems to bear on the challenges of each position.

Although I am highly regarded by my current employer and can provide outstanding personal and professional references at the appropriate time, I am interested in selectively exploring career opportunities with other telecommunications companies. However, I would appreciate your keeping my interest confidential until after we have had the chance to speak in person.

If you can use a highly skilled professional whose analytical and technical abilities have been proven in a variety of challenging environments, then I hope you will welcome my call soon, when I try to arrange a brief meeting to discuss your goals and how my background might serve your needs.

Sincerely,

Beatrice Ritter

BEATRICE RITTER

1110½ Hay Street, Fayetteville, NC 28305   •   preppub@aol.com   •   (910) 483-6611

OBJECTIVE

To benefit an organization that can use a skilled telecommunications professional with exceptional technical, communication, planning, and organizational abilities who offers an extensive background in network and transmission systems troubleshooting and restoration.

EDUCATION

Associate's in Electronics, Cleveland Institute of Electronics, Cleveland, OH, 2004.
Certificate in Computer Programming and CSC, University of Cincinnati, OH, 1994.

EXPERIENCE

With Verizon, advanced in the following "track record" of increasing responsibilities for this giant in the telecommunications industry:
2002-present: **NETWORK SURVEILLANCE ENGINEER II.** Cincinnati, OH. Promoted to this position after excelling as a Network Surveillance Engineer I; identify, isolate, and troubleshoot network events, quickly recognizing network degradation and system outages.
- Knowledgeable in NSTHS ticket priority and escalation procedures; drive issues to resolution, escalating as appropriate to facilitate resolutions for service outages.
- Monitor networks from T-1 to OC-192, as well as DXCs 1/0, 3/1, 3/3, Alcatel, Tellabs, and DSC in addition to RPS-370 and Pirelli Systems.
- Provide assistance to Restoration, using my working knowledge of signal flow to perform troubleshooting and reporting.
- Served as a member of the team that tested the Impact platform.
- Developed, suggested, and implemented a new design for the Daily Network Report (DNR) that was adopted for use throughout Transmission Surveillance.

2001-02: **NETWORK SURVEILLANCE ENGINEER I.** Cincinnati, OH. Utilized monitoring and database management systems to provide notification, dispatch, troubleshooting and repair assistance to minimize outages and restore service to the customer.
- Located cuts and failures on the transmission network during major outages, producing positive results and proving my ability to work under extreme pressure.
- Demonstrated my thorough understanding of Sonet/Sonet rings and digital radio as well as network and transmission system technologies while determining which network management tools were best suited to identifying and isolating degradation and outages.

Highlights of earlier experience:
COMMUNICATIONS OPERATOR & ARMY TELEPHONE SYSTEM PLANT TECHNICIAN. National Technologies, Cleveland, OH. Coordinated and tracked trouble reports, line records, and work orders to ensure that telephone and data circuits were tested, repaired, maintained, and updated within established deadlines.
- Maintained cable frame in support of outside technicians and other contractors; verified and tested lines to assure accurate cable location as well as line quality and availability.
- Programmed the GTD-5 switch to add and remove telephones from the system, change system features, and perform diagnostic testing.

TECHNICAL ASSISTANT. Ohio Power, Inc., Cleveland, OH. Utilizing NOMAD2 and SCI engineering software databases, coordinated and tracked requests for changes to drawings, recorded punch lists for modifications, and entered rewrites and changes to nuclear procedures for the facility. Directed background checks and fingerprinting of employees as well as obtaining, updating, and maintaining a database of security information, including clearances.

PERSONAL

Excellent personal and professional references are available upon request.

CAREER CHANGE

Date

Exact Name of Person
Title or Position
Exact Name of Company
Address
City, State, Zip

**NETWORKING
ENGINEER**

Dear Exact Name of Person: (or Dear Sir or Madam if answering a blind ad.)

I would appreciate an opportunity to talk with you soon about how I could contribute to your organization through my versatile management experience and proven abilities in the areas of developing, motivating, training, and molding employees into productive teams.

I have consistently found ways to improve morale and productivity while managing operations in organizations of as many as 500 employees. I have received numerous awards including four commendation and one meritorious service medals for my exceptional accomplishments in demanding leadership positions.

I am known as a dynamic leader who offers a talent for cutting through details and getting to the heart of a situation so that I can establish priorities and find the most effective solution. I am certain that I could apply my managerial and motivational abilities in a manner which could be beneficial to your organization.

I hope you will call or write me soon to suggest a time convenient for us to meet and discuss your current and future needs and how I might serve them. Thank you in advance for your time.

Sincerely yours,

Corey Bates

Alternate last paragraph:

I hope you will welcome my call soon to arrange a brief meeting to discuss your current and future needs and how I might serve them. Thank you in advance for your time.

COREY BATES

1110½ Hay Street, Fayetteville, NC 28305   •   preppub@aol.com   •   (910) 483-6611

OBJECTIVE

To contribute to an organization and gain additional experience in the field of networking administration and engineering.

EDUCATION & TRAINING

Bachelor's Degree, Networking Technologies, Columbus State University, Columbus, GA, 2004.

Graduate studies in **International Relations**, Central Texas College, Killeen, TX, 2001-02.

B.S. Management and Economics, University of North Carolina at Pembroke, NC, 1998.

EXPERIENCE

STUDENT. Columbus State University, Columbus, GA (2003-present). Maintain a 3.85 grade point average in Networking Technology curriculum, including the following courses:

Microcomputer Troubleshoot/Repair	Network System Performance
Intro to Programming in C++	Network Security
Network Management	Client/Server Design
Novell Network Fundamentals	UNIX Environment
Internet Architecture	Communication Protocol

Served as a U.S. Army officer with ending rank of Captain:

SPECIAL PROJECT MANAGER. U.S. Army, Fort Benning, GA (2003). Played a critical role in establishing procedures and setting priorities for a functional reorganization in response to government guidelines for downsizing the military.

- Advised a senior executive on issues relating to modernization, fielding new equipment, and the turn in of outdated equipment.
- Developed timeline and supervised the relocation of multimillion-dollar assets, including 22 helicopters, 60 vehicles, and 160 people to a renovated, consolidated facility.

LOGISTICS AND SUPPORT SERVICES MANAGER. U.S. Army, Germany (2002-03). Controlled a $3.4 million annual budget and more than $70 million worth of equipment while providing a 400-person organization with transportation, supply, maintenance, and other support functions.

- Planned and coordinated support for assets including 37 helicopters and 107 vehicles.
- Revitalized a company which had previously received unsatisfactory ratings in an important annual performance evaluation; earned commendable, error-free ratings.
- Conducted research which led to a $140,000 savings by establishing new procedures for identifying and turning in excess or unrepairable equipment.

GENERAL MANAGER. U.S. Army, Fort Hood, TX (2000-01). Took over a program which trained approximately 220 pilots annually and brought it back to a high level of productivity despite the drawbacks of operating at 70% staff strength.

- Implemented improvements to the company's safety program as part of a restructuring after the tragic death of the previous manager. Participated as a member of the Light Helicopter User Support Team for the Boeing/Sikorsky LH contractor.

TRAINING PROGRAM OPERATIONS MANAGER. U.S. Army, Fort Hood, TX (1999-00). Was promoted based on talents in handling details of allocating resources and planning operations for an organization with a $42 million annual budget, 500 people, and 225 aircraft.

PERSONAL

FAA-licensed commercial pilot with 2,000 hours of flight time and a Top Secret security clearance. Health conscious and physically fit marathon runner. Have traveled extensively.

CAREER CHANGE

Date

Exact Name of Person
Title or Position
Exact Name of Company
Address
City, State, Zip

**NUCLEAR &
MECHANICAL
ENGINEER**

Dear Exact Name of Person (or Dear Sir or Madam if answering a blind ad):

    With the enclosed resume, I would like to express my interest in exploring employment opportunities with your organization and make you aware of my broad base of management experience gained while advancing to the rank of Commander, U.S. Navy. While serving my country, I have become known as a senior military officer known for the ability to provide the vision and sound oversight needed to optimize the use of scarce human, material, and fiscal resources.

    As a senior officer, I have developed a reputation as an articulate, highly intelligent manager who excels in inspiring others to exceed expected standards. I was recently handpicked for a top-level consulting and strategic planning position as a Regional Director on the staff of the Commander of Submarine Forces for the U.S. Pacific Fleet. In my previous management position as a submarine Commanding Officer, I significantly improved morale and productivity of a 140-person workforce. I pride myself on my ability to lead by example, and I have been able to motivate junior associates through my strong personal example and commitment to the highest goals.

    Earlier positions on technical inspection teams, as a manager of maintenance and administrative services operations, and as an Engineering and Quality Control Officer allowed me to become known as a resourceful problem solver and innovative thinker. I am accustomed to overseeing and carrying out activities such as managing multimillion-dollar operating budgets; supervising operations support for complex billion-dollar technical activities; and coordinating large-scale projects which require a close eye on the details so that multiple organizations can work together. I hold a Top Secret SBI security clearance.

    If you can use a versatile and dynamic executive who meets challenges head on and obtains results through a positive, hands-on management style, I hope you will contact me soon to suggest a time when we might have a brief discussion of how I could contribute to your organization. I can provide excellent professional and personal references at the appropriate time.

Sincerely,

Eric Moses

ERIC MOSES

1110½ Hay Street, Fayetteville, NC 28305 • preppub@aol.com • (910) 483-6611

OBJECTIVE

To offer exceptionally strong management and problem-solving skills refined while controlling human, material, and fiscal resources worldwide along with a reputation as a positive and dynamic innovator who motivates, sets the example, and leads the way to quality results.

EDUCATION

B.S.M.E., Nuclear and Mechanical Engineering, Virginia Commonwealth University, Richmond, VA, 1992.

EXPERIENCE

While advancing as a senior officer to the rank of Commander, U.S. Navy, received numerous awards and honors in recognition of my ability to inspire personnel to exceed expected standards, provide sound fiscal oversight, and plan and manage complex billion-dollar technical and maintenance operations:

NUCLEAR AND MECHANICAL ENGINEER. Monterey, CA (2004-present). Consistently cited as having unlimited potential, insight, and vision, am credited with significantly improving morale and productivity of a 140-person workforce while directing maintenance activities on a submarine's nuclear power propulsion plant with expenditures of over $5 million annually.

- Manage a $1.5 million annual operating budget: have saved over $1 million through efforts to locate and procure "free asset" parts.
- Awarded a Meritorious Service Medal for conducting an extremely successful independent six-month special project in the Western Pacific, also planned and carried out two "flawless" projects, where my sub was the first to ever carry out a special operation.
- Am developing junior managers who excel in building groups of people with diverse skill levels into award-winning and productive teams of professionals.

TECHNICAL INSPECTION TEAM MANAGER. Monterey, CA (2000-03). Provided technical expertise and guidance for a team which developed operational scenarios and plans.

- Planned and carried out complex Tactical Readiness Evaluation (TRE) exercises which called for close cooperation between the U.S. Navy, Coast Guard, and Marine Corps.
- Described as an innovative evaluator and technical expert, provided feedback and identified trends which allowed the submarine community to improve performance.

MAINTENANCE AND ADMINISTRATIVE SERVICES MANAGER. Norfolk, VA (1998-00). Officially evaluated as "a rare, exceptional leader" who was "head and shoulders" above my peers, provided guidance and leadership through numerous special projects, inspections, exercise, and day-to-day operations of a nuclear powered submarine.

- Coordinated and led personnel smoothly through two major renovation projects and equipment upgrade projects including complicated refitting and unusual conditions.

TECHNICAL INSPECTOR. Norfolk, VA (1996-98). Cited for my tenacity and skills as a problem solver and troubleshooter, served as subject matter expert on submarine propulsion plants for the Navy's Nuclear Propulsion Examining Board.

Highlights of earlier U.S. Navy experience: Consistently singled out for praise in assignments as an Operations Manager, Navigator, and Engineering/Quality Control Officer.

HONORS

Received two prestigious Meritorious Service Medals and six Naval Commendation Medals.

PERSONAL

Known for my high personal ethics and standards, was entrusted with a **Top Secret/SBI security clearance**. Offer exceptional analytical and organizational abilities.

Date

Exact Name of Person
Title or Position
Name of Company
Address
City, State, Zip

PRODUCT ENGINEERING MANAGER
with experience as a plant engineer & process engineer

Dear Exact Name of Person: (or Dear Sir or Madam if answering a blind ad.)

I would appreciate an opportunity to talk with you soon about how I could add value to your organization through my versatile skills in both engineering and management.

Since receiving my B.S. degree in Engineering, I have excelled in jobs related to product design, manufacturing engineering, process engineering, and product engineering while earning a reputation as a resourceful technical problem solver who works well with people. I offer a strong "bottom-line" orientation and, in my most recent job, I generated new product margins and cost reductions which contributed more than $7.5 million annually. I have acquired expertise related to risk management legislation, patents and trademarks, UL/CSA certification procedures, and OSHA standards, and I have handled responsibility for OSHA, EPA, hazardous wastes, energy management systems, and computerized communication systems.

With a reputation as an engineer who works well with others and who can "translate" complex technical concepts into language non-engineers can understand, I am respected for my integrity and "common sense." I can provide outstanding personal and professional references.

In today's marketplace, I believe it makes sense for professionals to have as many areas of expertise as possible, and I can certainly offer you expert skills in both engineering and management. I sincerely enjoy working with people while handling the challenge of solving stubborn technical problems. A fast learner with the ability to rapidly master new bodies of knowledge in our fast-changing world, I would welcome the opportunity to help you carve out new niches and solve problems in emerging technologies as well as existing ones.

I hope you will welcome my call soon to arrange a brief meeting at your convenience to discuss your current and future needs and how I might serve them. Thank you in advance for your time.

Sincerely yours,

Christopher Bailey

Alternate last paragraph:
I hope you will call or write me soon to suggest a time convenient for us to meet and discuss your current and future needs and how I might serve them. Thank you in advance for your time.

CHRISTOPHER BAILEY

1110½ Hay Street, Fayetteville, NC 28305   •   preppub@aol.com   •   (910) 483-6611

OBJECTIVE

To contribute to an organization that can use a resourceful problem solver who offers a proven ability to manage people, products, programs, projects, finances, and operations.

EDUCATION

Bachelor of Science (B.S.) degree in Engineering, Hawaii Pacific University, Honolulu, HI, 1991.

EXPERIENCE

ENGINEER. Channel Products, Honolulu, HI (1993-2004). Excelled in this progression with a company that has recently decided to drastically decrease its new product engineering and design activities.

1999-04: PRODUCT ENGINEERING MANAGER. Was promoted to manage a department of professionals and support staff involved in engineering, designing, and determining specifications of consumer products.

- Generated new product margins and cost reductions which contributed more than $7.5 million annually to the bottom line. Planned and administered a budget of $1.5 million.
- Was regarded as the company's "internal expert" and representative in risk management legislation. Gained vast knowledge related to patents and trademarks; also acquired expertise related to UL/CSA and related agency certification procedures.
- Gained project scheduling (PC) experience, and was a consulting expert on many corporate projects. Traveled internationally in product sourcing and related activities.

1997-99: PLANT ENGINEER. Was responsible for OSHA, EPA, hazardous wastes, energy management systems, and computerized communications systems while managing the buildings and grounds, equipment, and maintenance for a 400ksf manufacturing facility.

- Coordinated the fielding/implementation of new construction/heavy equipment.
- Planned and budgeted for the expansion of capital assets.

1994-97: PROJECT ENGINEER. Was involved in a wide variety of projects related to product design while also redesigning/updating products and assuring their specifications conformed to UL/CSA standards. Figured out resourceful solutions to numerous technical problems. Was the Technical Representative to HVI for product standards and testing.

1993: PROCESS ENGINEER. Mastered time studies, performance standards, process/method selection, and layout; performed cost analysis and specifications documentation.

Other experience:

MANUFACTURING ENGINEER. O'ahu Computers, Honolulu, HI (1991-92). Was credited with making significant improvement to the bottom line through both labor savings and quality improvements in this job which involved me in coordinating new products during development and pilot production. Investigated and resolved rejected vendor materials issues.

MANUFACTURING ENGINEER. Kahana Manufacturing, Co., Honolulu, HI (1990-91). Constructed a high-speed production assembly line for automotive oil filters while coordinating project work between maintenance and manufacturing.

AFFILIATIONS

- Senior Member, Institute of Industrial Engineers
- Member, HVI Trade Association Technical Committees
- Member, AMCA Engineering and Technical Committees
- Member, Underwriters Laboratories Industry Advisory Councils

PERSONAL

Am respected for technical knowledge as well as integrity, principles, and "common sense."

Exact Name of Person
Exact Title
Exact Name of Company
Address
City, State, Zip

**PRODUCT LINE
ENGINEER**

earning degree in
electrical
engineering in his
spare time

Dear Exact Name of Person (or Dear Sir or Madam if answering a blind ad):

With the enclosed resume, I would like to express my interest in exploring employment opportunities with your organization.

As you will see from my resume, I have excelled in a track record of promotion with a company involved in the manufacturing of distribution and control products. I have earned a reputation as a gifted problem solver while performing as a Senior Engineering Technician, Design Engineer, and Product Line Engineer. Although I excelled in the engineering field, I did so without the benefit of formal education in engineering for several years. In 2000, I returned to college to earn my engineering degree in the evenings, and I will receive my B.S. in Electrical Engineering *summa cum laude* this May.

Although I am held in high regard by my current employer, the company is closing the plant where I work and relocating its product lines to a facility in Alabama. I have been offered a senior management position at the Alabama facility, but I am selectively exploring opportunities in other organizations. I would appreciate your holding my interest in your company in confidence at this time.

I believe that my success in the engineering field thus far has been due to my ability to look at each problem I encounter with a creative yet practical problem-solving approach. To use the vernacular, I am able to "think outside the box." I take pride in the numerous contributions I have made to my employer's bottom line, and I offer an ability to work effectively with others at all organizational levels.

I hope you will call or write me soon to suggest a time convenient for us to meet and discuss your current and future needs and how I might serve them. Thank you in advance for your time.

Sincerely,

Jared Coolidge

Alternate last paragraph:
I hope you will welcome my call soon to arrange a brief meeting to discuss your current and future needs and how I might serve them. Thank you in advance for your time.

JARED COOLIDGE

1110½ Hay Street, Fayetteville, NC 28305   •   preppub@aol.com   •   (910) 483-6611

OBJECTIVE

To add value to an organization that can use a product line engineer who offers extensive knowledge related to motor control application/design and electrical distribution equipment design along with extensive sales experience.

EXPERIENCE

ALABAMA D.C.B.U. (Distribution & Control Business Unit), purchased by SE Industries in 2004: *Began in the manufacturing area of this company and worked my way up into engineering and sales, 1991-present.* In February 2003, SE Industries announced its purchase of Alabama's distribution and control business unit. SE Industries decided to close its Birmingham, AL manufacturing plant and move the product lines to the Gadsden, AL facility.
- Received a corporate Quality Award for my role in this plant shutdown.

2004-present: PRODUCT LINE ENGINEER. After the buyout, was the person selected to transfer the front-end systems — engineering, order entry, and order processes — to Gadsden while also aiding in the shutdown of the Birmingham plant; played a key role in the transfer of production to this plant which produces electrical distribution equipment.
- After playing a key role in the smooth transition of product manufacturing, became involved in front-end process control, sales and design engineering.
- Skilled in developing quotations from customer-supplied information sources including schematics, single lines, and specifications.
- Received Quality Award for developing the Aftermarket Retrofit Program.

2001-03: SALES/DESIGN ENGINEER, AFTERMARKET PRODUCTS. Handled the sale of aftermarket products as well as the design of aftermarket retrofit products.
- Implemented the strategic goal of creating incremental growth by competitive market penetration with new products.
- Was commended for my role in helping the corporation exceed its original goal for new product: in 2003, five percent of all aftermarket sales resulted from these new products.
- Received Quality Award for implementing front-end product engineering system.

1997-00: SENIOR ENGINEERING TECHNICIAN. Was involved in the development of non-standard designs; provided guidance to a group of six engineering technicians.
- Handled specification for purchase of non-stock material. Received two Quality Awards for my role in the development of a computerized assembly program which cut costs.

1991-96: ENGINEERING TECHNICIAN. Developed bills of material and prepared electrical and shop drawings to instruct shop personnel in the fabrication of the product.
- Analyzed and utilized input from drawings, specifications, and sales quotations.

COMPUTERS

Skilled in using numerous software packages including Microsoft Word, Excel, PowerPoint, Adobe PageMaker, as well as software for internal engineering and quotations.

EDUCATION

Am working toward my goal of obtaining my degree in **electrical engineering**; enrolled in night classes at Gadsden State Community College, 2000-present.
Studied **Mechanical Drafting, Heating and Air Conditioning, and Plumbing** at Gadsden State Community College, 1989-93.

TECHNICAL TRAINING

In continuing technical education, studied commercial construction estimating, statistical process control, Autocad design and drafting, and other programming softwares.

Date

Exact Name of Person
Title or Position
Name of Company
Address
City, State, Zip

Dear Exact Name of Person: (or Dear Sir or Madam if answering a blind ad.)

I would appreciate an opportunity to talk with you soon about how I could contribute to your organization through my extensive background in quality control and engineering. I can provide outstanding personal and professional references upon your request, and I have won numerous awards for my resourceful problem solving as well as for my excellent work habits including perfect attendance.

As you will see from my resume, I have most recently made valuable contributions to the Coastal Corporation and, on my most recent annual performance evaluation, I received the highest rating given on every area of performance measured. While in this job I figured out, on my own initiative, a resourceful and low-cost method of disposing of hazardous chemical waste which is saving the company thousands of dollars annually. I have also developed a system of desk-top procedures which has become the model for similar sites. These 20 procedures are now being used in the U.S. and overseas and assure that field site depots are in audit-ready condition at all times. These and other procedures I have developed have led to more consistency on the job and far fewer errors. My job knowledge, creativity, problem-solving ability, and decision-making skills are at an exceptionally high level, and I feel I could make valuable contributions to your organization, too, as I have to Coastal Corporation.

You will also see from my resume that I previously "cut my teeth" on quality control inspection and testing. Even during college, while earning my degree in Business Administration, I worked as a quality control inspector for companies in North Carolina.

You would find me to be a congenial professional who is known for my ability to develop and maintain excellent working relationships. In my current job I have been credited with greatly improving internal communication and trust through my tactful communication skills and gracious style of dealing with people

I hope you will write or call me soon to suggest a time when we might meet to discuss your current or future needs and how I might serve them. Thank you in advance for your time.

Sincerely yours,

Kenneth Ables

Alternate last paragraph:
I hope you will welcome my call soon to arrange a brief meeting at your convenience to discuss your current and future needs and how I might serve them. Thank you in advance for your time.

KENNETH ABLES

1110½ Hay Street, Fayetteville, NC 28305　　•　　preppub@aol.com　　•　　(910) 483-6611

OBJECTIVE　　To apply my extensive knowledge related to quality control and engineering to an organization that can use a self-motivated self starter and team player with outstanding communication skills who offers a proven ability to develop new methods and reduce costs.

EXPERIENCE　　**SENIOR QUALITY ENGINEER**. Coastal Corporation. Various locations (1999-present). **Leesville, LA (2004-present)**. At one of the busiest U.S. military bases, have received the highest possible rating on every area of my performance measured: initiative ("self starter"); follow-through ("never any loose ends"); interpersonal relations ("outstanding rapport with management and engineering"); problem solving ("solves problems with minimum direction"); team work ("a team player"); and job knowledge ("performs tasks that are beyond scope").

- Supervise the receipt, in-process, and the final and shipping inspections of the Target Acquisition Designation Sight/Pilot Night Vision Sensor (TADS/PNVS) flight hardware related to the Apache helicopter; have become an expert in applying MIL-I-45208A in inspections, MIL-STD-45662 in calibrating electronic test equipment, and MIL-Q-9858A in processing flight hardware.
- On my own initiative, aggressively investigated hazardous chemical disposal options and devised a new method for disposing of expired chemicals/adhesives/paints that reduced annual costs from $10,000 to $200 at each field site; this led to Desk Top SOP-016 now being implemented at all Coastal Corporation sites.
- Developed a thoroughly documented system of 20 procedures for field site depots to assure audit-ready condition at all times; these procedures have become the model for all TADS sites and are being used by other quality representatives at Coastal Corporation depots throughout the U.S. and oversees; have been praised in writing for ensuring "more consistency on the job and far fewer errors."
- Developed and implemented an inspection system that ensures outstanding performance at field sites; this is a cost-effective system that exceeds both contractual and internal requirements. Designed and established a calibration system praised as thorough.

Iraq (2002-04). During the War on Terror, played a major role in operating a quality control center supporting Apache helicopters. Worked long hours seven days a week to produce an exceptionally high mission capability rate under harsh desert conditions.

- **1998-02:** Prior to my job in Iraq, attended the University of North Carolina full-time to complete my B.A. degree.

Charleston, SC (1990-98). Learned processes specific to electro-optical targeting/night vision equipment using engineering drawings, military specifications, and contracts.

- Established the inspection criteria for more than 300 manufacturing process plans (including circuit cards, subassemblies, and system level plans) utilizing engineering drawings, military specifications, and contracts. Dispositioned nonconforming hardware per MIL-Q-9858A determining root cause and corrective action.

EDUCATION　　**B.A., Business Administration**, University of North Carolina at Chapel Hill, NC, 2002
A.A., Business Administration, Fayetteville Technical Community College, NC, 1990

CERTIFICATIONS　Hand Solder, MIL-S-45743/MIL-STD-2000　　Cable & Harness, MIS-22129
Laser Eye Safety, ANSI Z136.1　　　　　　　　　ESD Sensitive, MIL-STD-1686A
Optics Cleaning/Handling　　　　　　　　　　Hazardous Waste

PERSONAL　　Member, American Society for Quality Control. Outstanding references available.

Exact Name of Person
Exact Title
Exact Name of Company
Address
City, State, Zip

PROTOTYPE ENGINEER

Dear Exact Name of Person (or Dear Sir or Madam if answering a blind ad):

With the enclosed resume, I would like to express my interest in exploring employment opportunities with your organization.

As you will see from my resume, I am currently excelling as a Prototype Engineer with a company in Atlanta, where I build one-of-a-kind high-speed manufacturing machines. I have provided significant input to teams which have programmed machines that produce carbon brushes for Ford, Craftsman, Toshiba, VTech, and others. Those machines have allowed key corporate giants to improve their products and profitability.

Although I am held in high regard in my current position and can provide outstanding references, I am selectively exploring opportunities in your city, where my wife has recently accepted a job in the medical field. I can provide outstanding references at the appropriate time, and I offer a reputation as a talented designer with a practical approach to problem-solving.

I hope you will call or write me soon to suggest a time convenient for us to meet and discuss your current and future needs and how I might serve them. Thank you in advance for your time.

Sincerely,

Alex Lymann

Alternate last paragraph:
I hope you will welcome my call soon to arrange a brief meeting to discuss your current and future needs and how I might serve them. Thank you in advance for your time.

ALEX LYMANN

1110½ Hay Street, Fayetteville, NC 28305 • preppub@aol.com • (910) 483-6611

OBJECTIVE

To offer my excellent engineering skills to an organization that is in need of a real go-getter with a positive mental attitude and a proven track record of success.

EXPERIENCE

PROTOTYPE ENGINEER. XYZ Manufacturers, Inc., Atlanta, GA *(2004-present)*. Design and build one-of-a-kind high-speed manufacturing machines. Work daily with in-house and other machine shops and suppliers, process engineers, production supervisors, mechanics, and other designers.
- Achieved an unbelievable success record and gained high praise for being able to successfully handle numerous projects at once.
- Redesigned and programmed machine that produces carbon brushes for all General Motors starters—speeding up existing process by 86% and producing a large cost savings.
- Programmed machines that produce carbon brushes for Ford, Craftsman, Toshiba, VTech, and others, improving production.

TECHNICIAN. Atlanta Daily News, Atlanta, GA (2003-04). Improved processes on production lines by new procedures, and improved design. Worked daily to improve presses, wrapping machines, inking machines, color and black and white copy machines, laser color separators, and film processors. Designed and installed plant security/surveillance system.
- Designed a three-side bundle wrap machine.
- Improved quality of black and white copy machines with improved toner collection.

OPERATIONS MANAGER. Georgian Security Systems, Savannah, GA (1999-03). Handled a wide variety of duties to include installation and troubleshooting of security, and access, and camera systems. Provided on-call troubleshooting for a vast array of equipment to include time locks, P.A. systems, injection and blow molding machines, reamers, presses, and others throughout the southeast.
- Secured a major contract for the U.S. government, at two military bases.

ELECTRONICS TECHNICIAN. Cingular, Savannah, GA (1996-99). Performed installation and troubleshooting on cellular telephones and the operating system.
- Achieved the highest efficiency rate throughout the company nationwide for two months.

EDUCATION

Electronics Engineering	**Digital Technology**
Machining	Welding
Drafting	AutoCad release 15

SKILLS

Wire/E.D.M. Machines	3 phase electrical
Ultrasonic welding	Online S.P.C.
All types of operator interfaces	Heat treat process
AC/DC motors	Servo and stepper motors
Robotics	Fabrication
CNC machining knowledge	Encoders and resolvers
Carbide tooling	Chemical mixing

Carbon, copper, lead, and graphite mixing and blending
Highly skilled at communication between machine and operator

LICENSES

Electrical License (GA)   *Commercial / General Contractor's License (GA)*
Refrigeration License (GA)   *Security License (GA)*
Level 2 Security Clearance (U.S. Government)

Date

Exact Name of Person
Title or Position
Name of Company
Address
City, State, Zip

**SECURITY
ENGINEER**

with extensive
project
management
experience

Dear Exact Name of Person: (or Dear Sir or Madam if answering a blind ad.)

I would appreciate an opportunity to talk with you soon about how I could contribute to your organization through my versatile skills related to security management and security engineering.

In one job as a security supervisor, I was cleared for a security clearance up to Secret/NATO Secret while clearing personnel for transportation of classified documents and maintaining security of an office complex. In another job I earned medals for superb performance of duty as a rifleman and for meticulous service as a gunner and ammunition bearer. I am skilled in firearms operation and maintenance and I am knowledgeable of numerous security systems.

You would find me to be an individual known for honesty and attention to detail as well as for my willingness to take on additional responsibilities. I can provide outstanding personal and professional references upon request.

I hope you will write or call me soon to suggest a time when we might meet to discuss your needs and goals and how I might serve them. Thank you in advance for your time.

Yours sincerely,

Jimmie John

Alternate last paragraph:
I hope you will welcome my call soon to arrange a brief meeting to discuss your current and future needs and how I might serve them. Thank you in advance for your time.

JIMMIE JOHN

1110½ Hay Street, Fayetteville, NC 28305   •   preppub@aol.com   •   (910) 483-6611

OBJECTIVE

To contribute to an organization that can use a versatile young professional who offers skills related to security management, personnel supervision, as well as engineering operations and maintenance coordination.

EXPERIENCE

TEAM MEMBER. Montana National Guard, Missoula, MT (2003-present). At multiple locations, provide equipment maintenance and teach battlefield survival skills to subordinates. Developed Standard Operating Procedures (SOP's) and field instructions.

ASSISTANT SUPERVISOR/PROJECT MANAGER. U.S. Army, Fort Leavenworth, KS (2003). Earned a prestigious medal for exceptional performance in controlling an extensive inventory of equipment while training, scheduling, and supervising up to 25 people; also assigned duties to personnel and evaluated their performance in this combat airborne engineer organization. Managed personnel in engineering projects; documented job site progress.
* Became known for my ability to motivate personnel to exceed performance goals.

ASSISTANT SUPERVISOR/PROJECT MANAGER. U.S. Army, Fort Wainwright, AK (2001-02). Was handpicked for this job normally held by a professional two ranks senior to me; scheduled personnel for work at numerous job sites while also organizing project layouts; trained and supervised up to 25 people and controlled equipment valued at thousands of dollars; received a prestigious medal for my performance.
* Ensured the smooth transition from construction engineering to combat engineering and then from light engineering to wheeled to mechanical.

SECURITY SUPERVISOR. U.S. Army, Germany (1999-01). Was cleared for a security clearance up to SECRET/NATO SECRET in a job which involved me in clearing personnel for transportation of classified documents, performing as courier of classified documents, and maintaining security of office complex to prevent unauthorized entry of personnel or extraction of information. Received a respected award for superior job performance and was commended for ensuring zero security breaches in this two-year period.

ASSISTANT SUPERVISOR. U.S. Army, U.S. and Korea (1996-99). In an engineering organization and in an infantry regiment, assisted in the organization of project layouts while training and supervising up to 25 people.

ACTING SUPERVISOR, GUNNER, AMMUNITION BEARER, & RIFLEMAN. U.S. Army, Fort Drum, NY (1993-96). Earned medals for "superb performance of duty as a rifleman" and for "meritorious service as a gunner and ammunition bearer" while earning rapid promotion into management positions at the world's busiest U.S. military base.
* Taught battlefield survival skills to subordinates.
* Ensured general maintenance/readiness of equipment.

EDUCATION

More than two years of college-level technical and management training, U.S. Army.

OTHER SKILLS

Hardware: PC computers; various printers
Software: Enable, Windows, Adobe PageMaker, Quick Books Pro
Security systems: JSIIDS security systems and monitoring devices

PERSONAL

Am known for my honesty and attention to detail. Always take on additional responsibilities on my own initiative. In my spare time enjoy reading and working with computers.

Date

Exact Name of Person
Exact Title
Exact Name of Company
Address
City, State, Zip

SENIOR FIELD
TECHNICIAN

Dear Exact Name of Person (or Dear Sir or Madam if answering a blind ad):

With the enclosed resume, I would like to express my interest in exploring employment opportunities with your organization.

As you will see from my resume, I have worked in the environmental field as a Senior Field Technician. While supervising 14 agricultural scouts, I performed liaison with farmers and, in the non-growing season, I supervised a three-person soil sampling crew. In prior employment, I worked for the Maine Department of Transportation and assisted state geologist in activities that supported highway and bridge construction.

With an outstanding personal and professional reputation, I am selectively investigating opportunities in your industry.

I hope you will call or write me soon to suggest a time convenient for us to meet and discuss your current and future needs and how I might serve them. Thank you in advance for your time.

Sincerely,

Arthur Chase

Alternate last paragraph:
I hope you will welcome my call soon to arrange a brief meeting to discuss your current and future needs and how I might serve them. Thank you in advance for your time.

ARTHUR CHASE

1110½ Hay Street, Fayetteville, NC 28305   •   preppub@aol.com   •   (910) 483-6611

OBJECTIVE

To benefit an organization through my education in geography and city planning, my experience in the engineering field, my computer knowledge, as well as my excellent communication skills and ability to work well independently or with others.

EDUCATION

Earned a **Bachelor of Science degree in Geography** with a concentration in the area of **City Planning,** St. Joseph's College, Standish, ME, 2003.

TRAINING

Completed a 330-hour internship in the Engineering Department of the Maine Works Department for the City of Orono, ME, May-August 2003.
- Gained exposure in a variety of operational areas and practical knowledge with an emphasis on utilizing computers for word processing and database applications, surveying, and tax research.

COMPUTER KNOWLEDGE

Through training and experience, have become familiar with the use of computers for the following applications and with the following software:
applications: computer mapping, word processing, maintaining databases, spreadsheets
software: Microsoft – Word, Excel, and PowerPoint
other: am familiar with GIS, internet applications

EXPERIENCE

SENIOR FIELD TECHNICIAN. Maine Technical Services, Orono, ME. (2004-present). Supervised 14 agricultural scouts, collected and processed data from scouts for consultant, worked as a liaison between consultant and clients (farmers). In non-growing season, supervised three-person soil sampling crew. Also manually drew soil zones from eyesight, topographic maps, and aerial photos. Used Ph meter to run tests on soil samples to make recommendations to clients.

GEO-TECHNICAL ASSISTANT. Maine Department of Transportation, Bangor, ME. (2004). Assisted state geologist and other crew members (2) in drilling/probing soil to test for ability to support highway/bridge construction. Operated state vehicles, worked in many areas of ME east of I-95. Also performed relatively simple survey work, i.e. turning angles, shooting benchmarks, and obtaining elevations. Performed maintenance on job-related equipment.

Highlights of earlier experience: Learned to deal with the public in a sales job.
COOK. Denny's, Orono, ME. Earned the respect of management personnel for my hard work, customer service orientation, and ability to get along with my co-workers and supervisors. Trained new employees.
FARM WORKER. Local farm, Orono, ME. Grew up on a farm and at an early age was taking responsibility for a wide range of daily activities related to hog and cow production and animal care.

VOLUNTEER EXPERIENCE

Contributed my time in volunteer activities which included:
SPORTS OFFICIAL. Officiated for a men's basketball league and a youth baseball league. Coached high school boys' church basketball team.
CHORUS MEMBER. Sang at the Kodak Theater with my high school chorus and later in college toured the east coast with the St. Joseph's College Concert Choir.

PERSONAL

Am a responsible young professional known for my strong work ethic. Through my family background growing up on a farm, learned sound management principles, judgment, and initiative. Excellent personal and professional references.

TWO-PAGE RESUME

BRYCE VERSE

1110½ Hay Street, Fayetteville, NC 28305 • preppub@aol.com •
(910) 483-6611

STRUCTURAL ENGINEER

with experience as a director of marketing & operations

EDUCATION
Bachelor of Science in Structural Engineering, University of Idaho, Moscow, ID, 1989.

CONTINUING EDUCATION
In asbestos abatement, air monitoring, hazmat training in chemical first response and clean up.
OSHA TRAINING machinery and machine guarding standards, basic instructor course in occupational safety and health standards for the construction industry; compliance in industrial hygiene.

COMPUTERS
Highly computer literate. Proficient in the use of many popular computer operating systems and software applications.

SUMMARY OF QUALIFICATIONS
In all position where I served as Director of Marketing or Marketing & Operations, have been entrusted with responsibilities and achieved measurable results in areas which include:

- **Personnel Management**: Supervised construction and maintenance crews of up to 500 employees, including engineers, architects, project managers, contractors, and subcontractors, as well as all office and support staff.
- **Budget Management**: Developed and managed project budgets for maintenance, construction, and renovation projects ranging from $20 to $200 million; was responsible for 10,000 multi-family housing units, 5,700 buildings, and construction of new facilities.
- **Profitability**: Averaged between 26 and 35% return on expenses.
- **Logistics**: Supervised the redistribution of equipment, supplies, fixtures, and personnel while overseeing the closing and restructuring of various military bases and training facilities.
- **Purchasing**: Contacted vendors and manufacturers worldwide to obtain necessary equipment, fixtures, and supplies.

In the last fifteen years, have managed projects with a total new worth of more than **$3.5 billion**.

PROFESSIONAL & BUSINESS HISTORY
DIRECTOR OF MARKETING & OPERATIONS. American Services Corporation, Seattle, WA (2004-present). Oversee all aspects of the marketing and operations divisions of this large company which provides contracted engineering services for government projects.

- Conduct negotiations with various government agencies, subcontractors, vendors/suppliers, union representatives, and commercial concerns.
- Apply my extensive knowledge of FARs, Contract Law, and GAO procedures governing contract administration and interpretation.
- Analyze potential profitability of new projects and other business opportunities and make bid/no bid recommendations.
- Manage the corporate total quality management (TQM) program and provide TQM training as needed.

DIRECTOR OF OPERATIONS. National Energy Engineering, Co., San Diego, CA (2000-04). Oversaw all aspects of the marketing and operations divisions of this large company which provides contracting services for government projects.

- Conducted negotiations with various government agencies, subcontractors, vendors and suppliers, union representatives, and commercial concerns. Analyzed profitability of new projects and other business opportunities and made bid/no bid recommendations.
- Developed and implemented innovative and effective marketing strategies to increase sales and profitability of the business; incorporated these strategies into company's business plan.
- Managed the corporate total quality management (TQM) program and provided TQM training. Performed human resource functions including recruiting, interviewing, and hiring, administration of benefits, and employee administration.

DIRECTOR OF MARKETING & OPERATIONS and **ASSISTANT to the PRESIDENT.** Crates Corporation, Inc., Cheyenne, WY (1995-00). Aggressively recruited by Crates to create and organize their new Marketing Division; tasked with capturing a significant share of the available Department of Defense market.

- Developed initial marketing studies which identified and prioritized available opportunities and developed successful strategies for winning an improved market share.
- Established the business unit that was responsible for capturing six long-term O & M contracts worth more than $34.2 million dollars in its first ten months of operation.
- Key player in each of these awards developing the initial opportunity and strategies for successful bidding and capture.

DIRECTOR OF MARKETING. Electronics Services, Inc., Boulder, CO (1992-95). Oversaw all operational aspects of the marketing department for this large contracting company; responsible for researching and preparing bid proposals on government contracts as well as editing technical and cost proposals.

- Reviewed solicitations and made bid/no bid recommendations.
- Investigated subcontractors and subcontract agreements for new business opportunities; conducted negotiations on Joint Venture Agreements.
- Functioned as technical writer on a variety of programs.

DIRECTOR OF MARKETING. Western Services, Inc., Seattle, WA (1990-92). Responsible for managing and directing marketing efforts to acquire new business in the facilities O & M field, particularly Government programs. Functional duties included planning and conducting marketing research, analyzing available data, participating in the bid/no bid decision making process, and managing proposal preparation process including development of operational and pricing strategies.

MARKETING and **PROJECT MANAGER.** American Company, Inc., Washington, DC (1987-89). Manager Housing and Grounds Maintenance operations for 5,400 units located at military bases nationwide. Prepared proposals and conducted marketing research in development of new business. Duties include drafting proposals, developing proposal strategies, participation in the bid/no bid decision process, attending site visits, negotiating joint venture agreements, and representing the company in business development situations.

PROJECT MANAGER. Country Lands, Co., Wilmington, DE (1985-87). Responsible for day-to-day operations of the family housing maintenance and construction scheduling.

PERSONAL   Excellent references upon request. Versatile individual with strong problem-solving skills.

Date

Exact Name of Person
Title or Position
Exact Name of Company
Address
City, State, Zip

SYSTEMS ENGINEER

with experience as a
director of operations

Dear Exact Name of Person (or Dear Sir or Madam if answering a blind ad):

With the enclosed resume, I would like to express my interest in exploring employment opportunities with your organization.

As you will see from my resume, I have established a background of accomplishments as an effective resources manager while advancing to the rank of Colonel in the U.S. Army. A graduate of the U.S. Military Academy at West Point, NY, with a degree in General Engineering, I have subsequently earned Master of Science degrees in Systems Technology and National Security. Although I am considered to be on "the fast track" and have been strongly encouraged to remain in military service with a good possibility of promotion to General, I have decided to seek opportunities in the profit-making sector.

My management ability has been displayed in assignments which have culminated in my present position as Director of Operations for a counterdrug task force. In this capacity, I have gained recognition as a key figure in planning and coordinating operational, technical, and intelligence support, and I have been credited with bringing these activities "up to a new level of performance." In a previous line management position, I controlled a $1 million budget while providing leadership for a 600-person organization. In a prior assignment, I played a key role in the assignment and career management of military officers.

Consistently described as a visionary who excels in making the most of scarce resources while guiding personnel to set and exceed high performance standards, I have been selected for management positions which required a top-notch leader and problem-solver. I have earned numerous honors for my strong leadership style as well as my ability to mentor and develop others. Cited as a top-notch planner and problem-solver, I have improved productivity, morale, and efficiency in every organization in which I have worked. I hold a Top Secret security clearance.

If you can use a highly motivated management professional who thrives on meeting challenges head on, I hope you will contact me soon to suggest a time we might meet to discuss how I could contribute to your organization. I will provide excellent professional and personal references at the appropriate time. Thank you for your time and consideration.

Sincerely,

Ronald Hall

RONALD HALL

1110½ Hay Street, Fayetteville, NC 28305 • preppub@aol.com • (910) 483-6611

OBJECTIVE

To contribute to an organization that can use a seasoned management and engineering professional with excellent human resources and operations knowledge.

EDUCATION & TRAINING

M.S., National Security, Texas A & M International University, Laredo, TX, 2004.
M.S., Systems Technology, Texas A & M International University, Laredo, TX, 1994.
B.S., General Engineering, U.S. Military Academy, West Point, NY, 1984.
Completed intense military training including the Airborne Course and Ranger School, the military "stress test" of an individual's mental and physical limits.

EXPERIENCE

Advanced to the rank of Colonel in the U.S. Army based on exceptional skills as a strategic thinker and sound resource manager with the vision to see the "big picture" while attending to the details of planning and directing programs and projects:
DIRECTOR OF OPERATIONS. Fort Stewart, GA (2004-present). Credited with accomplishments which have brought counterdrug efforts "up to a new level of performance," develop, guide, and manage organizations and individuals involved in operations throughout the continental U.S.; supervise and guide members of a 50-person task force.

- Develop, synchronize, and integrate operational, technological, and intelligence support utilizing military personnel and assets into civilian law enforcement activities at the state, local, and national agency levels in support of more than 400 missions annually.
- Am recognized as a driving force in integrating technological advances and maximizing training opportunities which result in significant advances in effectiveness.

GRADUATE STUDENT. Texas A & M International University, Laredo, TX (2003-04). Completed a graduate-level program which culminated in a M.S. degree in National Security.

GENERAL MANAGER and **TECHNICAL OPERATIONS CENTER MANAGER.** Fort Riley, KS (2001-03). Controlled a $1 million annual budget and directed all operational, technical, administrative, and management support for a 600-person organization.

- Praised for my vision and successful leadership style which focused on "empowering junior leaders," challenged them to exceed high standards while earning recognition as "the best" manager at my level.
- Developed administrative support programs focusing on financial management, quality of life, and environmental initiatives which became recognized as the model to emulate.

ASSISTANT DIRECTOR. Department of Defense, Washington, DC (1998-01). Officially evaluated as a productive and versatile manager "with boundless potential," assisted in coordinating policies and programs related to the career management of military officers.

- Applied sound judgment and a positive management style while involved in policy formulation, the interpretation of directives, and management of staff activities.
- Was cited for my energetic, enthusiastic personality as well as my ability to manage the details of scheduling and implementing a wide range of special actions.

PLANNING AND OPERATIONS MANAGER. Italy (1995-98). Advanced in management roles within a field artillery organization where my versatile knowledge allowed me to achieve results while planning and managing activities for a large organization.

PERSONAL

Top Secret security clearance. Honors include five Meritorious Service Medals as well as U.S. Army and Joint Services Commendation Medals. Proficient with Internet and Microsoft applications to include PowerPoint and Word. Outstanding references on request.

Date

Exact Name of Person
Exact Title
Exact Name of Company
Address
City, State, Zip

Dear Exact Name of Person (or Dear Sir or Madam if answering a blind ad):

I would appreciate an opportunity to talk with you soon about how I could contribute to your organization through my education, experience, and knowledge.

As you will see from my enclosed resume, I received my B.S. in Electrical Engineering from Southern University & Agricultural & Mechanical College in Baton Rouge, LA. In order to complete this rigorous degree program, I was required to pass graduate-level courses in Digital Signal Processing, Project Management for Engineers, Introduction to Neural Processing, and Switching Theory. Since earning my degree I have supplemented my education with additional courses in AUTOCAD V.14 (Parts 1 and 2) and C Programming.

I earned rapid advancement with Howell Corporation located in New Orleans, LA, and am currently working at the Howell Corporation's Automotive Division located in Baton Rouge. Originally hired by Howell Corporation in March 2003 as a Production Technician, I rapidly advanced to a shift supervisor's job before my selection as a Quality Technician. In 2004 I received a promotion to Team Leader at a facility in Baton Rouge.

My strongest skills are my ability to anticipate problems, analyze situations, and develop the solutions which will result in increasing productivity and profitability. In earlier jobs in shipping and receiving operations, as well as in technical jobs with Howell, I initiated changes which reduced man hours and lowered costs.

If you can use a positive, results-oriented professional with strong technical skills related to automation and production operations, I would enjoy an opportunity to meet to discuss your needs. I can assure you in advance that I have an excellent reputation and can provide outstanding references.

Sincerely,

Allen Baker

ALLEN BAKER

1110½ Hay Street, Fayetteville, NC 28305 • preppub@aol.com • (910) 483-6611

OBJECTIVE

To offer my technical abilities to an organization that can benefit from my outstanding problem-solving, decision-making, and leadership skills.

EDUCATION & TRAINING

B.S. in Electrical Engineering, Southern University & Agricultural & Mechanical College, Baton Rouge, LA, 2002.
- To complete this rigorous degree program, was required to pass the following graduate-level courses: Digital Signal Processing, Project Management for Engineers, Introduction to Neural Processing, and Switching Theory.
- Completed additional course work which includes:
C Programming, Delagdo Community College, New Orleans, LA, 2000
AUTOCAD V.14, Parts I and 2, Loyola University, New Orleans, LA, 2004

EXPERIENCE

Advanced with the Howell Corporation in the following "track record":
2004-present: TEAM LEADER & ELECTRICAL ENGINEER. Baton Rouge, LA. Was handpicked as Team Leader of a team which ensures quality, productivity, safety, and customer service for this operation. Supervise as many as eight workers manufacturing climate control modules for automotive air conditioning systems.
- Participate in operations including hand assembly, calibration, testing, and packaging.
- Use hand and power tools, machines, and charging equipment as well as precision gauges and measurement devices to complete assembly operations.
- Member of the team that achieved QS-9000 certification for this facility.

2003-04: PRODUCTION TECHNICIAN, QUALITY TECHNICIAN, AND SHIFT LEADER. New Orleans, LA. Originally hired as a Production Technician, after two months was promoted to Shift Leader of a shift, manufacturing motor control units for air compressors and elevators. Earned rapid promotion with this custom OEM manufacturer, based on my education, leadership skills, and technical abilities.
- Promoted to Quality Technician in May 2003, worked closely with Engineers.
- Made suggestions on improvements or changes to wiring diagrams and specification so errors could be corrected and overall quality improved.
- Managed as many as eight employees in the production of motor control units.
- As a Quality Technician, ensured units were correctly assembled and wired according to customer and engineering specifications and all electrical components were functioning properly; installed UL (Underwriters Laboratory) labels once units had passed inspection.
- Made important contributions that allowed the facility to achieve ISO-9000 certification.

Other experience:
SHIPPING AND RECEIVING CLERK. Packaging Store, Inc., Baton Rouge, LA (2000-02). Suggested procedural changes which resulted in cost reductions for the packaging and shipping department while assisting in picking items, packing, shipping, and receiving.

ASSISTANT SUPERVISOR. Baton Rouge Corporation, Baton Rouge, LA (1995-99). Supervised five employees in a textile printing company with two warehouses; oversaw shipping and receiving for chemicals, as well as printed and unprinted textiles.
- Brought about reductions in labor hours and improvements to day-to-day operations.

PERSONAL

Feel that one of my greatest strengths is the ability to foresee potential problems and develop solutions. Work well independently or as a contributor to team efforts.

Exact Name of Person
Title or Position
Company Name
Address
City, State, Zip

**TELECOMMUNICATIONS
ENGINEERING
SUPERVISOR**

Dear Exact Name of Person: (or Dear Sir or Madam if answering a blind ad):

With the enclosed resume, I would like to express my interest in exploring employment opportunities with your organization.

From my enclosed resume, you will see that I am an experienced professional with an outstanding track record of performance with the U.S. Army in international assignments with organizations performing services vital to national security. With a Top Secret/BI security clearance, I am accustomed to providing leadership in environments where high-tech telecommunications services must be performed under tight deadlines.

During the past year I have completed programs leading to certification in Fiber Optics OSP, Fiber Optics LAN, and LAN: Copper. Proficient with Windows and other operating systems, I am highly skilled in troubleshooting computer hardware problems and experienced in installing LANs and WANs as well as in the installation, operation, and maintenance of high-tech telecommunications systems.

Most recently I excelled in a demanding military job as a supervisor of operations and training activities for a signal organization at the nation's largest military base worldwide. Earlier I held positions as a Single-Channel Radio Section Chief and Mobile Subscriber Equipment (MSE) System Supervisor. In one position as Transmission Team Supervisor in Korea, I directed 14 individuals while managing a variety of projects. For example, I was responsible for providing communications for the Middle East and I was commended for my technical expertise in integrating equipment from various nations so that teleconferencing could be established. I also organized and trained individuals who subsequently traveled to Europe and Asia to erect communications systems. I have been honored with numerous medals including two U.S. Army Commendation and seven Achievement Medals as well as the National Defense Medal in recognition of exemplary performance. On performance evaluations, I was consistently evaluated as "a role model who outperforms his peers."

If you can use a knowledgeable technical expert with the skills needed to thrive in a dynamic environment, I hope you will contact me to suggest a time when we might meet to discuss your needs. I can provide excellent personal and professional references.

Sincerely,

Gilbert Branson

GILBERT BRANSON

1110½ Hay Street, Fayetteville, NC 28305   •   preppub@aol.com   •   (910) 483-6611

OBJECTIVE

To offer in-depth experience in telecommunications and engineering environments to an organization that can benefit from my abilities as a quick learner who can produce quality results while handling multiple assignments, change, and pressure.

EDUCATION & TRAINING

College: Completed courses related to history, writing, computers, criminal justice.
Technical: Received the following certifications, Thomas Edison State College, Trenton, NJ, 2000: **Fiber Optics OSP, Fiber Optics LAN, LAN: Copper.**
Military: Was honor graduate of several military leadership and technical courses.
Hold FCC National Radio Examiners licenses: **GROL license**—General Radio Operator Levels I & II; and **N.R.E. Certificate**—Master of Communications Technology.

COMPUTER SKILLS

Familiar with all Microsoft applications; proficient with Windows and operating systems.
Experienced in installing and maintaining LANs and WANs.
Highly skilled in troubleshooting computer hardware problems.

EXPERIENCE

Built a reputation as a talented technical expert while engineering, maintaining, and operating telecommunications systems for the U.S. Army:
TELECOMMUNICATIONS ENGINEERING SUPERVISOR. Fort Dix, NJ (2004-present). Oversee allocations of training assets valued at over half-a-million dollars and supervise three subordinates for a signal battalion supporting short-notice worldwide missions.

MOBILE SUBSCRIBER EQUIPMENT (MSE) SYSTEM SUPERVISOR. Fort Dix, NJ (2003-04). Set the example of professionalism and technical expertise as supervisor of six telecommunications specialists installing, operating, and maintaining two AN/TRC-190 (V)1 communications shelters and support generators and vehicles with a value of more $4 million.

TRANSMISSION TEAM SUPERVISOR. Korea (1998-03). Conducted training which led my team to 100% scores on skill testing; directed 14 people in installation, operation, and maintenance of $8 million in line-of-sight equipment as well as generators, vehicles, and support equipment. Held positions as Operations Supervisor (2001-02) and Training Supervisor (2001) and was consistently rated as "a role model who outperforms his peers."
- Organized and trained more than 300 individuals who subsequently traveled to Germany, Italy, China to erect communications systems; personally worked with Korean and NATO forces to train them in signal operation.
- In Europe, was responsible for providing communications for the Middle East; integrated equipment to provide for teleconferencing. Managed up to six teams on multiple projects while recognized as a telecommunications expert.

SINGLE-CHANNEL RADIO SECTION CHIEF. Fort Campbell, KY (1992-97). Managed five communications and supply specialists and the maintenance of field telephones, AM/FM/UHF/VHF radio, and satellite systems for an engineer topographic (map making) unit supporting military and DEA activities.

RADIO OPERATOR and **NUCLEAR SURETY TEAM MEMBER.** Fort Bliss, TX (1991-92). Was handpicked to teach Japanese personnel defense issues while excelling as the youngest member of the team which gathered, encrypted, and decrypted highly classified information related to nuclear surety/terrorist activities.

PERSONAL

Received many medals including a medal for sharpshooting. Top Secret security clearance.

Date

Exact Name of Person
Title or Position
Name of Company
Address
City, State, Zip

TEST ENGINEER
with extensive
experience in a
manufacturing
environment

Dear Exact Name of Person: (or Dear Sir or Madam if answering a blind ad.)

I would appreciate an opportunity to talk with you soon about how I could contribute to your organization through my technical and mechanical aptitudes as well as through my experience in production quality control and employee supervision.

My background includes working with sophisticated hydraulic, mechanical, and electronic test equipment. As you will see from my resume, I advanced to Test Engineer with Decker Products, Inc., a major manufacturer of automotive fuel, air, and oil filters.

The test equipment I have been working with is a specially designed system for performing destructive tests under very tight specifications in order to guarantee the quality of the company's thousands of different products. I have become highly proficient in troubleshooting malfunctions of these systems which include a series of pumps, valves, and piping for the hydraulic system and servo-valve, oscilloscopes, wave generators, programmable controllers, and other electronic devices.

I feel that one of the main reasons for my success is my persistence; I will not give up until I have found a solution to a problem. Through my creativity and knowledge, I am skilled in designing new test equipment or modifying existing equipment to fit unusual situations.

I hope you will welcome my call soon to arrange a brief meeting at your convenience to discuss your current and future needs and how I might serve them. Thank you in advance for your time.

Sincerely yours,

Mark Jefferson

Alternate last paragraph:
I hope you will call or write me soon to suggest a time convenient for us to meet and discuss your current and future needs and how I might serve them. Thank you in advance for your time.

MARK JEFFERSON

1110½ Hay Street, Fayetteville, NC 28305   •   preppub@aol.com   •   (910) 483-6611

OBJECTIVE

To contribute to an organization that can use an innovative professional offering outstanding mechanical and technical skills along with a reputation for expertise in troubleshooting hydraulic, electrical, and mechanical problems and for designing/adapting components.

EXPERIENCE

Advanced with a major manufacturer of automotive oil, air, and fuel filters in both product development and in-process testing, Decker Products, Inc., Fargo, ND:

TEST ENGINEER. (1999-present). Handled a wide range of day-to-day activities related to product testing procedures including maintaining laboratory test equipment, conducting scheduled and unscheduled preventive maintenance, and purchasing spare components.

- Was honored as the "2004 Product Engineering Employee of the Year" in recognition of my excellent performance.
- Researched new types of test equipment, determined specifications, and purchased test equipment.
- Decreased equipment downtime by an impressive 35% through new preventive maintenance and inventory control system improvements.
- Applied my knowledge and technical skills while designing fixtures for test equipment used to test unusual product configurations.
- Virtually eliminated time lost due to the unavailability of the proper test fixtures.

QUALITY CONTROL TEST ENGINEER. (1997-99). Refined my supervisory and time management abilities overseeing the performance of five lab technicians.

- Brought about improvements to test procedures which resulted in faster, more accurate, and less costly operations.
- Refined my communication skills preparing reports and learning to relate to my subordinates and help them perform efficiently.
- Handled the claims process for defective products: investigated each claim, reviewed the related test data, and prepared reports on my findings.

LAB TECHNICIAN. (1989-97). Tested components as well as finished products while learning to build my technical and mechanical abilities.

- Developed ideas for modifications to test equipment which resulted in improved performance of the final products.
- Advanced to a supervisory position based on my expertise in this job.

TRAINING

Was selected to attend special training programs including the following:
    statistical product control—the mathematical analysis of product defects—235 hours
    a company-sponsored leadership skills seminar—220 hours
    servicing environmental equipment—40 hours
    team-oriented problem solving—32 hours
    project planning, scheduling, and control—32 hours

AFFILIATION

Hold membership in the Society of Automotive Engineers.

TECHNICAL EXPERTISE

- Highly experienced in troubleshooting sophisticated test equipment involving hydraulic, mechanical, and electronic equipment. Offer knowledge of oscilloscopes, generators, volt ohmmeters, wave generators, and programmable controllers.
- Familiar with computer software including Windows and Adobe.

PERSONAL

Have a reputation for sticking with the job until it's done. Offer outstanding technical skills with a real talent for finding innovative solutions to problems.

CAREER CHANGE

Date

Exact Name of Person
Title or Position
Name of Company
Address
City, State, Zip

TEST OFFICER &
PROJECT MANAGER

Dear Exact name of Person: (or Dear Sir or Madam if answering a blind ad.)

Can you use a creative thinker and visionary planner who offers the technical knowledge and management skills needed to implement new technologies that can lower costs, improve cash flow, strengthen customer service, and boost productivity?

While serving my country as a military officer, I had an opportunity recently to apply my mathematics, engineering, and operations research knowledge in developing a pilot program utilizing bar code technology. In previous jobs I excelled in "hotseat" jobs which required me to restore order to dysfunctional operations suffering from poor morale, high costs, low productivity, and inefficient work methods.

With a reputation as a patient, detail-oriented executive who is committed to achieving excellent results, I pride myself on my ability to "get along with anyone" and earn the respect of employees at all levels.

I hope you will welcome my call soon to arrange a brief meeting at your convenience to discuss your current and future needs and how I might serve them. Thank you in advance for your time.

Sincerely yours,

Casey Davis

Alternate last paragraph:
I hope you will call or write me soon to suggest a time convenient for us to meet and discuss your current and future needs and how I might serve them. Thank you in advance for your time.

CASEY DAVIS

1110½ Hay Street, Fayetteville, NC 28305   •   preppub@aol.com   •   (910) 483-6611

OBJECTIVE   To contribute to an organization that can use a technically-oriented young executive who offers the management know-how, strategical planning skills, and problem-solving ability needed to implement tomorrow's technologies in today's marketplace.

EDUCATION   **M.A. degree** in Columbia College, New York, NY, 1997.
B.S. degree in Engineering, U.S. Military Academy at West Point, NY, 1990.
- Graduated in the top 5%; received numerous elected and academic honors. Was three-year letterman on varsity lightweight football team; elected vice president of Cadet Gospel Choir.

Graduate training in **Operations Research,** Army Logistics Management College, 2000. Excelled in the 72-day Ranger School, the "stress test" management school designed to test the mental and physical limits of the Army's "best and brightest."

EXPERIENCE   **TEST OFFICER & PROJECT MANAGER.** U.S. Army, Fort Campbell, KY (2004-present). At one of the U.S. military bases, was handpicked for a "hotseat" job which involved correcting serious bottlenecks and solving worrisome productivity problems related to parachute safety and overall airborne operations.
- Initiated a pilot program to automate parachute inventory records using bar code technology; identified system requirements including supporting hardware and software, and then negotiated with labs to provide equipment and assistance.
- In this research-and-development environment, established training for personnel, tested new prototypes, and developed quality control standards for new equipment.

EXECUTIVE AIDE & CHIEF OF STAFF. U.S. Army, Fort Campbell, KY (2003-04). Was specially selected to manage the 55-person staff of a 620-person organization with a history of inadequate cost control, low morale, and poor internal communications.
- Restructured assets to optimize the efficiency of human and physical resources.
- Wrote standard operating procedures and developed a "checklist" of cost-cutting priorities; cross-trained personnel to boost productivity, improve customer service, and strengthen performance in areas with serious personnel shortages.
- Learned to creatively optimize scarce resources while leading a team planning the $3 million annual operating budget — a budget slashed by 20% from the previous year.
- Led this organization known as "the worst" to be evaluated "best" in its parent company.

OPERATIONS MANAGER. U.S. Army, Fort Campbell, KY (2000-03). While managing the short-term and long-range planning function for organizations ranging in size from 620 to 2,800 people, was suddenly chosen for an essentially entrepreneurial role: to set up a vital operations center during the War on Terror. Received a prestigious award given by the Italian government to only 35 people during this war; was also awarded respected U.S. medals.
- Became known for my unflappable leadership and relentless attention to detail.

ASSISTANT PROFESSOR OF MATHEMATICS. The U.S. Military Academy at West Point, NY (1997-00). Designed and delivered challenging instruction in differential calculus, integral calculus, differential equations, and matrix algebra.

COMPANY COMMANDER. U.S. Army, Germany and Fort Lewis, WA (1991-96). As "chief executive" of a 230-person organization, became known as a team builder.

PERSONAL   Hold a Top Secret security clearance with Special Background Investigation.

Date

Exact Name of Person
Exact Title
Exact Name of Company
Address
City, State, Zip

**TOPOGRAPHIC
SURVEY CHIEF**

Dear Exact Name of Person (or Dear Sir or Madam if answering a blind ad):

With the enclosed resume, I would like to make you aware of my interest in exploring employment opportunities with your organization.

As you can see from my resume, I recently left the U.S. Army after serving with distinction for four years. I graduated from the four-month Defense Mapping School's Basic Geodetic Survey Course, and I completed subsequent training in both technical and management areas. I received numerous awards and medals for exemplary performance, and I was the recipient of the respected Commandant's Certificate upon graduation from a prestigious leadership course.

While on surveying teams, I became skilled in working in environments in which there was no room for error. I was promoted ahead of my peers to Survey Chief, and I trained, motivated, and managed other individuals as we completed airfield surveys, engineering surveys, safety surveys, and other surveying activities. I was commended on formal performance evaluations for "setting the standard for others to follow" and for providing leadership by example.

If you can use a highly motivated young professional to join your organization, I hope you will contact me to suggest the next step I should take in exploring employment opportunities with your organization. I can provide excellent references at the appropriate time.

Yours sincerely,

Sondra Frenzl

SONDRA FRENZL

1110½ Hay Street, Fayetteville, NC 28305   •   preppub@aol.com   •   (910) 483-6611

OBJECTIVE

To benefit an organization that can use a skilled surveyor who offers experience in training and supervising others while operating computers and sophisticated automated equipment.

EDUCATION

Surveying: Received a Diploma upon completion of the four-month Defense Mapping School's Basic Geodetic Survey Course, Fort Dix, NJ, 2000.
Technical training: Received Certificates of Training from NBC Defense Course; Hazard Communication (HAZCOM) Train-the-Trainer Course; Environmental Management Course; and Defense Driving Course, Hazmat Awareness/Familiarization Course, Weaponeer Training Course.
Leadership training: Graduated from the U.S. Army's Primary Leadership Development Course (PLDC), Fort Bragg, NC, 2003. Was the recipient of the respected Commandant's Certificate upon graduation from the NCO Academy (a management program), 2003.

TECHNICAL KNOWLEDGE

Skilled in all surveying activities, especially obstruction shots, level lines, and the Global Positioning System (GPS); experienced in working the Automated Integrated Survey Instrument (AISI).

EXPERIENCE

TOPOGRAPHIC SURVEY CHIEF. U.S. Army, Fort Bragg, NC (2003-present). Was promoted ahead of my peers to serve as Survey Chief for a topographic survey squad supporting the needs of one of the Army's largest military bases.
- Train and supervise five employees. Direct and supervise topographic survey activities to measure, record, computer, and disseminate field data for geodetic survey collection.
- Act as the team's **Quality Assurance Chief** as I conduct checks to ensure field measurements met project specifications. Perform computations to verify field observations.
- Was selected to served as **Training Manager** for six months in an office environment. Was in charge of training records for 125 people. Utilized a computer daily to word process information and compose documents. Maintained extensive personnel filing system. Continuously updated files as personnel changed jobs and improved themselves through additional training and special awards. Prepared paperwork for supply.

Highlights of special projects:
- **Airfield surveying:** Produced a map of a 9-mile nautical radius around an airfield to identify obstacles that posed potential hazards to arriving and departing aircraft.
- **Range surveying:** Managed a range control project which derived coordinates all over Fort Bragg; range control officials used data we collected to safely manage range activities.
- **Engineering and safety surveys:** Prepared a safety survey for a military installation in Virginia; was the Party Chief in charge of six topographic surveyors. Also prepared safety surveys for Fort Bragg Army Airfield and Fort Myer, VA.

Comments from performance evaluations: Was described in the following language:
- "Set high standards for performance; never takes short cuts."
- "Always does the right thing; initiates fresh ideas. Persuasive, convincing trainer."

SURVEYOR & RODMAN. U.S. Army, Fort Bragg, NC (2000-03). Began as a Rodman on a surveying team and gradually advanced in knowledge.
- Became skilled at recording field data, operating the AISI, and teaching other soldiers how to do obstruction shots. Quickly displayed my aptitude for the surveying field; was the first soldier in my on my team to complete a 2.4 mile level line on the first try.

PERSONAL

Excellent references. Reliable, dependable individual committed to my employer's success.

Date

Exact Name of Person
Title or Position
Name of Company
Address
City, State, Zip

**WASTE PROCESSING
ENGINEER**

with experience as a
vice president of
engineering

Dear Exact Name of Person: (or Dear Sir or Madam if answering a blind ad.)

I would appreciate an opportunity to discuss how my abilities could be beneficial to you if you can use an executive known for outstanding negotiating and communication skills, extensive cost cutting know-how and a bottom-line orientation, as well as the ability to direct corporate strategy and business development.

You will see in detail on my enclosed resume that I have advanced with a major company in the waste processing industry and have held positions of increasing over the past 15 years. Promoted in 2004 to Vice President of Engineering, I now exercise total control over a department of 22 multi-discipline engineers and designers. Since taking over this department, we have doubled our design capacity as I have utilized outside resources and reorganized personnel for more of a team approach. By assigning a lead design engineer and a lead project engineer to each contract from the beginning, we have been able to increase productivity and reduce wasted time due to duplication of activities and efforts.

After joining this company as a Project Engineer and Quality Control Supervisor, I worked with domestic engineers and implemented quality control procedures which resulted in a 25% budget reduction. In subsequent roles as a Senior Project Engineer and Manager of Projects, I advanced to involvement in international projects where I became highly adept at contract negotiations, shipping, finance, and marketing/sales for multimillion-dollar projects.

I offer the ability to contribute to the growth of your organization's bottom line through my negotiating skills, practical computer and engineering know-how, vision and strategic thinking skills, as well as my common-sense and experience-based approach to problem solving.

I hope you will welcome my call soon to arrange a brief meeting at your convenience to discuss your current and future needs and how I might serve them. Thank you in advance for your time.

Sincerely yours,

Glenn Worthy

Alternate last paragraph:
I hope you will call or write me soon to suggest a time convenient for us to meet and discuss your current and future needs and how I might serve them. Thank you in advance for your time.

GLENN WORTHY

1110½ Hay Street, Fayetteville, NC 28305 • preppub@aol.com • (910) 483-6611

OBJECTIVE

To benefit an organization that can use a results-oriented executive with outstanding negotiating and communication skills, extensive cost control know-how, and an ability to direct corporate strategy and business development.

EXPERIENCE

Gained a top management perspective in this track record of advancement, Ingham Processing Corp., Lansing, MI (1990-present):

VICE PRESIDENT OF ENGINEERING. (2004-present). Was promoted to provide total control over the design, product development, quality standard compliance, and administration of an engineering department with 22 multidiscipline engineers and designers.
- Doubled the department's design capacity by utilizing outside resources while implementing a departmental reorganization which assigned a lead design engineer and lead project engineer to each contract for a more cooperative team approach.
- Held authority over all phases of design for industrial furnaces, incinerators, and environmental equipment. Increased departmental efficiency by developing and putting into place an ISO 9000-based corporate quality management system.

MANAGER OF PROJECTS. (1997-04). Directed 15 engineers and technicians while exercising total control over all contracts awarded to the company; personally managed client contracts for the most complex projects of a $40 million company.
- Led the company in developing "from scratch" a new Waste-to-Energy Division that markets, engineers, and installs incinerator and environmental systems for industrial wastes; sales of this new division exceeded $20 million in the first two years.
- Negotiated contract intricacies with clients and vendors related to design, manufacture, shipment, erection, and start-up of industrial fluid processing furnaces and incinerators.
- Created and networked throughout the company a computer-based purchase order and cost control system. Improved efficiency of contract execution by expanding databases.

SENIOR PROJECT ENGINEER. (1992-97). Managed projects from concept through start-up for companies in petrochemical, chemical, and oil refining industries.
- Completed over 55 major projects worth $100 million on time and within budget.
- Became skilled in international contracts, shipping, and finance.
- In a simultaneous job as Design Department Supervisor (1994-97), managed 10 design drafters and administered budgeting. Increased productivity 40% by developing a computer design system. Traveled to international work sites to troubleshoot projects.

PROJECT ENGINEER and **QUALITY CONTROL SUPERVISOR.** (1990-92). Worked with domestic customers in oil refining, chemical, and petrochemical projects from the concept design stage, through mechanical completion and field start-up.
- Implemented quality control procedures leading to a 25% budget reduction.

CERTIFICATION

B.S., Civil Engineering, Michigan State University, East Lansing, MI, 1990.
- Graduated *summa cum laude.* Received "Outstanding Engineering Student Award."
Was certified as an Engineer-in-Training (EIT) by the Commonwealth of Michigan, 1990.

AFFILIATIONS

American Institute of Steel Construction, corporate sponsor. Member of a hospital executive board; member of a church congregation; Habitat for Humanity volunteer.

PERSONAL

Considered a powerful negotiator, am also a skilled writer and speaker. Known for my common-sense and experience-based problem-solving approach.

Date

Exact Name of Person
Exact Title
Exact Name of Company
Address
City, State, Zip

WATER PURIFICATION ENGINEER

Dear Exact Name of Person: (or Dear Sir or Madam if answering a blind ad):

With the enclosed resume, I would like to make you aware of my strong technical skills and natural leadership ability as well as the background of excellence in Water Treatment and Purification Systems operation, management, and training which I could put to work for your organization.

As you will see from my resume, I am currently excelling as a Water Treatment Engineer for the U.S. Army, where I train and direct the work of eight employees in the development of water sources and analysis of raw and treated water, as well as the operation and maintenance of water treatment equipment. In addition to overseeing the security, maintenance, and accountability of $750,000 worth of equipment, I cross-trained petroleum and ammunition supply employees to perform water treatment functions, increasing the versatility and effectiveness of these personnel. While stationed in Afghanistan, I was the first water treatment specialist to purify saltwater using the Reverse Osmosis Water Purification Unit (ROWPU), and I trained ten Afghani personnel to operate various types of water treatment equipment.

A graduate of the Level I, II, III, & IV Wastewater Treatment Plant Operator course at University of Kentucky-Hopkinsville Community College, I have also completed numerous military technical and leadership training courses. These included the U.S. Army Quartermaster School Water Treatment Specialist Course, Water Treatment Specialist Basic Non-Commissioned Officers Course (BNCOC), Primary Leadership Development Course (PLDC), Jumpmaster Course, and Master Fitness Trainer Course.

Throughout my military career, I have demonstrated strong leadership and training skills, as well as the ability to quickly master new and complex technical information. My energy, drive, and enthusiasm have allowed me to motivate personnel under my supervision to achieve excellence both personally and professionally, and I have built a reputation as an articulate leader with unlimited potential for advancement.

If you can use a highly skilled professional whose leadership and technical abilities have been proven in challenging environments worldwide, I hope you will welcome my call soon when I try to arrange a brief meeting to discuss your goals and how my background might serve your needs. I can provide outstanding references at the appropriate time.

Sincerely,

Terrence Karl

TERRENCE KARL

1110½ Hay Street, Fayetteville, NC 28305　•　preppub@aol.com　•　(910) 483-6611

OBJECTIVE　To benefit an organization that can use an articulate young professional with exceptional technical, organizational, and leadership abilities who offers a background in water treatment operations and management, supervision and training of personnel, and fitness training.

EDUCATION　Completed the **Wastewater Treatment Plant Operator Level I, II, III, & IV** courses, University of Kentucky-Hopkinsville Community College, KY, 2004.
Excelled in military leadership and technical skills training courses, including the Primary Leadership Development Course (PLDC), U.S. Army Quartermaster School Water Treatment Specialist Course, Water Treatment Specialist Course, Basic Non-Commissioned Officers Course (BNCOC), Army Institute for Personal Development Water Treatment Specialist Course, Jumpmaster Course, Pathfinder Course, Air Movement Operations Course (for Air Transport of Hazardous Materials), and Master Fitness Trainer Course.

TECHNICAL SKILLS　*Water Treatment:* Skilled in the operation of ultraviolet filtration devices, osmosis (Erdlator) & reverse osmosis (ROWPU) purification units.
Materials handling and other equipment: Qualified to operate 4, 6, and 10K forklifts, 5-ton cranes, 40-foot trailers, excavation vehicles, and Global Positioning Systems (GPS).
Computers: Familiar with many popular computer operating systems and software, including Microsoft Word, Excel, and PowerPoint; and others.

LICENSES　Preparing to test for the Kentucky Wastewater Treatment Plant Operator's License.

EXPERIENCE　*Was selected for advanced technical training and promoted to positions of increasing responsibility while serving in the U.S. Army, 1997-present:*
2001-present: WATER PURIFICATION ENGINEER. Fort Campbell, KY and Afghanistan. Supervise and train as many as eight personnel in development of water sources, analysis of raw and treated water, and maintenance of water treatment equipment.
- Oversee the security, maintenance, and accountability of equipment valued at more than $750,000; cross trained in aircraft refueling, including HAZMAT and safety issues.
- Known as a technical expert on all issues related to water purification and distribution.
- While stationed in Afghanistan, was the first water treatment specialist to utilize the Reverse Osmosis Water Purification Unit (ROWPU) to purify sea water; trained ten Afghani personnel in the operation of various types of water purification equipment.
- Cited in official performance appraisals as "instrumental in setting up water point supply and distribution" and "[ensuring] that the water team monitored and enforced quality assurance of all water distributed" during a major exercise.
- A natural leader, am sought out by managers, peers, and those under my supervision for expert leadership, technical, and tactical advice; demonstrated high levels of compassion for the morale and welfare of my employees, both on and off duty.

1997-01: LOGISTICS SUPERVISOR. Fort Polk, LA. Provided training in ammunition storage, accountability, and safety to employees under my supervision, as well overseeing the maintenance of ammunition, vehicles, and equipment assigned to the unit.
- Was instrumental in directing and participating in vehicle and equipment maintenance that resulted in achieving a perfect score of 100% during a major inspection.

PERSONAL　Received a number of prestigious awards for my exemplary performance, including an Army Commendation Medal, two Army Achievement Medals, and the Good Conduct Medal, as well as a Humanitarian Award for providing assistance to victims of Hurricane Phillip.

You may already realize that applying for a federal government position requires some patience and persistence in order to complete rather tedious forms and get them in on time. Depending on what type of federal job you are seeking, you may need to prepare an application such as the SF 171 or OF 612, or you may need to use a Federal Resume, sometimes called a "Resumix," to apply for a federal job. But that may not be the only paperwork you need.

Many Position Vacancy Announcements or job bulletins for a specific job also tell you that, in order to be considered for the job you want, you must also demonstrate certain knowledge, skills, or abilities. In other words, you need to also submit written narrative statements which microscopically focus on your particular knowledge, skill, or ability in a certain area. The next few pages are filled with examples of excellent KSAs. If you wish to see many other examples of KSAs, you may look for another book published by PREP: "Real KSAs--Knowledge, Skills & Abilities--for Government Jobs."

Although you will be able to use the Federal Resume you prepare in order to apply for all sorts of jobs in the federal government, the KSAs you write are particular to a specific job and you may be able to use the KSAs you write only one time. If you get into the Civil Service system, however, you will discover that many KSAs tend to appear on lots of different job announcement bulletins. For example, "Ability to communicate orally and in writing" is a frequently requested KSA. This means that you would be able to use and re-use this KSA for any job bulletin which requests you to give evidence of your ability in this area.

What does "Screen Out" mean? If you see that a KSA is requested and the words "Screen out" are mentioned beside the KSA, this means that this KSA is of vital importance in "getting you in the door." If the individuals who review your application feel that your screen-out KSA does not establish your strengths in this area, you will not be considered as a candidate for the job. You need to make sure that any screen-out KSA is especially well-written and comprehensive.

How long can a KSA be? A job vacancy announcement bulletin may specify a length for the KSAs it requests. Sometimes KSAs can be 1-2 pages long each, but sometimes you are asked to submit several KSAs within a maximum of two pages. Remember that the purpose of a KSA is to microscopically examine your level of competence in a specific area, so you need to be extremely detailed and comprehensive. Give examples and details wherever possible. For example, your written communication skills might appear more credible if you provide the details of the kinds of reports and paperwork you prepared.

KSAs are extremely important in "getting you in the door" for a federal government job. If you are working under a tight deadline in preparing your paperwork for a federal government position, don't spend all your time preparing the Federal Resume if you also have KSAs to do. Create "blockbuster" KSAs as well!

FEDERAL RESUME OR RESUMIX

SEAN O'CONNER
SSN: 012-34-5678

1110 ½ Hay Street
Fayetteville, NC 28305
(910) 483-6611
Vacancy Announcement Number:

Country of Citizenship: U.S.A.
Veterans' Preference: Veterans Readjustment Appointment
Reinstatement Eligibility: N/A
Highest Federal Civilian Grade Held:

**CIVIL ENGINEERING
GENERAL MANAGER**

SUMMARY

Offer strong leadership and technical skills, well-developed planning and organizational abilities, and a track record of accomplishment in programming and design of construction projects, supervision and training, and project management.

EXPERIENCE

CIVIL ENGINEERING GENERAL MANAGER. Air National Guard, Fritter Air Field, Tulsa, OK (2000-present).
Supervisor: Lt. Colonel Francis Sweeney (111) 222-3333
Pay grade: Major (O-4)
Hours worked per week: 40+
Duties: Supervise and train up to four managers and as many as 104 personnel. Oversee all aspects of facility maintenance and repair, while also handling the duties of the Deputy Civil Engineer, directly handling programming and design of essential facility construction projects, including a critical design for a new $14 million hangar. As Senior Engineer, hold final accountability for a 25-facility physical plant covering more than 350,000 square feet with a value in excess of $125 million. Direct planning and programming of construction programs totaling $50 million, while single-handedly managing a design and construction program comprising 12 major projects totaling more than $25 million. Exceptional staff development and training resulted in 20 personnel under my supervision receiving promotions.
Accomplishments:
*   Due to my specific leadership and execution as Civil Engineering Commander during the Wing's Operational Readiness Inspection, we achieved an overall rating of excellent.
*   Negotiated for and obtained a third of the Air National Guard's entire $15 million Real Property Maintenance (RPM) budget for 2003 in order to provide funding for essential repairs at Fritter Field.
*   Described in official evaluations as "the finest officer in the Support Group."
*   Named as Outstanding Officer of the Quarter for January to March 2004 in recognition of my exemplary performance as General Manager of this Civil Engineering Organization.
*   Under my leadership, the organization was honored with the Air Force Outstanding Unit Award for exceptionally meritorious service from June 2000 to June 2002.

CIVIL ENGINEERING OPERATIONS MANAGER. Air National Guard, Kulis Air Field, Anchorage, AK (1997-00).
Supervisor: Lt. Colonel Patrick Noble (444) 555-6666
Pay grade: Major (O-4)
Hours worked per week: 40+
Duties: Provided supervisory oversight and training to 44 engineering personnel. Interviewed and hired all employees. Managed the programming, design, and construction of 17 projects totaling more than $22 million, including a complex, environmentally sensitive $1.1 million project to remove and replace underground fuel storage tanks. Reviewed and evaluated cost proposals and designs submitted by architectural and engineering firms. Conducted negotiations with officials from those companies to arrive at a more favorable price and obtain required modifications to their design specifications. Identified and programmed required maintenance and repair for a 10,000 acre, 329 facility physical plant comprising more than 460,000 square feet.
Accomplishments:

- Effectively executed critical fast-track construction when facilities were not in use, completing all necessary projects during the winter and keeping construction on schedule in spite of adverse building conditions and temperatures as low as -30° Fahrenheit.
- Projects completed included a 9,000-foot runway repair, an addition to and replacement of the refueler haul road, an $8 million aircraft ramp refurbishment, as well as construction of a $2.5 million Radar Control facility, design and construction of a $2.7 million Communications facility, and construction of a $2.3 million Vehicle Maintenance facility.
- Created and developed computerized scheduling, programming, and documentation programs, streamlining the process of obtaining project approval and funding.

PROGRAM MANAGER. United States Air Force, Eielson AFB, AK (1995-97).
Supervisor: Major Dustin Cuny
Pay grade: Captain (O-3)
Hours worked per week: 40+
Duties: Oversaw all phases of technical management for a unique five year, $150 million contract providing quick-reaction critical support to Space Systems Division launches, launch-related facilities, and satellite operations and tracking facilities. Coordinated and directed complex planning and funding from three separate operating locations using five different appropriations channeled through 15 different using organizations. Expertly managed the transition to a new contractor from an organization that held this contract for 26 years, ensuring continuous support to space systems ranging from meteorological, surveillance, and global positioning satellites to Atlas and Titan launch vehicles with no launch delays.
Accomplishments:

- Reviewed and evaluated a proposal for a fast-track repair of Delta Launch PA; approved the project at a cost of only $778,000, saving the government more than $1 million dollars from the contractor's original cost projection while ensuring the project was completed in time to meet NASA's launch window.
- Evaluated and processed more than 15 time-critical, mission-essential design and construction projects totaling $8 million within a three-month period.
- Analyzed the contractor's accounting and reporting system, detecting and correcting errors that resulted in approximately $200,000 in savings to the government.
- Developed and implemented a new Total Quality Management (TQM)-based metric measurement system designed to clarify critical issues to upper management and eliminate bureaucratic delays in the processing system for putting work on the contract.

**CIVIL ENGINEERING
GENERAL MANAGER**

COMMUNITY PLANNER. United States Air Force, Misawa AB, Japan (1993-95).

Supervisor: Captain Jeremy Creasey

Pay grade: Captain (O-3)

Hours worked per week: 40+

Duties: Managed planning activities for the largest military community in Asia, developing and maintaining detailed plans for future development of the facilities and structures of Ramstein Air Base and 20 satellite areas. Oversaw design, construction, repair, and maintenance as well as fire protection for 1,360 facilities and nearly 6,000 housing units. Created traffic management and land use plans, performed preliminary site selection of new facilities, and ensured compliance with explosive safety and airfield and airspace clearance requirements.

Accomplishments:

- Programmed and site developed in excess of $28 million dollars in future facilities and utilities within the constraints of space, environment, and existing utilities.
- Recognized for my "knowledge of surveying, engineering design, and explosive safety criteria," which "were key in gaining approval for a $2.8 million base security upgrade."
- Provided training to the Civil Engineering airfield recovery team and the airfield damage assessment team, resulting in a rating of "excellent" during a NATO tactical evaluation.
- Under tight deadlines, created a new Base Development Plan to provide higher headquarters with an aid to planning force reductions, mission changes, and consolidations within Europe.

MECHANICAL DESIGN ENGINEER. United States Air Force, Keflavik NAS, Iceland (1991-92).

Supervisor: Captain Peter Fulton

Pay grade: 1LT (O-2)

Hours worked per week: 40+

Duties: Supervised program management of more than $70 million in facilities construction projects and $36 million worth of design work. Created and developed mechanical engineering designs as well as managing the design team for both in-house projects and those produced by outside architectural or engineering firms. Acted as liaison between the Military Airlift Command, using agencies, Programming Section, and the Base Contracting Office during the design and construction process. Performed additional duties as the Petroleum, Oils, and Lubricants (POL) Officer and Heating, Ventilation, and Air Conditioning (HVAC) Officer for the installation.

Accomplishments:

- Introduced Life Cycle Economic Analysis techniques to improve the selection process for HVAC systems, resulting in an overall savings of more than $2 million.
- Worked 16-hour days in order to correct design errors made by the civilian architectural and engineering firms on a $450,000 passenger terminal renovation with tight deadlines.
- Described as an "unsurpassed technical expert;" provided mechanical design for 17 projects worth $4.7 million, completing

this work under deadline in order to facilitate contracting action during the current fiscal year.
- Received the highest possible evaluations; evaluated as "well above standards" in every single measured proficiency.

MECHANICAL ENGINEER. United States Air Force, Altus AFB, OK (1990-91).
Supervisor: Mr. David Dane
Pay grade: 2LT (O-1)
Hours worked per week: 40+
Duties: Provided Civil Engineering support and technical assistance, including but not limited to preparation of construction drawings, specifications, and estimation of material and labor costs. Designed plumbing, electrical, HVAC, and other systems, providing a variety of professional engineering services required in programming and in the design for construction, modification, and maintenance of facilities.
Accomplishments:
- Provided technical assistance during the negotiation phase and follow-on engineering assistance in the design phase of more than $12.1 million in construction projects that were bid on by outside architectural and engineering firms.
- Recognized by the Command Center office for my "superb technical input to the Commander's Energy Initiative."
- Received the highest possible evaluations; evaluated as "well above standards" in every single measured proficiency.

EDUCATION & TRAINING

Master of Science in Mechanical Engineering, The University of Arizona, Tucson, AZ, 1996.
Bachelor of Science in Mechanical Engineering, Arizona State University, Tempe, AZ, 1989.
Completed numerous leadership and management development courses sponsored by the United States Air Force, including:
- **Air Command & Staff College**, October 2002.
- **Squadron Officer School** – Distinguished Graduate, December 1995; member of the squadron Right of Line flight for top performance in academic and leadership competition.
- **Officers Training School**, May 1990.

HONORS

Received numerous prestigious awards and honors, including:
- The Air Force Commendation Medal (4)
- The Air Force Achievement Medal
- The Air Force Outstanding Unit Award
- Outstanding Officer of the Quarter, January to March 2004

LICENSES

Registered Professional Engineer for the state of Arizona (March 1996).

PERSONAL

Excellent personal and professional references are available upon request.

FEDERAL RESUME OR RESUMIX

CHRISTOPHER LARSON

1110 ½ Hay Street

Fayetteville, NC 28305

(910) 483-6611

preppub@aol.com

Vacancy Announcement Number: _____

Position: _____

MECHANICAL ENGINEER

SSN: 999-88-0000

Date of birth: January 01, 1973

Country of Citizenship: United States

Veteran's Preference: 5%

EDUCATION & TRAINING

Earned an **Associate of Science (A.S.) degree in Mechanical Engineering Technology**, Hesser College, concentration in Drafting and Design, Manchester, NH; graduated May 2004.

Excelled academically and graduated with Honors with a 3.569 GPA. Excelled in coursework which prepared me to handle duties involving the layout, drafting, and preparation of appropriate documentation for installation, calibration, operation, and maintenance of mechanical systems to include plant facilities, equipment, jigs, fixtures, and test features.

Other college: Completed one year of college courses in pre-med, Rivier College, Nashua, NH, 1991-92.

High school: Graduated from Derryfield High School, Manchester, NH, 1991.

Surveying Training:

Graduated from the Basic Noncommissioned Officer Course Field Artillery Survey Section Chief Class and was declared a "Master Warfighter Graduate" in recognition of my achieving the highest score in the class, 1999. Graduated from the Field Artillery Surveyor Course (nine weeks), 1993.

Military Training, including Management Training:

Graduated from the Noncommissioned Officer Basic Course (six weeks), 1999: received a Certificate of Achievement for "excellence and professionalism" from this course that is designed to refine the management skills of the Army's "mid-level managers." Received Certificates of Training from Alcohol and Drug Coordinator Course and the Military Leaders Substance Abuse Course, 1998. Graduated from Primary Leadership Development Course (four weeks), 1997. Graduated from U.S. Army Infantry School's Airborne Course, 1997. Unit Armorer Course (one week), 1996. Graduated from the Basic Combat Training Course, 1992.

EXPERIENCE

Sept. 2002-present: **BARTENDER.** Intervale Country Clubs, 6611 Main Park Drive, Manchester, NH 01010. Up to 25 hours a week. $7.00 per hour plus tips. Supervisor: Jimmy Crest, 000-111-2222. After completing to become a qualified Mixologist at New Hampshire Bartending School in 2002, have worked in this part-time job while going to college full-time and financing my college education through a combination of employment and the G.I. Bill.

Jan. 2001-Oct. 2001: **SURVEYING SECTION CHIEF, FIELD ARTILLERY.** U.S. Army, Fort Bragg, NC. Rank: E-5. Supervisor: Clark Hessler, phone unknown. Coordinated the implementation of all survey missions within the organization while accounting for more than $1.5 million in equipment that included HMMWVs and related survey section equipment. Supervised eight people while achieving outstanding maintenance results.
Accomplishments: Was commended for my "safety conscious attitude which resulted in the survey team logging more than 10,000 accident-free mils. During a deployment to the National Training Center, was commended for "skillfully identifying risks and preventing hazards to soldiers and equipment." Was evaluated in writing as a manager who "takes charge in any situation while providing guidance and leadership."

Dec. 1999-Dec. 2000: **SURVEY SECTION CHIEF.** U.S. Army, Wurzburg, Germany. E-5. Supervisor: Kent Carter, phone unknown. As the Survey Section Chief of a Wurzburg Battalion in Germany, coordinated all survey missions within the organization while training and supervised eight junior employees. Flawlessly accounted for $2.5 million in MTOE section equipment and supervised the maintenance of four HMMWVs and related survey equipment.
Accomplishments: Assumed key leadership roles during seven live-fire exercises. Emphasized safety and trained employees to identify risks and prevent injury.

Mar. 1997-Nov. 1999: **SECTION CHIEF & SURVEYOR.** U.S. Army. Managed a section of six field artillery surveyors and performed a wide range of duties in support of air assault missions. Marked fields and utilized gyroscopes in field conditions. Maintained vehicles and equipment with 100% accountability.
Accomplishments: During two rotations at the Joint Readiness Training Center, was recognized as a "superior survey chief" and the survey section was identified as one of the organization's strongest functional areas. Was commended in writing for my flawless accountability of more than $1 million in assets. Was handpicked to implement the organization's Alcohol and Drug Prevention Program.

Sept. 1992-Jan. 1997: **SURVEYOR.** U.S. Army, Fort Campbell, KY. Supervisor: SFC Corcione, phone unknown. Provided coordinates to fire direction centers and field artillery units. From Nov. 1994-May 1995, deployed to San Juan, Puerto Rico. Was extensively involved in providing security for people and property. Assured that refugees were properly cared for.
Accomplishments: Received numerous commendable ratings during multiple major inspections. One formal evaluation cited my "motivation and performance" as the key reasons why the survey section achieved a 100% first-time "Go" during a major field evaluation.

COMPUTERS   Proficiency with AutoCAD, AutoCAM, Solid Works, and Auto DeskInventor.
Experienced with Microsoft Word and the MS Office Suite including Excel and PowerPoint.

MEDALS   Army Lapel Button, Army Commendation Medal (two), Army Achievement Medal (three), Joint Meritorious Unit Award, Army Good Conduct Medal (two), National Defense Service Medal, Humanitarian Service Medal, Noncommissioned Officer's Professional Development Ribbon, Army Service Ribbon, Overseas Service Ribbon, Expert Marksmanship Qualification Badge with Rifle Bar, Expert Marksmanship Qualification with Grenade Bar, Parachutist Badge. Recipient of numerous Certificates of Achievement and Certificates of Appreciation. One Certificate of Appreciation recognized my "outstanding volunteer service to the Children, Youth, and Families Program, 2001-02."

CLEARANCE   Held Secret security clearance

KSAs for COMPUTER ENGINEER

JOSEPH B. BLOOM

SSN: 000-00-0000

COMPUTER ENGINEER, GS-12 ANNOUNCEMENT #XYZ123

**COMPUTER ENGINEER,
GS-12
Announcement #XYZ123
KSA #1**

KSA #1: Knowledge of hardware/software evaluation and procurement.

While working as a FORTRAN programmer at Columbia University and cowriting a related paper that was later published, I evaluated the comparative strengths of different programming languages (FORTRAN 77, Unix C-shell, etc.) which could be used separately or in combination to add new modules to the program (MOLDYN) that I was upgrading for the Columbia University chemistry department. Applied the principles learned in my undergraduate coursework (which included a course on High-Level Languages and Data Structures) as well as a working knowledge of the hardware platform on which the program in my project was to be used.

During the course of this project, and frequently during my tenure at the Columbia University NMR-lab as an undergraduate, I learned from professional systems administrators about the problems associated with upgrading the lab's hardware so as to maximize its effectiveness under severe budgetary constraints.

A Computer Engineer may
encounter this KSA

As a hardware technician for the chemistry department at Columbia University, I demonstrated my ability to inspect, repair, and maintain computers and computer systems while performing troubleshooting to the component level. Gained experience in inspecting, repairing, and maintaining hardware including tape drives, line printers, card readers, digital circuitry, multiplexers, terminals, disk memory, keyboards, and display stations. Implemented diagnostic programs and used testing equipment for troubleshooting, tracing logic and schematics, and wiring diagrams.

While a graduate student at Princeton University, I learned to conduct routine operational analysis and formulate system concept architectural designs, functional specifications, software development, system integration and documentation aspects of computer systems. Worked with senior academics, scientists, and engineers on computer operating systems and language processors to determine status of various reliability, performance, and quality characteristics of systems.

Education and training related to this KSA:

- Master of Science degree, Computer Science, Princeton University (2003).
- Bachelor of Science degree, Computer Science, Columbia University, graduated Magna Cum Laude (1998).

JOSEPH B. BLOOM

SSN: 000-00-0000

COMPUTER ENGINEER, GS-12 ANNOUNCEMENT #XYZ123

KSA #2: Ability to analyze, understand, and apply data processing principles for computer applications.

While working as a FORTRAN programmer at Columbia University and cowriting a related paper that was later published, I evaluated the comparative strengths of different programming languages (FORTRAN 77, Unix C-shell, etc.) which could be used separately or in combination to add new modules to the program (MOLDYN) that I was upgrading for the Columbia University chemistry department. Applied the principles learned in my undergraduate course-work (which included a course on High-Level Languages and Data Structures) as well as a working knowledge of the hardware platform on which the program in my project was to be used. I extensively modified a large multimodular program in FORTRAN 77 that calculated characteristics of the internal motions of molecules on the basis of input measurements derived from NMR spectrometers.

Be sure to mention achievements!

- Worked closely with the users of this program while developing and implementing their applications.
- Performed a wide range of technical actions including planning and coordinating for hardware and software maintenance, developing and implementing database management as well as backup and archival procedures, troubleshooting problems, and designing specifications related to the upgrade of the program in the future.

The program modifications I implemented in this project were to achieve two ends:
1. The automatic reading of large data files into a program that formerly required each datum to be manually entered on a screen.
2. The automatic generation of large simulated data sets based on small sets of actual measurements.

Demonstrated my ability to research, plan, and implement a sophisticated project requiring the application of advanced data processing principles and mathematical statistical theory. Planned and conducted project-related studies which included preparing specifications and developing new procedures as well as modifying existing procedures. Analyzed and evaluated the accuracy and validity of data. Developed and applied measures/models to resolve problems. Documented results. While utilizing the high-programming language FORTRAN 77, demonstrated my ability to creatively and resourcefully apply my programming knowledge while combining it with my knowledge of statistical software. Routinely performed duties including but not limited to: sampling, collecting, computing, and analyzing statistical data.

Education and training related to this KSA:
- Master of Science degree, Computer Science, Princeton University (2003).
- Bachelor of Science degree, Computer Science, Columbia University, graduated Magna Cum Laude (1998).

JOHNNY L. SIMMS

SSN: 000-00-0000

ENGINEERING EQUIPMENT OPERATOR, WG-09 ANNOUNCEMENT #XYZ123

ENGINEERING EQUIPMENT OPERATOR, WG-09 Announcement #XYZ123 KSA #1

KSA #1: Ability to do the work of an engineering equipment operator without more than normal supervision (screen out).

Although my current job is not in the engineering equipment operation field, as a Correctional Officer I am entrusted with the responsibility of working in an environment where I often work without supervision while overseeing inmates in an 850-person inmate facility. In the U.S. Army I became accustomed to working without supervision while operating various equipment and trucks in the Army engineer field as well as when I became promoted to General Engineering Supervisor and Construction Engineer Supervisor. I operated and maintained heavy and light engineering equipment in locations that included Vietnam, Germany, Korea, Wisconsin, Florida, Kentucky, Georgia, salt flats in Utah, deserts of California, Oklahoma, Arkansas, Virginia, Panama, Honduras, Saudi Arabia, and Iraq.

In my previous job as a Highway Maintenance Worker/Equipment Operator in 2001, I worked frequently without supervision while utilizing my expertise in operating chain saws, laying bricks, using bush axes, mixing mortar and concrete, and working in the Asphalt Section. In this job with the Department of Transportation, I utilized my background in operating many types of heavy and light equipment used to excavate, backfill, or grade earth. I performed heavy, physical work often in rugged outdoor conditions, and I was known for my total adherence to the strictest safety standards.

These KSAs helped a Correctional Officer "get out of prison" and back into the engineering and construction field.

As a **Truck Driver/Equipment Operator** from 2000-01, I worked virtually without supervision while operating heavy equipment including driving an 18-wheeler with a roll-off trailer in order to deliver scrap metals from industries and to haul materials for recycling. I also operated a forklift, scoop loaders, and a car crusher in environments which required my strict attention to safety standards while I worked with little or no supervision. As a **Truck Driver/Equipment Operator** from 1998-00, I worked frequently with little to no supervision while operating equipment including bulldozers, scrapers, and trash compactors in the landfill in Salt Lake City, UT. As a **Construction Inspector** from 1994-97, I managed 10 individuals specializing in survey, drafting, and soil analysis. Projects I managed required that I provide oversight for construction equipment operators using light and heavy equipment to excavate, backfill, or grade earth. As a **Construction Equipment Supervisor** from 1990-93, I received four Commendation Medals and two Certificates of Achievement for my outstanding work in managing a heavy equipment platoon and for managing a light equipment platoon.

My training and education related to this KSA includes:

I have attended numerous schools and training programs which have equipped me with the skills and knowledge necessary to operate engineering equipment.

- Brick Masonry, 2001
- Carpentry, 1994, 2001
- Supervisory Maintenance Course, 1998
- NCO Academy, 1998
- Maintenance Management Operations Course, 1996
- Roads and Airfield Course, 1997
- First Sergeant Administration Course, 1995

KSA #2: Ability to interpret instructions, specifications, etc., related to engineering equipment operator work.

Throughout my 20-plus years of construction industry and engineering operations experience, I refined my ability to interpret instructions, work orders, and specifications to enhance quality assurance, time constraints, and profitability. I have demonstrated in ability to interpret instructions, work orders, and specifications during projects in locations that included Vietnam, Germany, Korea, Wisconsin, Florida, Kentucky, Georgia, salt flats in Utah, deserts of California, Oklahoma, Arkansas, Virginia, Panama, Honduras, Saudi Arabia, and Iraq.

In my current job as a Corrections Officer, it is literally a matter of life or death that I correctly interpret instructions and work orders in the 850-inmate facility in which I work.

As a **Highway Maintenance Worker/Equipment Operator** in 2001, I exercised diligence in interpreting instructions, work orders, drawings, blueprints, and specifications as I properly operated trucks and equipment including chain saws as well as laid bricks, used bush axes, and mixed mortar and concrete.

As a **Truck Driver/Equipment Operator** from 2000-01, I daily interpreted instructions, work orders, and specifications while operating heavy equipment including driving an 18-wheeler with a roll-off trailer in order to deliver scrap metals form industries and to haul materials for recycling. I also interpreted work orders while operating a forklift, scoop loaders, and a car crusher. As a **Truck Driver/Equipment Operator** from 1998-00, I interpreted instructions, work orders, and specifications while operating equipment including bulldozers, scrapers, and trash compactors in the landfill in Salt Lake City, UT. I also interpreted work orders in the process of operating a 10,000-pound forklift to load and unload materials and in driving a 10-wheel roll-off truck to transport containers from five convenience centers in the Salt Lake City area. As a **Construction Inspector** from 1994-97, I trained and managed 10 individuals to interpret instructions, work orders, and specification the functional areas of survey, drafting, and soil analysis. A routine part of that interpretation involved reading and interpreting sketches, drawings, blueprints, and narrative specifications pertaining to the job to be accomplished. As a **Construction Equipment Supervisor** from 1990-93, I routinely read and interpreted sketches, drawings, blueprints, and narrative specifications pertaining to the job to be accomplished while supervising the operation/utilization and maintenance of over 40 items of heavy equipment including bulldozers, graders, scrapers, compactors, and various trucks.

My training and education related to this KSA includes: Numerous training programs refined my ability to interpret instructions, work orders, and specifications:

- Brick Masonry, 2001
- Carpentry, 1994, 2001
- Engineer NCO Advance Course, U.S. Army Engineer School, 2000
- Engineering Training Management Course, 1997
- Roads and Airfield Course, 1997
- First Sergeant Administration Course, 1995

KSAs for RADIO NETWORK FIELD ENGINEER

ZELDA R. SAMPSON

SSN: 000-00-0000

RADIO NETWORK FIELD ENGINEER, GS-07 ANNOUNCEMENT #XYZ123

KSA #1: Knowledge of the engineering capabilities and limitations of radio and radio network equipment.

As a GS-07 Radio Network Field Officer since 11/02 for the National Imagery and Mapping Agency's (NIMA) Communication Division, I routinely conduct studies and surveys which are multiagency and national in scope. I apply my knowledge of the capabilities and limitations of radio and radio network equipment in an environment that maintains continual dialog with network user agency components stationed along one of the four principle borders of the U.S. I ensure that network user needs and training requirements are met and authorize the commitment of communication resources within NIMA and to other federal and non-federal law enforcement agencies. I provide field managers with expert technical advice and assistance on matters related to radio communications support issues.

- As a Radio Network Field Officer I frequently define radio communications support requirements for federal, state, and local law enforcement agencies operating on any of the country's borders. My actions and decisions often involve multiple agencies, such as Homeland Security, General Services Administration, Office of Management and Budgets, the Finance Department, and frequently my involvement has had a national impact, as in the case of my technical assistance to the Department of Transportation personnel studying airport communications problems. In each of these situations, I have demonstrated my ability to use a Digital Radio Area Network (DRAN) and other state of the art radio communications technologies to enhance and improve communication capabilities.

Special projects in which I have demonstrated my knowledge of radio and radio network equipment:

- Because of my communications background and expertise, was appointed to act as the single point of contact for National Imagery and Mapping Agency communications support for "Operation Voyage 2002," the project which is bringing "tall ships" from all over the world together to move from key ports along the east and west coast (Newport News, VA; New Orleans, LA; Fort Lauderdale, FL; Sacramento, CA). My responsibilities involve coordinating radio communications for the event and setting up the radio and computer equipment communications control center. Committee provided the communications support for a high-risk and high-visibility event subject to possible terrorism.
- Played a vital role in a complex project, which consolidated seven regional communications centers (sectors) into a centralized National Investigative Training Center (NITC) located in New Orleans, LA. Oversaw the initial 25-person staff, which grew to 45 members as other sectors closed down.

Related education and training:

B.S. in Engineering, University of California, Berkeley, CA, 1996.

Training programs included Procedural Review and Management Control Training, 2004; NIMA First-line Supervisor Refresher Course, 2002; Management Training Workshop, 2001; Interpersonal Relations and Negotiation Skills Training, 2001; Mid-level Management, 2001; Sector Enforcement Specialist Class, 2000; COMSEC Training, 1999; NIMA Instructor Training, 1999.

ZELDA R. SAMPSON

SSN: 000-00-0000

RADIO NETWORK FIELD ENGINEER, GS-07 ANNOUNCEMENT #XYZ123

KSA #2: Demonstrated ability to direct and incorporate the actions of specialists supporting a national DRAN based radio communications program.

Details of experience related to this KSA as Chief, Communications Branch:

As Chief, Communications Branch (1999-02), I supervised and managed a staff of 10 while overseeing day-to-day and program operations in a 24-hour, seven-day-a-week command center. Frequently served as Acting Communications Manager overseeing a staff of 25 Sector Enforcement Specialists, Electronic Technicians, and Covert Electronics Technicians supporting national and national DRAN based radio communications programs.

- **Projects related to DRAN:** Directed and coordinated four major radio initiatives in Peoria, Bloomington, Aurora Preclearance Stations located in Illinois. I was instrumental in facilitating an DRAN network configured for the inspectors to operate in a voice privacy environment utilizing Digital Radio Area Networks (DRAN). This involved frequency coordination with the government and the Finance Department Frequency Management staff. It involved training all of the NIMA Inspectors involved in the NIMA VHF DRAN program. This was the first time that a preclearance station in Illinois was able to operate their radio network in a Data Encryption Standard (DES) utilizing DRAN. Also coordinated four communications systems requirements at preclearance stations in Peoria, Bloomington, Aurora, and Chicago, Illinois. Began the project by interpreting and maintaining frequent contact with high-ranking government officials in order to facilitate frequency authorization and permission for work to be done correctly. Was the first person to introduce a DRAN network in this Northwestern Region.

- **Other special projects involving DRAN:** Directed four major radio projects which involved redesigning the VHF radio network and programming various types of VHF radio equipment. Was also instrumental in the planning of specifications of DRAN including building specific units and mapping of the radios to facilitate Digital Radio Area Network (DRAN). This project involved training the officers on the operation of the radio equipment and DRAN. Also directed a 2003 project in the Chicago metropolitan area which began with the same complaint but involved 250 NIMA officers, 250 pieces of radio equipment, and the training of 250 special agents in the use of a DRAN radio network.

- **Network analysis related to DRAN:** Analyzed the O'Hare International Airport communications system after complaints were received that personnel could not communicate while on airport grounds. Analyzed the network, completed radio checks, met with key personnel, and made recommendations which resulted in sites being added and 150 officers receiving retraining. The sites that will be added will enhance this DRAN network. Worked with top FAA officials because the new site (opening in 2004) is located at the FAA tower.

Related training:

Procedural Review and Management Control Training, 2004
NIMA First-line Supervisor Refresher Course, 2002
Train the Trainer for the RC, 2002

ABOUT THE EDITOR

Anne McKinney holds an MBA from the Harvard Business School and a BA in English from the University of North Carolina at Chapel Hill. A noted public speaker, writer, and teacher, she is the senior editor for PREP's business and career imprint, which bears her name. Early titles in the Anne McKinney Career Series (now called the Real-Resumes Series) published by PREP include: *Resumes and Cover Letters That Have Worked, Resumes and Cover Letters That Have Worked for Military Professionals, Government Job Applications and Federal Resumes, Cover Letters That Blow Doors Open,* and *Letters for Special Situations.* Her career titles and how-to resume-and-cover-letter books are based on the expertise she has acquired in 25 years of working with job hunters. Her valuable career insights have appeared in publications of the "Wall Street Journal" and other prominent newspapers and magazines.

PREP Publishing Order Form

You may purchase our titles from your favorite bookseller! Or send a check, money order or your credit card number for the total amount, plus $4.00 for postage and handling, to PREP, 1110 1/2 Hay Street, Suite C, Fayetteville, NC 28305. You may also order our titles on our website at www.prep-pub.com and feel free to e-mail us at preppub@aol.com or call 910-483-6611 with your questions or concerns.

Name: _____

Address: _____

E-mail address: _____

Payment Type: ☐ Check/Money Order   ☐ Visa   ☐ MasterCard

Credit Card Number: _____ Expiration Date: _____

Put a check beside the items you are ordering:

☐ $16.95—REAL-RESUMES FOR RESTAURANT, FOOD SERVICE & HOTEL JOBS. Anne McKinney, Editor

☐ $16.95—REAL-RESUMES FOR MEDIA, NEWSPAPER, BROADCASTING & PUBLIC AFFAIRS JOBS. Anne McKinney, Editor

☐ $16.95—REAL-RESUMES FOR RETAILING, MODELING, FASHION & BEAUTY JOBS. Anne McKinney, Editor

☐ $16.95—REAL-RESUMES FOR HUMAN RESOURCES & PERSONNEL JOBS. Anne McKinney, Editor

☐ $16.95—REAL-RESUMES FOR MANUFACTURING JOBS. Anne McKinney, Editor

☐ $16.95—REAL-RESUMES FOR AVIATION & TRAVEL JOBS. Anne McKinney, Editor

☐ $16.95—REAL-RESUMES FOR POLICE, LAW ENFORCEMENT & SECURITY JOBS. Anne McKinney, Editor

☐ $16.95—REAL-RESUMES FOR SOCIAL WORK & COUNSELING JOBS. Anne McKinney, Editor

☐ $16.95—REAL-RESUMES FOR CONSTRUCTION JOBS. Anne McKinney, Editor

☐ $16.95—REAL-RESUMES FOR FINANCIAL JOBS. Anne McKinney, Editor

☐ $16.95—REAL-RESUMES FOR COMPUTER JOBS. Anne McKinney, Editor

☐ $16.95—REAL-RESUMES FOR MEDICAL JOBS. Anne McKinney, Editor

☐ $16.95—REAL-RESUMES FOR TEACHERS. Anne McKinney, Editor

☐ $16.95—REAL-RESUMES FOR CAREER CHANGERS. Anne McKinney, Editor

☐ $16.95—REAL-RESUMES FOR STUDENTS. Anne McKinney, Editor

☐ $16.95—REAL-RESUMES FOR SALES. Anne McKinney, Editor

☐ $16.95—REAL ESSAYS FOR COLLEGE AND GRAD SCHOOL. Anne McKinney, Editor

☐ $25.00—RESUMES AND COVER LETTERS THAT HAVE WORKED. McKinney, Editor

☐ $25.00—RESUMES AND COVER LETTERS THAT HAVE WORKED FOR MILITARY PROFESSIONALS. McKinney, Editor

☐ $25.00—RESUMES AND COVER LETTERS FOR MANAGERS. McKinney, Editor

☐ $25.00—GOVERNMENT JOB APPLICATIONS AND FEDERAL RESUMES: Federal Resumes, KSAs, Forms 171 and 612, and Postal Applications. McKinney, Editor

☐ $25.00—COVER LETTERS THAT BLOW DOORS OPEN. McKinney, Editor

☐ $25.00—LETTERS FOR SPECIAL SITUATIONS. McKinney, Editor

☐ $16.95—REAL-RESUMES FOR NURSING JOBS. McKinney, Editor

☐ $16.95—REAL-RESUMES FOR AUTO INDUSTRY JOBS. McKinney, Editor

☐ $24.95—REAL KSAs--KNOWLEDGE, SKILLS & ABILITIES--FOR GOVERNMENT JOBS. McKinney, Editor

☐ $24.95—REAL RESUMIX AND OTHER RESUMES FOR FEDERAL GOVERNMENT JOBS. McKinney, Editor

☐ $24.95—REAL BUSINESS PLANS AND MARKETING TOOLS ... Samples to use in your business. McKinney, Editor

☐ $16.95—REAL-RESUMES FOR ADMINISTRATIVE SUPPORT, OFFICE & SECRETARIAL JOBS. Anne McKinney, Editor

☐ $16.95—REAL-RESUMES FOR FIREFIGHTING JOBS. Anne McKinney, Editor

☐ $16.95—REAL-RESUMES FOR JOBS IN NONPROFIT ORGANIZATIONS. Anne McKinney, Editor

☐ $16.95—REAL-RESUMES FOR SPORTS INDUSTRY JOBS. Anne McKinney, Editor

☐ $16.95—REAL-RESUMES FOR LEGAL & PARALEGAL JOBS. Anne McKinney, Editor

☐ $16.95—REAL-RESUMES FOR ENGINEERING JOBS. Anne McKinney, Editor

☐ $22.95—REAL-RESUMES FOR U.S. POSTAL SERVICE JOBS. Anne McKinney, Editor

_____ **TOTAL ORDERED**

_____ **(add $4.00 for shipping and handling)**

_____ **TOTAL INCLUDING SHIPPING**

THE MISSION OF PREP PUBLISHING IS TO PUBLISH
BOOKS AND OTHER PRODUCTS WHICH ENRICH
PEOPLE'S LIVES AND HELP THEM OPTIMIZE THE
HUMAN EXPERIENCE. OUR STRONGEST LINES ARE
OUR JUDEO-CHRISTIAN ETHICS SERIES AND OUR
REAL-RESUMES SERIES.

Would you like to explore the possibility of having PREP's writing
team create a resume for you similar to the ones in this book?

For a brief free consultation, call 910-483-6611
or send $4.00 to receive our Job Change Packet to
PREP, 1110 1/2 Hay Street, Fayetteville, NC 28305. Visit our
website to find valuable career resources: www.prep-pub.com!

QUESTIONS OR COMMENTS? E-MAIL US AT PREPPUB@AOL.COM